PIANTA DELLA CITTA'
DI NAPOLI
come esiste nel presente Anno
MDCCXC.
L E P A L U D I
Pasconcello
Strada Regia di Portici
Ponte della Maddalena
BORGO DI LORETO
Strada Nuova

GIULIANO BUGIALLI'S

Foods of Naples

AND CAMPANIA

PHOTOGRAPHS BY ANDY RYAN

STEWART, TABORI & CHANG
NEW YORK

Endpapers: Map of Naples, seventeenth century, courtesy of Voyage Pittoresque,
Via Vittoria Colonna, Naples, Italy

Images on pages 65, 144, 204, 226, 230, 233, 250, 261 from *Usi e Costumi de Napoli e Contorni descritti e dipinti*, Francesco de Bourcard (1866), courtesy Biblioteca Nazionale, Palazzo Reale, Naples, Italy

Published in 2003 by
Stewart, Tabori & Chang
A Company of La Martinière Groupe
115 West 18th Street
New York, NY 10011

Export Sales to all countries except Canada, France,
and French-speaking Switzerland:
Thames and Hudson Ltd.
181A High Holborn
London WC1V 7QX England

Canadian Distribution:
Canadian Manda Group
One Atlantic Avenue, Suite 105
Toronto, Ontario M6K 3E7 Canada

Library of Congress Cataloging-in-Publication Data
Bugialli, Giuliano
Giuliano Bugialli's foods of Naples / by Giuliano Bugialli.
p. cm.
Includes index.
ISBN 1-58479-211-6
1. Cookery, Italian. 2. Cookery—Italy—Naples. I. Title: Foods of Naples. II. Title.

TX723 .B767 2002
641.5944'73—dc21 2002067011

The text of this book was composed in Mrs. Eaves and Avenir.

Design by Lynne Yeamans
Graphic Production by Kim Tyner

Printed in Japan by Toppan Printing Co.

10 9 8 7 6 5 4 3 2 1

First Printing

PAGE 1: *The view down Via San Gregoria.*
PAGES 2–3: *The beautiful Bay of Naples.*
PAGE 4: *Mount Vesuvius as seen from Naples.*
PAGE 5: *A typical street scene in Campania.*
PAGE 13: *This is an inscription in a copy of Harold Acton's history,* The Bourbons of Naples.

I want to dedicate this book to the memory of my brother Paolo. He was a wonderful writer and a superb reporter. A real Florentine, his tongue was sharp as a knife. He pretended not to understand why I was writing about food, but I understood him better than that.

This book gave me the opportunity to explore a subject the way he did, with a journalist's eyes, and no city was better for this exploration than Naples. Neapolitans enjoy spending their lives in the streets, eating in the streets and doing business there. Everywhere the sacred and profane are united.

So I started to look around me with the goal of locating and combining the food, my most beloved subject, and lifestyle of the Neapolitans *in punta dei piedi* (in a humble way). Hopefully, I was able to capture the spirit of the people and the place.

contents

list of recipes (*** means that recipe is mentioned only)

homemade ingredients

breads

pasta and sauces

appetizers

first courses

vegetables

main courses

FISH

main courses

MEAT

desserts

my naples

I fell in love with Naples before I ever visited the city. Listening to the tales of three very special people, I came to understand and eventually love the city through their eyes.

Although I try to forget how many years ago this happened, I cannot forget the friends who made it possible: Sir Harold Acton, the great historian of Naples, and Nicky Mariano, who, with her sister, achieved fame for organizing the professional activities (or, as the Italians say, *mettevano ordine*) of the great art historian Bernard Berenson.

Sir Harold and "the sisters" had deep ties to Naples. The descendant of another famous Lord Acton, who had played a central role in keeping Naples out of the hands of Napoleon—thus gaining Neapolitan citizenship for the family—Sir Harold lived in Florence, but frequently visited friends in the south.

In those days, the rapid train had just been introduced, connecting Milan to Naples via Florence and Rome. Sir Harold was a frequent passenger, always traveling with one or both of the Mariano sisters. This was the only fast train that stopped at Mergellina Station in Naples, from which they could continue by boat to their Neapolitan residences. In addition to the sisters, Lord Acton would always bring along at least one guest, and I was flattered to have an open invitation to join them.

The train included a special Pullman car that featured a few individual armchairs in place of the standard seats, and their preferred mode of travel was to occupy *il salottino*, a small room with four armchairs facing each other, separated from the other seats in the car. I believe this was the first traveling artistic salon, which came to be called the *salotto letterario*, or literary salon, because the guests included the poet Edith Sitwell, John Constable's grandson, who was a painter himself, as well as many other eminent art historians.

We talked about everything in the course of these journeys, but Naples was the principle subject of conversation—Naples as seen through the native eyes of Sir Harold and Nicky Mariano. They shared the love that the great German poet Goethe had for the city, rather than the derision expressed by the Italian poet Leopardi. Their amusing stories of adventures and misadventures in Naples were informed by their observation that all of life there—business, eating, even sleeping—took place in the middle of the streets.

Their stories, so alive and fascinating, were just the beginning of my love affair with Naples and its people. Through the years, I have come to agree with the Italian writer Mario Stefanile, who said that if you eat a *sfogliatella*, you do not need a tourist guide to understand the essence and the poetry of Naples.

The old kingdom of Naples included six now separate regions: Campania, Abruzzi, Molise, Basilicata, Apulia, and Calabria. With the exception of Abruzzi, these regions share much common history, and their customs are similar, though distinct. The same can be said for the different cities and small towns that make up the region of Campania, immediately surrounding Naples.

As the capital of the entire kingdom, Naples—much like Paris in France—became a repository for the food traditions of the entire area. However, different towns developed their own versions of some of these dishes. In the chapters that follow, several versions of certain recipes will be given to show how fascinating these differences can be.

Indeed, I am sometimes convinced that many dishes moved from other parts of the kingdom to Naples, rather than vice versa. We cannot forget that Naples was once second only to London as the largest European port, and as an international city Naples happily absorbed dishes not only from the other Italian states, but from other countries as well. To this mix, we can add the influence of the English, French, and Spanish, who all ruled Naples at one time or another throughout its complicated history. And so, in the early classic cookbooks of Cavalcanti and Corrado we find many recipes described as *alla Fiorentina*, *alla Bolognese*, *alla Genovese*, *alla Francese*, *alla Spagnola*, and so on.

Despite all these outside influences—and there were many—what is most surprising is that the Neapolitans have created a cuisine with a completely unique personality, rather than a bastardized cuisine with a very strong foreign influence. The dishes and their traditions have been well documented through the centuries, in literature that describes not only the food itself, but the everyday life of the people of Naples. Beginning with Boccaccio (1313–1375), who spent time in Naples and used it as a locale in many of his short stories, and continuing through Dumas, Goethe, and Stendahl, each of whom wrote about different aspects of life in the city, and, most important, de Bourcard, whose *Usi e Costumi di Napoli* contains vivid descriptions of the food and the character of the street vendors, bringing the Naples of the mid-nineteenth century to life.

And so we can say that if the life of Naples is lived on its streets, then food plays such an important part in the lives of Neapolitans that it often assumes the lead role in the *commedia*. Neapolitans themselves say that they do not eat to satisfy their needs, but as a "devotion"—a particular dish must be eaten at that specific moment because of a religious notion, or a superstition that will bring good luck or thwart the bad. This is why Neapolitan cookbooks do not include a large number of recipes: More text is devoted to the lengthy and complex reaction to the eating of a specific dish than to the directions for cooking it.

Therefore, to better present the Neapolitan approach to food, the recipes in this book have been arranged in a more Neapolitan manner, emphasizing ingredients and techniques rather than courses. Some of these recipes are well known, but they are presented here in their authentic versions, with all the "fads" removed. Others are not familiar outside their native region, and these retain their original integrity.

al caro amico
con tanti auguri
da un anglo-napoletano
Harold Acton.

CHAPTER ONE

how to make the *real* neapolitan food

It is not difficult to reproduce authentic Neapolitan food outside of Naples: You must simply set aside your own way of thinking and follow not only the step-by-step instructions of the recipes, but the Neapolitan approach to each dish as well.

This is a cuisine that is prepared deliberately, whether in the slow and tedious simmering of a sauce or in the rapid creation of the beloved fried dishes.

The ingredients that are combined to form a Neapolitan dish all maintain their individual personality. Even after many hours of cooking a sauce, the wonderful aromas of the tomatoes and of all the different herbs come through.

For authentic flavor, it also helps if you prepare a selection of homemade condiments to keep in your pantry to use in many of the classic Neapolitan dishes. To this day, many Neapolitan families prepare some basic signature ingredients that are considered staples of the pantry. For example, even if a commercial tomato paste is used as the basis for a *ragù*, some homemade tomato paste (the *conserva*) must be added or the sauce won't taste right.

In this chapter, you will find recipes for the most typical homemade ingredients. Any real Neapolitan kitchen has these essential condiments on hand.

LEFT: *The famous lemons from Sorrento, known to make the best* limoncello *(page 26).*
PRECEDING PAGES: *A view of modern Naples.*

Red wine vinegar requires just two ingredients: wine and the starter, or "mother," which is generally a few pieces of white bread. You can see the dark, thick layer created by the starter in the homemade red wine vinegar shown below. If you want to make your wine vinegar stronger, pour it into a plastic container and place it in the freezer. As it freezes, some excess water will rise to the top; discard the water and the vinegar underneath will be more concentrated.

Although Neapolitans use a lot of vinegar, they prefer lemon as a dressing for simple salads. Typically the lemon is served in slices on top rather than squeezed onto the salad.

aceto di vino

RED WINE VINEGAR

MAKES ABOUT 3½ CUPS

2 slices white bread, crusts removed

4 cups dry red wine

Put the bread in a glass jar, then pour the wine over it. Place a piece of cheesecloth over the top of the jar and set the jar aside in a cabinet or on a countertop away from direct sun.

Let the jar rest for about 25 days: In this period of time, the bread will turn very dark in color and become almost gelatinous. This is the so-called mother of the wine vinegar. Carefully drain and filter the wine that has become vinegar into a bowl, then pour it into a bottle. The vinegar is now ready to be used.

You can add more wine to the jar containing the mother of the vinegar. This time, the process of changing the wine into vinegar will be much faster, about 1 week.

ABOVE: *Homemade red wine vinegar, ready for use. Note the dark, thick layer of the starter at the bottom.*

Peppers preserved in wine vinegar are a Neapolitan staple used in a variety of dishes. Here, as in most of the recipes in this book, I use the readily available bell pepper, but in Neapolitan markets, it is sometimes possible to find a smaller, rather round, usually red pepper called a *papacelle* (see photo, pages 28–29). These peppers are also sold seasoned, mainly with hot pepper, and preserved in wine vinegar. In Neapolitan slang, *paparuolo* means sweet pepper and *papavero* means poppy, so *papacelle* combines the two words to reflect the fact that these sweet peppers are red as a poppy. *Papacelle* preserved in vinegar is served as a vegetable or used as the main ingredient in a sauce.

peperoni all'aceto

PEPPERS PRESERVED IN RED WINE VINEGAR

SERVES 6 AS AN APPETIZER
OR 3 AS A VEGETABLE

3 large red bell peppers

3 large yellow bell peppers

1/4 cup extra-virgin olive oil

1 large clove garlic, peeled and cut into slivers

1/2 cup red wine vinegar, preferably homemade (page 17)

Salt and freshly ground black pepper

1/2 cup cold water

Large pinch of dried oregano

Roast, peel, and cut the peppers into strips according to the directions on page 57, then place the peppers on a serving platter and set aside.

Heat the oil in a small saucepan over medium heat. When the oil is lukewarm, add the garlic and sauté for a few seconds; the garlic should be very light in color. Pour in the vinegar, season with salt and abundant black pepper, and simmer for 2 minutes. Add the cold water and simmer until the liquid has reduced by two-thirds. Season with the oregano, mix very well, and pour everything over the peppers.

Let the peppers marinate for at least 2 hours before serving.

RIGHT: Papacelle *as they are sold in the market.*

Eggplants are particularly versatile gastronomically because they so easily absorb the different flavors of the other ingredients in a dish. Naples and the Campania region primarily grow the long, dark purple variety of eggplant.

melanzane all'aceto

EGGPLANT PRESERVED IN RED WINE VINEGAR

SERVES 6 TO 8 AS AN APPETIZER OR 3 TO 5 AS A VEGETABLE

6 medium-sized eggplants, about 8 ounces each

Coarse-grained salt

1 quart not very strong red wine vinegar, preferably homemade (page 17)

5 cloves garlic, peeled and cut into slivers

Fresh or dried oregano leaves to taste

Hot red pepper flakes to taste

About 2 cups extra-virgin olive oil

Peel the eggplants and cut them into 1/2-inch-thick slices. Arrange the eggplant slices on a serving platter, sprinkle with coarse salt, and place another serving platter over them as a weight. Let rest for 1 hour.

Drain the eggplant and rinse it under cold running water to remove all the salt. Bring the vinegar to a boil over medium heat, add the eggplant, and cook for 4 minutes. Remove the eggplant slices and pat them with paper towels to remove some of the vinegar.

Arrange a layer of the eggplant on the bottom of a crockery or glass bowl. Sprinkle some of the garlic, oregano, and red pepper flakes over the eggplant, then drizzle with 2 tablespoons of the olive oil. Repeat, making several layers of eggplant and seasonings. Pour the remaining olive oil over the top layer of eggplant.

Press the eggplant slices by placing a dinner plate on top, inserted into the bowl. Cover and refrigerate overnight. Bring to room temperature before serving.

peperoni sottaceto

PEPPERS MARINATED IN WHITE WINE VINEGAR

SERVES 6 AS AN APPETIZER
OR 3 AS A VEGETABLE

- 3 red bell peppers, cleaned, seeded, with tops, stems, and all filaments removed
- 3 yellow bell peppers, cleaned, seeded, with tops, stems, and all filaments removed
- 2 quarts cold water
- 2 quarts white wine vinegar
- Coarse-grained salt

ABOVE: *Peppers Marinated in Wine Vinegar. Note that the red peppers have given their color to the white wine.*

These peppers are used for a variety of dishes, such as Insalata di Rinforzo *(page 252), and can be used outside of Italy as a substitute for* papacelle.

Soak the peppers for 30 minutes in a bowl of cold water. Bring a pot containing the 2 quarts cold water to a boil over medium heat; add 2 cups of the vinegar and coarse salt to taste. When the acidulated water returns to a boil, drain the peppers and add them to the pot.

Simmer for 5 minutes. Use a strainer-skimmer to transfer the peppers to a cutting board lined with a thick layer of paper towels. Let the peppers rest until they are very well drained.

Place the peppers in a glass jar. Heat the remaining vinegar over medium heat until it is warm, then pour it into the jar containing the peppers.

Let the vinegar cool completely, about 2 hours, then close the jar and refrigerate. After 2 days, the peppers are ready to be used.

la giardiniera

MIXED VEGETABLES PRESERVED IN WINE VINEGAR

MAKES ABOUT 4 CUPS

About 2 pounds mixed vegetables (some combination of the following):

- Carrots, scraped and cut into 1-inch disks
- Bell peppers, cleaned, seeded, all filaments removed, cut into 2-inch pieces
- Pearl onions, cleaned and left whole
- Cauliflower, cleaned and cut into florets
- Gherkins (tiny, dark green cucumbers), cleaned and left whole

PLUS

3 quarts cold water

Coarse-grained salt

About 4 cups white vinegar

2 tablespoons superfine sugar

5 white peppercorns

5 black peppercorns

A staple of the Neapolitan pantry, this mixture of pickled vegetables is a part of the antipasto all year round, but is also a main ingredient of Insalata di Rinforzo *(page 252), a salad that is served with a traditional Christmas meal.*

Wash all the vegetables and cut them as described at left, then let them soak for 30 minutes in a bowl of cold water.

Bring the 3 quarts cold water to a boil in a large saucepan over medium heat; add coarse salt to taste, then 1 cup of the vinegar. Drain the vegetables, add them to the pot, and cook for 30 seconds. Using a strainer-skimmer, transfer the vegetables to a mason jar.

Bring the remaining 3 cups of vinegar to a boil in a small saucepan over medium heat, stir in the sugar, and simmer for 2 minutes.

Pour the hot vinegar into the jar containing the vegetables, making sure the liquid covers the vegetables completely. Add the white and black peppercorns. Let the vinegar cool completely before tightly closing the jar.

Store the jar in a cool, dark place, or better still, in the refrigerator. You can use the *giardiniera* after it has marinated for about 2 weeks.

concentrato di pomodoro

HOMEMADE TOMATO PASTE

YIELD VARIES (SEE NOTE)

2 pounds ripe tomatoes, preferably San Marzano-type plum tomatoes, or 2 pounds canned tomatoes, preferably imported Italian

OPPOSITE: *Caserta, a short distance from Naples, is the site of the Royal Palace of the Old Kingdom of Naples. The palace was built for Carlo III di Borbone by L. Vanvitelli to parallel the luxury of Versailles.*

The history of Naples was for long periods tied to the Bourbon family. In 1734, through a series of treaties, Carlo III di Borbone, son of the Bourbon king of Spain and his Italian queen, Elizabetta Farnese, heir to the Italian duchies Parma and Piacenza, became the first king of a newly independent kingdom of Naples, which included Sicily and the entire southern portion of Italy. The Bourbon kings were very popular among the Neapolitans, and included several enlightened rulers and great builders who did much to beautify the city and the rest of the kingdom.

However, Naples lost its attempts to unify Italy to the Piedmontese, who had been Naples' principal rival since Eleonora Gonzaga convinced her husband, the king of Spain, to create an independent Italian kingdom in southern Italy under her son. (She hoped to create an Italian confederation in Naples). But the next king of Spain was the son of a Savoia, who ruled Piedmont. Over the years, Piedmont's strength was increased until the Piedmont kings were able to create a unified Italy in 1860.

This tomato concentrate is an essential ingredient in any meat sauce. In Naples, even if commercial tomato paste is used, a little of the homemade concentrato *will be added or else "it will not taste right."*

If you are using fresh tomatoes, cut them into pieces. Place the fresh or canned tomatoes in a nonreactive casserole, preferably flameproof terra-cotta, over medium heat and simmer for 35 minutes. Pass the cooked tomatoes through a food mill into a crockery or glass bowl, using the disk with the smallest holes.

Return the tomatoes to the casserole and simmer over low heat for 1 hour, stirring every so often with a wooden spoon to make sure it does not scorch on the bottom. The sauce should become very thick and homogenous. Transfer it to a crockery or glass bowl to cool completely, about 1 hour.

Pour the tomato concentrate into ice-cube trays and freeze until completely hard. Remove the cubes from the tray and store in freezer bags.

When needed, remove the necessary number of tomato paste cubes and let them defrost completely before use.

NOTE: Depending on how much water is in the tomatoes, the quantity derived from 2 pounds of tomatoes will vary.

conserva di peperoni dolci

SWEET BELL PEPPER PASTE

MAKES ABOUT 1½ CUPS

4 large red bell peppers

1 heaping teaspoon fine salt

1 flat teaspoon hot red pepper flakes

Extra-virgin olive oil

This conserva *can be used to give more body to a spicy tomato sauce.*

Carefully clean the peppers, removing the stems, seeds, and filaments. Cut the peppers into 1-inch-wide strips and let them soak in a bowl of cold water for 30 minutes.

Lightly drain the peppers and place them in a heavy casserole that will hold them in two or three layers. Season the peppers with the salt and red pepper flakes. Cover the casserole and set it over medium heat. With the heat, the peppers will produce some liquid. Cook about 20 minutes, until all the liquid is absorbed; that is the moment when the peppers are soft enough to pass them through a food mill. Pass them, using the disk with the smallest holes, into a crockery or glass bowl and let stand for about 1 hour.

Once the *conserva* is cool, it is ready to be used. You can keep the *conserva* in a glass jar in the refrigerator, with a little olive oil poured over the top, for as long as 2 or 3 months.

scorze di arancia candite

CANDIED ORANGE PEEL

MAKES 32 PIECES

2 large, thick-skinned oranges, washed in lukewarm water and dried with a cotton dish towel

Large pinch of coarse-grained salt

FOR THE SYRUP

2 cups cold water

1 cup granulated sugar

2 drops freshly squeezed lemon juice

PLUS

1 cup granulated sugar

The flavor of these delicious homemade candies is far superior to any commercial version. They can be used in any number of desserts, from cannoli *to* pastiera *(pages 226 and 248), and will keep for several months in an airtight container.*

Cut off the tops and bottoms of the oranges, then use a paring knife to cut the peel of each orange from top to bottom, first into fourths, then eighths, then sixteenths. Still using the paring knife, detach each piece of orange peel. Scrape out the inner white part and soak the peels in a bowl of cold water for 1 hour, changing the water twice.

Bring a small pot of cold water to a boil over medium heat, add the coarse salt, then drain the peels and add them to the boiling water. Simmer for 2 minutes. Drain the peels, rinse them under cold running water, and place them in a crockery or glass bowl. Refrigerate, covered, until needed.

PREPARE THE SYRUP: Put the cold water, sugar, and lemon juice in a small saucepan over low heat and cook for about 1 hour, or until a thin syrup, still light in color, forms. Add the orange peels to the pan, mix very well, and remove the pan from the heat. Let the orange peels rest in the syrup until cool, about 1 hour.

Use a pair of tongs to transfer the orange peels to a crockery or glass bowl; set aside. Return the saucepan containing the leftover syrup to low heat and cook until the syrup thickens; a very thin string should form when pouring the syrup from a spoon. Pour this syrup over the orange peels and let them rest until cool, about 1 hour.

Transfer the orange peels to a piece of parchment paper, arranging them so they do not touch. Let the candied peels stand for about 1 hour, then toss them in the cup of sugar and place them in a glass jar. They are now ready to be used.

limoncello

LEMON LIQUEUR

The making of liqueurs at home is still a common activity all over Italy; however, limoncello *is made exclusively in Naples. Grain alcohol, which is most often used as the base, is perfectly legal and widely available.*

MAKES 4 CUPS

- 1 very large lemon, or 2 medium-sized lemons, washed in lukewarm water and dried with a cotton dish towel
- 1 quart pure grain alcohol or unflavored vodka
- 2 cups cold water
- 1 to 3 cups granulated sugar
- 3 or 4 drops freshly squeezed lemon juice

Wrap the lemon or lemons in a piece of cheesecloth and tie like a package, using rather strong string and leaving about 6 inches of string on both ends.

Pour the alcohol into a crockery or glass cookie jar. Holding the package by the two ends of the string, hang it in the jar, making sure the lemon does not touch the alcohol. Wrap the string ends around the mouth of the jar and tie tightly. Close the jar tightly and seal the lid by wrapping the seam with adhesive tape. Leave the jar in a cool, dark place for 1 month.

When ready, prepare a syrup combining the cold water, the 1 to 3 cups of sugar (adjust the amount according to how sweet you want the liqueur to be), and the lemon juice. Simmer over medium heat until the mixture is reduced by half, about 1 hour. Allow the syrup to rest until completely cool.

Unseal the cookie jar, remove and discard the lemon, and pour the flavored alcohol into a large jar, along with the syrup. Mix very well and pour the mixture into a bottle, filtering it through a coffee filter.

Cork the bottle and let it rest in the refrigerator for at least 1 week before using it. Serve the *limoncello* in ice-cold glasses.

ABOVE: *To make* limoncello, *lemons are suspended in a tightly sealed jar over alcohol for a month.* **RIGHT:** *Campania produces a walnut liqueur called* Nocino *that is made in Emilia-Romagna as well. Following the old custom, fresh walnuts that have not yet hardened are marinated—still in the shell—in pure grain alcohol, along with nutmeg, cinnamon, and other spices. Once the liqueur is ready, the fresh shell becomes soft enough to eat, and it is traditional to serve the shell, cut into small pieces, along with the liqueur.* **OPPOSITE:** *Glasses of* limoncello *on the incredibly beautiful roof garden of the Excelsior Hotel, which overlooks the Bay of Naples.*

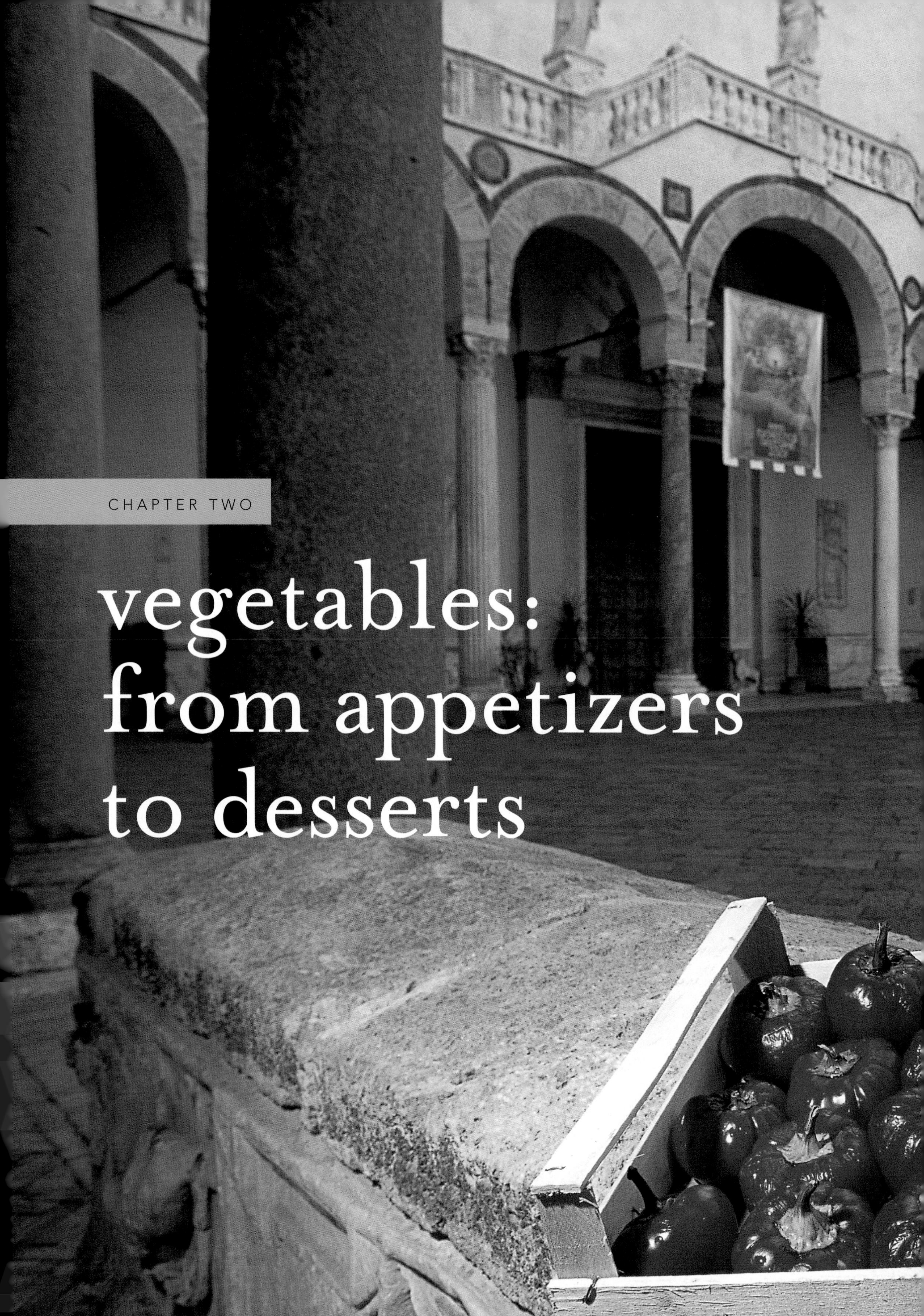

CHAPTER TWO

vegetables: from appetizers to desserts

Before becoming the absolute headquarters of the commercial dried pasta industry, Naples was known for its vegetables, and Neapolitans were known for the many ways they used them. Because their dinners were so often based on vegetables, they were given the name *mangiafoglie*, or *magnafoglie* in Neapolitan, which means leaf eaters. It is possible that this choice was a reflection of the region's conditions; they ate what was locally available. When dried pasta was developed, no other region in Italy could match the many combinations of pasta and vegetables, particularly pasta and legumes. But vegetables always have been available in this area in an incredible and wonderful variety.

Campania Felix was the name given to this region by the ancient Romans; the word *felix* means lucky more than happy in this context. The Campanians are lucky, indeed, that their soil and climate enables them to produce the best tomatoes, peppers, eggplant, and artichokes in Italy. What is even more surprising is their ability to prepare so many different dishes with these ingredients and other regional vegetables, from appetizers to main dishes and even desserts.

Both broccoli and cauliflower, including the purple cauliflower that is slowly gaining popularity beyond Naples, were developed in Campania. Although the varieties of broccoli used in Campania are unequaled elsewhere, if we want to choose the most characteristic vegetables of the region, we must name eggplant and peppers. Both are prepared in a multitude of ways: baked, fried, and stuffed—sweet and sour. Here you will even see eggplant paired with chocolate and served as a dessert (see *Parmigiana di Melanzane alla Cioccolata*, page 48).

Note that throughout Italy, a vegetable dish is never served on the same plate as a piece of meat or fish: A vegetable is always served separately. Dishes that generally go under the "vegetable" category in the United States are considered appetizers or even main courses in Campania.

It is quite common to add capers, pitted Gaeta olives, and even some anchovies preserved in oil, which have been drained and cut into small pieces, to the almost cooked artichokes. Escarole is prepared in the same way: boiled, then sautéed in olive oil (with or without garlic) and seasoned with salt and pepper, with the capers, olives, and anchovies added at the last moment. The same method is used for curly endive as well.

A smooth bunch of escarole stuffed with the same ingredients and seasonings as above makes a popular dish during the Christmas season. Bunches of escarole are parboiled in salted water, then opened like a flower, and stuffed. The bunch is closed and tied like a package and cooked through in oil and broth. This famous dish is known as *Pie' di Scarola.* There is also the *Involtini di Scarola,* for which escarole leaves are parboiled and then placed on a flat surface in the shape of several squares. The same stuffing is placed on each square, which is then rolled up like a common involtino. The cooking is finished in oil, garlic, and broth.

carciofi al tegame

ARTICHOKE CASSEROLE

SERVES 6

- 3 large artichokes
- 1 lemon, cut in half
- 1/4 cup extra-virgin olive oil
- 1 pound yellow onions, cleaned and thinly sliced
- 15 sprigs Italian parsley, leaves only
- 3 cloves garlic, peeled
- 3 tablespoons very fine unseasoned bread crumbs, preferably homemade, lightly toasted
- Salt and freshly ground black pepper
- Hot red pepper flakes to taste (optional)
- 2 medium-sized all-purpose potatoes, peeled, cut into 1-inch cubes, and left soaking in a bowl of cold water
- 1 cup lukewarm water

OPPOSITE: *Fresh cannellini beans are called* "spullicarielli" *in the Neapolitan dialect, which comes from the verb* "spulleca," *meaning to shell.*

PRECEDING PAGES: *A box of* papacelle *in the courtyard of the Cathedral of Salerno. These peppers are used in dishes fresh, sautéed with seasonings, or preserved in wine vinegar.*

Soak the artichokes for 30 minutes in a large bowl of cold water containing the squeezed lemon halves. Clean the artichokes, removing the tough outer leaves, chokes, and hair (see page 263), and cut them into eighths. Return the artichokes to the acidulated water until needed.

Using 1 tablespoon of the oil, heavily grease the bottom of a casserole and arrange all the onions in it. Drain the artichokes, place them on top of the onions, and drizzle with the remaining oil.

Finely chop the parsley and garlic together on a cutting board, then transfer them to a small crockery or glass bowl. Add the bread crumbs and season with salt, pepper, and the red pepper flakes if using. Mix very well.

Drain the potatoes and distribute them among the artichoke pieces, then sprinkle the parsley mixture all over.

Place the casserole over medium heat for 2 minutes, without stirring, then add the lukewarm water, cover the casserole, and cook it for 25 minutes. By this time, all the vegetables should be cooked.

Gently mix the vegetables, transfer them to a serving platter, and serve hot.

carciofi ripieni

STUFFED ARTICHOKES

SERVES 6

- 6 large artichokes
- 1 large lemon, cut in half
- 2 extra-large eggs, lightly beaten
- 20 sprigs Italian parsley, leaves only, finely chopped
- 5 tablespoons freshly grated Parmigiano or Pecorino Romano cheese
- 4 slices (about 2 ounces) white bread, crusts removed
- Salt and freshly ground black pepper
- 6 tablespoons extra-virgin olive oil
- 12 large scallions, white parts only, cut into thin disks then coarsely chopped
- 1 1/2 to 2 cups water, or 2 cups completely defatted chicken broth, preferably homemade

Soak the artichokes for 30 minutes in a large bowl of cold water containing the squeezed lemon halves. Clean the artichokes, removing the tough outer leaves, chokes, and hair (see page 263).

Cut off the stems of the artichokes and coarsely chop them, returning the top part of the artichokes to the cold water. Place the chopped artichoke stems, eggs, parsley, and Parmigiano in a crockery or glass bowl and mix very well. Cut up the bread and add it to the bowl. Season with salt and pepper, add 2 tablespoons of the oil, and mix again. Let the bread soak for 10 minutes.

Remove the artichokes from the water, dry them with paper towels, and then lightly season the insides with salt. Place one-sixth of the stuffing in the cleaned pocket of each artichoke.

Place the scallions in a heavy casserole that is large enough to hold all the artichokes standing up in one layer. Add the remaining 4 tablespoons oil and set the casserole over medium heat. Sauté the scallions for 2 minutes; then arrange the artichokes over them. Add 1 1/2 cups of the water or broth, cover the casserole, and continue to cook the artichokes over medium heat for 45 minutes, or more if needed. The artichokes should become very soft. Be sure they do not stick to the bottom of the casserole; add the other 1/2 cup water if needed.

Ladle some of the juices, with the scallions, over each artichoke. Remove the casserole from the heat and let the artichokes rest for 5 minutes before serving warm (or at room temperature) with some of the juices.

OPPOSITE: *Large artichokes, perfect for* Carciofi Ripieni.

carciofi a "fungetiello"

ARTICHOKES IN THE STYLE OF MUSHROOMS

SERVES 6

4 large artichokes

1 large lemon, cut in half

1/4 cup extra-virgin olive oil

2 tablespoons (1 ounce) unsalted butter

2 large cloves garlic, peeled and left whole

Salt and freshly ground black pepper

About 1/2 cup chicken broth, preferably homemade

1/4 cup capers preserved in wine vinegar, drained

1/4 pound Gaeta olives or Calamata olives, pitted; if using the Calamata, cut into pieces

10 sprigs Italian parsley, leaves only, coarsely chopped

Soak the artichokes for 30 minutes in a large bowl of cold water containing the squeezed lemon halves. Clean the artichokes, removing the tough outer leaves, chokes, and hair (see page 263), and cut the artichokes into fourths or eighths, depending on how big they are. Put them back in the acidulated water.

Heat the oil and butter in a heavy casserole, preferably flameproof terracotta or enamel-coated, over medium heat. When the oil is lukewarm, drain the artichokes and add them to the casserole along with the garlic. Season with salt and pepper and lightly sauté for 2 minutes. Cover the casserole, lower the heat, and cook for about 15 minutes, turning the artichokes several times and adding a few tablespoons of the broth each time as needed.

By this time, the artichokes should be almost cooked and still very juicy. Add the capers and olives, and cook for 2 to 3 minutes more. Just before removing the casserole from the heat, sprinkle the parsley over the artichokes and mix very well.

Transfer the contents of the casserole to a warmed serving platter, and serve hot.

tubetti e cavolfiore

PASTA AND CAULIFLOWER

SERVES 4 TO 6

1 large head cauliflower, cleaned, all green leaves removed, cut into florets

1/2 cup extra-virgin olive oil

4 large cloves garlic, peeled and cut into thirds

Freshly ground black pepper

Fine salt

20 sprigs Italian parsley, leaves only

Coarse-grained salt

1/2 pound dried short tubular pasta, such as *tubetti* or *pennette* (small penne), preferably imported Italian

TO SERVE

Freshly ground black pepper

15 fresh basil leaves, torn into thirds

ABOVE: *At the market of Porta Nolese, cauliflower, kale, and "friarelli," a leafy green that is similar to broccoli raab.* **OPPOSITE:** *A platter of* Finocchi al Sugo. **FOLLOWING PAGES:** *The view from the famous Villa Angelina of the Achille Lauro. The peninsula, which is covered with vines, orange and lemon trees, was ceated by Lauro, who was a shipping magnate, in the shape of a boat. Here is the prow! Capri, Ischia, and Procida may be seen across the bay.*

Soak the cauliflower florets in a bowl of cold water for 30 minutes. Place a large skillet containing the oil over medium heat, and when the oil is lukewarm, add the garlic and sauté until lightly golden, less than 2 minutes. You may discard or keep the garlic in the oil, to your taste.

Transfer the cauliflower from the water to the hot oil, trying to retain a few drops of water on the cauliflower. Be very careful because the oil will splash a little bit. Immediately cover the skillet and cook for 3 minutes. Season with pepper and mix very well.

Cover again and cook for about 15 minutes more, or until the florets are completely cooked but still retain their shape and are lightly golden. If the lid to the skillet fits tightly, you will have enough steam so you won't need to add any water; otherwise, add a few drops of cold water as needed. When the cauliflower is almost ready, season with fine salt, sprinkle the parsley all over, and mix very well.

While you cook the cauliflower, bring a large pot of cold water to a boil. Add coarse salt to taste, then add the pasta and cook it for 8 to 11 minutes (1 minute less than for al dente). Drain the pasta and add it to the skillet, still over the heat. Mix very well and cook for 1 minute more.

Transfer the contents to a warmed serving platter. At this point, many of the florets will come apart to form a sauce. Serve topped with more freshly ground black pepper and the basil leaves.

finocchi al sugo

FENNEL CASSEROLE

SERVES 6

6 fennel bulbs, cleaned, all the feathery leaves removed

1 lemon, cut in half

6 tablespoons extra-virgin olive oil

3 large cloves garlic, peeled and finely chopped or left whole

Salt and freshly ground black pepper

1/2 cup cold water

10 sprigs Italian parsley, leaves only, finely chopped

This is a clean preparation, with very surprising results. As it cooks, the fennel loses its licorice taste and becomes very sweet, with a mellow aftertaste.

Cut the fennel bulbs into eighths and soak them for 30 minutes in a bowl of cold water containing the squeezed lemon halves.

Heat the oil in a large skillet over medium heat, and when the oil is warm, lightly drain the fennel and add it to the skillet, along with the garlic. Sauté the fennel until lightly golden on both sides, and season with salt and pepper.

Add the cold water, cover the skillet, and cook for 10 minutes more, shaking the pan several times to be sure the fennel does not stick.

By this time, the fennel should be almost cooked and soft. Sprinkle it with the parsley, cover the skillet again, and cook for 1 minute more. The fennel should be very soft but still retain its shape; almost no liquid should be left in the pan.

Transfer the fennel to a serving platter and serve hot.

Most beans were brought to Europe from Latin America after the discovery of the New World, but fava beans are indigenous to the Middle East and the Mediterranean region. Dried fava beans are available year-round, while the fresh ones have only a short season during early spring. Look for tender, fresh beans, still in the pods, at grocery stores with large produce sections or at gourmet markets. When choosing fresh favas, select those with pods that aren't bulging with beans, as this indicates age.

fave fresche al tegame

FRESH FAVA BEAN CASSEROLE

SERVES 4

2 pounds fresh fava beans, unshelled, to yield about 1 pound, shelled

Coarse-grained salt

1/4 cup extra-virgin olive oil

2 large cloves garlic, peeled and left whole

Salt and freshly ground black pepper

Large pinch of hot red pepper flakes

10 sprigs Italian parsley, leaves only, finely chopped

Soak the shelled beans in a bowl of cold water containing a large pinch of coarse salt for 30 minutes. This will remove the bitter taste if the beans are not very fresh. Heat the olive oil in a skillet over medium heat, add the garlic, and sauté it for 1 minute or until very light in color.

Drain the beans, rinse them under cold running water, and add them to the skillet. Season with salt, pepper, and the red pepper flakes. Sauté the beans, stirring them frequently with a wooden spoon, for 15 minutes or longer, until they are rather soft but still retain the light green skins attached to the pulp. Add a little warm water as needed.

Sprinkle the parsley over the beans, mix, and transfer the casserole to a serving platter. Serve hot.

insalata di fagioli serpenti alla napoletana

LONG BEAN SALAD

SERVES 6 TO 8

2 pounds long beans or string beans

Coarse-grained salt

3 large cloves garlic, peeled and cut in half

Large pinch of hot red pepper flakes

2 tablespoons red wine vinegar

1 large yellow onion, cleaned and sliced into thin rings

6 tablespoons extra-virgin olive oil

Salt and freshly ground black pepper

1/4 pound pitted Gaeta or Calamata olives

15 sprigs Italian parsley, leaves only, coarsely chopped

Soak the beans in a bowl of cold water for 30 minutes. Bring a large pot of cold water to a boil over medium heat, adding coarse salt to taste. Meanwhile, drain the beans, and if you are using long beans, cut them into thirds. Add the beans to the boiling water along with the garlic, red pepper flakes, vinegar, and onion. Simmer until the beans are cooked but still have a very light bite, 6 to 10 minutes depending on their thickness.

Drain the beans, garlic, and onion and transfer them to a serving platter. Season with the oil and salt and pepper to taste, and add the olives. Mix very well, sprinkle with the parsley, and serve hot.

melanzane "a scapece"

MARINATED EGGPLANT

SERVES 8 TO 10

6 medium-sized eggplants, about 8 ounces each

Coarse-grained salt

3 large cloves garlic, peeled and finely chopped

Salt and freshly ground black pepper

Several pinches of hot red pepper flakes

Several pinches of dried oregano

1/2 cup extra-virgin olive oil

3 tablespoons strong red wine vinegar

Clean the eggplants and cut them horizontally into 1/2-inch-thick slices. Bring a large casserole of cold water to a boil over medium heat, add coarse salt to taste, then the eggplant slices, and simmer for 4 minutes or longer, depending on their size. The eggplants must be cooked but still perfectly retain their shape.

Transfer the eggplant slices to one or two serving platters lined with paper towels. Let them rest a little while to be sure most of the water is absorbed.

Make a layer of eggplant in a crockery or glass bowl. Sprinkle with some of the chopped garlic, followed by salt, pepper, red pepper flakes, and oregano to taste. Finally, drizzle over some of the oil and vinegar. Repeat, making layers of eggplant and seasonings, until all the eggplant is used up. Cover the bowl and refrigerate it at least overnight before serving.

The marinated eggplant will last several days in the refrigerator.

"mulignane picchi-pacchio"

STEWED EGGPLANT

SERVES 6 TO 8

6 medium-sized eggplants, about 8 ounces each

Coarse-grained salt

2 pounds cherry tomatoes

1/2 cup extra-virgin olive oil

2 cups vegetable oil (preferably a mixture of half sunflower oil, half corn oil)

About 1 cup unbleached all-purpose flour

3 large cloves garlic, peeled and cut into slivers

Salt and freshly ground black pepper

Fresh basil leaves, or fresh or dried oregano

Peel the eggplants and cut them into strips about 4 inches long and 1/2 inch thick. Arrange the eggplant on a platter, scatter with coarse salt, and place another platter on top as a weight. Let rest for 1 hour.

Meanwhile, preheat the oven to 375°F. Place the cherry tomatoes in a baking dish and bake for 20 minutes. (In this way, the cherry tomatoes become firmer, much closer to the texture of the ones we find in Italy, which have much thinner skins.)

Heat half the olive oil and all the vegetable oil in a large skillet over medium heat. Rinse the eggplant pieces under cold running water and pat them dry with paper towels. Very lightly flour the pieces by placing them, a few at a time, in a colander with a little of the flour and shaking the colander so the excess flour falls out.

When the oil is hot (about 375°F), add some of the eggplant pieces and fry them until light in color all over, about 2 minutes. Transfer the eggplant to a serving platter lined with paper towels to absorb excess oil. Fry all the eggplant in the same way.

Meanwhile, prepare the sauce: Heat the remaining 1/4 cup olive oil in a large casserole over medium heat, and when the oil is warm, add the garlic and lightly sauté for a few seconds; the garlic should still be very light in color. Add the cherry tomatoes, raise the heat, season with salt and pepper, and cook for 15 minutes, mixing every so often with a wooden spoon.

Add the eggplant, mix very well, and cook for 2 minutes more. Add the basil or oregano and mix again. The tomatoes should break up into pieces but not form a uniform sauce.

Taste for salt and pepper, mix again, and transfer to a serving platter. Serve hot.

panini di melanzane

EGGPLANT "SANDWICHES"

SERVES 8 AS AN APPETIZER

2 medium-sized eggplants, about 8 ounces each

Coarse-grained salt

1 all-purpose potato, about 6 ounces

About 1 1/2 cups vegetable oil (preferably a mixture of half sunflower oil, half corn oil)

Unbleached all-purpose flour

1 extra-large egg, lightly beaten

3 tablespoons freshly grated Parmigiano

5 sprigs Italian parsley, leaves only, finely chopped

Fine salt and freshly ground black pepper

TO FRY THE "SANDWICHES"

2 extra-large eggs

Pinch of fine salt

Unbleached all-purpose flour

TO SERVE

Salt

1 large lemon, cut into thin slices

Peel and clean the eggplants, discarding the ends. Cut each one lengthwise into four thick slices and arrange them on a platter. Sprinkle with coarse salt, put a platter on top as a weight, and let stand for 30 minutes.

Meanwhile, boil the potato in salted water until very soft, about 25 minutes.

Drain the eggplant slices, rinse them under cold running water, and pat them dry with paper towels. Heat the oil in a skillet over medium heat, and when it reaches 375°F, lightly flour the eggplant slices and fry them until lightly golden on both sides, about 2 minutes total. Transfer the eggplant to a serving platter lined with paper towels to absorb excess oil. Leave the oil in the skillet.

Peel the potato and pass it through a potato ricer into a crockery or glass bowl, using the disk with the smallest holes. Add the egg, Parmigiano, parsley, and salt and pepper to taste. Mix very well with a wooden spoon. Spread the potato mixture over four slices of the eggplant, then cover them with the remaining four slices. Cut each "sandwich" into two pieces.

FRY THE "SANDWICHES": Using a fork, lightly beat the eggs and the fine salt in a bowl. Reheat the oil in the skillet, and when it is hot, about 375°F, lightly flour each sandwich, dip it in the eggs, and fry on both sides until lightly golden.

Transfer the sandwiches to a serving dish lined with paper towels to absorb all the excess oil, then lift them off the paper and serve sprinkled with a little salt, with the lemon slices.

crostini di melanzane

EGGPLANT CANAPÉS

SERVES 6

1 very large round eggplant, about 1 1/2 pounds

2 large cloves garlic, peeled and finely chopped

1 1/2 teaspoons fine salt

1/2 teaspoon freshly ground black pepper

1/4 cup extra-virgin olive oil

Large pinch of dried oregano

TO BAKE THE EGGPLANT

2 tablespoons cold water

1 tablespoon extra-virgin olive oil

Salt and freshly ground black pepper

TO SERVE

3 slices country-style bread, each cut into 4 pieces, lightly toasted on both sides if desired

5 sprigs Italian parsley, leaves only, coarsely chopped

Preheat the oven to 375°F. Wash the eggplant very well and dry it with paper towels.

Add the garlic, fine salt, pepper, oil, and oregano to a small crockery or glass bowl and mix very well. Use an apple corer to make holes of different depths, from 1 inch to a maximum of 2 inches, all over the eggplant. Do not discard the pieces of eggplant that remain inside the apple corer, because they will become the "corks" for the holes. Insert the garlic mixture in the different holes and close each one with its cork.

BAKE THE EGGPLANT: Mix the water and oil together in a small bowl. Place the eggplant in a glass baking dish, brush it with the oil mixture, and season it with salt and pepper. Bake for 1 hour, or until the eggplant is very soft to the touch.

Transfer the eggplant to a cutting board, peel off the skin, and put the pulp on a plate. Use a fork to mix and smooth the eggplant pulp; then while it is still very warm, spread some of the pulp mixture over each slice of bread.

Serve warm, sprinkled with the parsley.

RIGHT: *Eggplants, a regional favorite, for sale in an open-air market.*

melanzane all'aglio

EGGPLANT IN GARLIC SAUCE

SERVES 6

3 long thin eggplants, no larger than 6 ounces each, stems removed

About 12 tablespoons extra-virgin olive oil

Fine salt

FOR THE SAUCE

3 cloves garlic, peeled and finely chopped

1/4 cup red wine vinegar, preferably homemade (page 17)

2 tablespoons extra-virgin olive oil

Salt and abundant freshly ground black pepper

20 large fresh mint leaves, torn into thirds

Cut the eggplants in half lengthwise. Use a paring knife to make a diamond pattern on each cut side, and sprinkle with a little fine salt.

Place 3 tablespoons of the oil in a skillet that has a lid and is large enough to hold the six eggplant halves in one layer, and set it over medium heat. When the oil is hot, arrange the eggplants in the skillet with the cut sides down. Cover the skillet and sauté for 1 minute, adding a little more oil when the previous oil is completely absorbed by the eggplant and using a metal spatula to shift the eggplant halves so they do not stick to the skillet.

Cover again and repeat, adding oil as needed, until the cut sides are golden and the eggplants are almost cooked through.

Turn the eggplant halves over, cover again, and cook until the rounded sides are completely soft, 4 minutes or more depending on the size of the eggplants. Transfer the eggplants to a serving platter with the cut sides facing up.

PREPARE THE SAUCE: Mix the garlic, vinegar, and oil together; season with salt and abundant pepper, and add the mint leaves. Mix again, then pour the sauce over the eggplant.

Let rest for at least 15 minutes before serving. The eggplant may be prepared in advance and kept, covered, in the refrigerator; remove from the refrigerator 1 hour before serving.

melanzane alla pizzaiola

EGGPLANT, *PIZZAIOLA* STYLE

SERVES 4 TO 6

4 eggplants, about 6 ounces each

Coarse-grained salt

5 tablespoons extra-virgin olive oil

3 large cloves garlic, peeled and cut into slivers

1 1/2 pounds ripe tomatoes, blanched (see page 263), skin and seeds removed; or 1 1/2 pounds drained canned tomatoes, preferably imported Italian, all seeds removed

Salt and freshly ground black pepper

1 1/2 cups vegetable oil (preferably a mixture of half sunflower oil, half corn oil)

1 cup unbleached all-purpose flour

About 20 large fresh basil leaves, torn into thirds

1 flat tablespoon fresh oregano leaves, or 1 scant teaspoon dried oregano

Peel the eggplants and cut them into thirds lengthwise. Place the slices on a platter in layers, sprinkling coarse salt over each layer. Cover the eggplant with a heavy platter and let rest for 1 hour.

To prepare the sauce, heat the olive oil in a nonreactive saucepan over medium heat. When the oil is lukewarm, add the garlic and lightly sauté for a few seconds; the garlic should still be light in color. Add the tomatoes and season with salt and pepper. Let the sauce cook over medium heat for about 5 minutes, leaving the tomatoes in chunks; this is not a smooth sauce. Let rest until needed.

Preheat the oven to 375°F.

Drain the eggplant and rinse it very well under cold running water to remove all the salt; then pat it dry with paper towels.

Heat the vegetable oil in a large skillet over medium heat, and when it is hot, about 375°F, lightly flour the eggplant and fry it, a few slices at a time, until golden on both sides, about 2 minutes.

Transfer the eggplant to a serving platter lined with paper towels to absorb excess oil.

Lightly oil a glass baking dish and arrange all the eggplant in it, in as many layers as needed. Sprinkle the eggplant with the basil and oregano, then pour the tomato sauce on top. Bake for 15 minutes or until the sauce is rather reduced.

Serve directly from the baking dish.

melanzane ripiene

STUFFED EGGPLANT

SERVES 6

Coarse-grained salt

3 long thin eggplants, not more than 6 ounces each, stems removed

FOR THE STUFFING

3 whole anchovies preserved in salt, boned and rinsed under cold running water; or 6 anchovy fillets packed in oil, drained

4 heaping tablespoons capers preserved in wine vinegar, drained

3 medium-sized cloves garlic, peeled

Freshly ground black pepper

1 tablespoon extra-virgin olive oil

TO BAKE THE EGGPLANTS

3 tablespoons extra-virgin olive oil

Salt and freshly ground black pepper

Bring a large pot of cold water to a boil and add coarse salt to taste, then add the whole eggplants and simmer for 10 minutes. Transfer the eggplants to a plate, cover with paper towels dampened in cold water, and let stand until cool, about 30 minutes.

Preheat the oven to 375°F.

PREPARE THE STUFFING: Finely chop the anchovies, capers, and garlic all together on a cutting board. Transfer to a small bowl and add black pepper to taste and the oil. Mix very well.

There are two methods for stuffing the eggplants. Either use an apple corer to make holes of different depths, from 1 inch to a maximum of 2 inches, all over the cooled eggplants. Reserve the pieces of eggplant that remain inside the apple corer to use as "corks." Insert the stuffing in the various holes and close each one with its cork.

Alternatively, cut each of the eggplants in half vertically, spread the stuffing onto three of the cut halves, then reassemble the eggplants, tying them like a salami (see page 263).

BAKE THE EGGPLANTS: Place the stuffed eggplants in a glass baking dish, pour 1 tablespoon of the oil over each, and season with salt and pepper. Bake for 35 minutes, or until the eggplants are very soft.

Transfer the eggplants to a serving platter and let rest for at least 15 minutes before serving.

"mulignane a scarpone"

EGGPLANT SHAPED LIKE A BOOT

SERVES 6

6 long thin eggplants, about 6 ounces each, stems removed

Coarse-grained salt

1 large clove garlic, peeled

10 sprigs Italian parsley, leaves only

6 tablespoons extra-virgin olive oil

Salt and freshly ground black pepper

3 tablespoons capers preserved in wine vinegar, drained

3 ounces Gaeta or Calamata olives, pitted and cut into small pieces

2 whole anchovies preserved in salt, boned and rinsed under cold running water, and cut into small pieces; or 4 anchovy fillets packed in oil, drained and cut into small pieces

3 tablespoons very fine unseasoned bread crumbs, preferably homemade, lightly toasted

TO BAKE THE EGGPLANTS

1/4 cup extra-virgin olive oil

1/2 cup cold water

Cut the eggplants in half vertically. Place the eggplant halves, cut sides facing up, on a platter.

Sprinkle some coarse salt over the eggplants, cover them with a second heavy platter, and let rest for 1 hour.

Rinse the eggplants well under cold running water to remove all the salt, and pat them dry with paper towels. Use a spoon to scoop out the pulp from the eggplants, being careful to leave the skins intact, with no holes. Reserve the skins (the *scarponi*) to be stuffed later.

Coarsely chop all the eggplant pulp and save it for the stuffing. Finely chop the garlic and parsley together on a cutting board.

Heat the oil in a medium-sized casserole over medium heat. When the oil is warm, add the parsley mixture and sauté for 1 minute. Put in the eggplant pulp and cook for 15 minutes, stirring every so often with a wooden spoon, and season with salt and pepper to taste. Add the capers, olives, and anchovies, and cook for 2 minutes more. Add half of the bread crumbs and mix well, then transfer the contents of the casserole to a crockery or glass bowl and let cool completely, about 30 minutes.

BAKE THE EGGPLANTS: Preheat the oven to 375°F and lightly oil a baking dish. Stuff each eggplant shell with the cooled eggplant mixture. Arrange the eggplants in the baking dish, and pour the 1/4 cup oil over them. Pour the water into the baking dish (but not over the eggplant). Bake for 40 minutes, or until the tops are lightly golden and the stuffing is still very soft to the touch. Sprinkle with the remaining 1 1/2 tablespoons bread crumbs.

Transfer the eggplants to a serving platter and serve hot, or after a few hours, at room temperature.

melanzane in dolce e forte

EGGPLANT IN A SWEET-AND-SOUR SAUCE

SERVES 4

4 long thin eggplants, about 6 ounces each

1 tablespoon coarse-grained salt

1 cup vegetable oil (preferably a mixture of half sunflower oil, half corn oil)

1/2 cup extra-virgin olive oil

6 tablespoons strong red wine vinegar, preferably homemade (page 17)

Salt and freshly ground black pepper

2 teaspoons superfine sugar

TO SERVE

Fresh basil leaves

Italian parsley leaves

Peel the eggplants and cut them horizontally into 1/2-inch-thick slices. Arrange the eggplant slices on a platter and sprinkle with the coarse salt. Place a second platter on top as a weight and let rest for 1 hour.

Drain the eggplant and rinse the slices well under cold running water to remove all the salt; pat them dry with paper towels.

Heat the vegetable oil in a skillet over medium heat, and when it is hot, about 375°F, fry the eggplant slices, a few at a time, until golden all over. Transfer the eggplant to a serving platter lined with paper towels to absorb excess oil.

Discard the vegetable oil in the skillet and add the olive oil while the pan is still very hot; set it over medium heat. Add the vinegar and salt and pepper to taste. When the vinegar is half evaporated, add the sugar, mix very well, and after removing the paper towels beneath the eggplant slices, immediately pour the sauce over the eggplant.

Let the eggplant marinate in the sauce for at least 1 hour, sprinkle it with the basil and parsley leaves, and serve at room temperature.

parmigiana di melanzane alla cioccolata *or* timballini di melanzane al cioccolato

LITTLE EGGPLANT TIMBALES STUFFED WITH CHOCOLATE

MAKES 6 TIMBALES

4 eggplants, about 6 ounces each

1 tablespoon coarse-grained salt

1 cup unbleached all-purpose flour

Very large pinch of ground cinnamon

About 1 cup extra-virgin olive oil

FOR THE STUFFING

8 ounces semi-sweet chocolate, cut into small pieces

1/3 cup heavy cream

4 ounces candied citron, cut into small pieces

2 ounces finely ground Italian ladyfingers *(savoiardi)*

FOR THE SYRUP

1 cup cold water

1/2 cup sugar

2 drops freshly squeezed lemon juice

TO BAKE THE TIMBALES

Unsalted butter and sugar, for the molds

FOR THE SAUCE (OPTIONAL)

8 ounces semi-sweet chocolate, cut into small pieces

1/3 cup heavy cream

TO SERVE

2 tablespoons superfine sugar (optional)

Candied orange peel, preferably homemade (page 25)

Peel the eggplants and cut them vertically into very thin slices. Place the slices in a bowl of cold water with the coarse salt and let them soak for 30 minutes.

Mix the flour with the cinnamon and spread it over a pastry board. Drain the eggplant slices, pat them dry with paper towels, and lightly coat them with the aromatic flour.

Heat the oil in a skillet over medium heat and when it is hot, about 375°F, lightly fry all the eggplant slices, a few at a time, and transfer them to a platter lined with paper towels to absorb excess oil.

PREPARE THE STUFFING: Place the chocolate and heavy cream in a small saucepan and set the saucepan next to a lighted burner on low heat for about 15 minutes. In this way, the chocolate will melt very slowly, incorporating the heavy cream to form a smooth and rather dense sauce.

PREPARE THE SYRUP: Combine the cold water, sugar, and lemon juice in a skillet over medium heat. Simmer for about 10 minutes; the syrup should not be very thick and should still be very light in color. Brush the tops of the eggplant slices with the syrup; repeat twice.

When the chocolate mixture is smooth, remove it from the heat and add the candied citron and ground ladyfingers. Mix very well.

BAKE THE TIMBALES: Preheat the oven to 375°F. Lightly butter the insides of six custard cups or ramekins and coat them with sugar. Line the sides and then the bottom of the molds with the eggplant slices, the syrup-coated sides facing inward. Fill each mold halfway with stuffing, top with a thin layer of eggplant, add the remainder of the stuffing, and finish with another thin layer of eggplant. Let the molds rest for a few minutes before baking them.

Bake the *timballini* for 25 minutes. Meanwhile, if desired, prepare a chocolate sauce by slowly melting together the chocolate and heavy cream as described in the directions for the stuffing above.

When the *timballini* are done, unmold them onto a dessert plate and let them cool for a few minutes. Sprinkle with the superfine sugar or drizzle with the chocolate sauce, and top with the candied orange peel. Serve immediately.

ABOVE: *These eggplant timbales are stuffed with chocolate and may be topped with superfine sugar or a chocolate sauce and candied orange peel.*

scaloppine di melanzane

EGGPLANT *SCALOPPINE*

SERVES 4 TO 6

4 eggplants, no larger than 6 ounces each

About 1 tablespoon coarse-grained salt

2 extra-large eggs

Fine salt and freshly ground black pepper

Large pinch of dried oregano

2 cups vegetable oil (preferably a mixture of half sunflower oil, half corn oil)

1 cup unbleached all-purpose flour

1 cup very fine unseasoned bread crumbs, preferably homemade, lightly toasted

TO SERVE

Fine salt

1 lemon, cut into wedges

Peel the eggplants and cut them vertically into slices a little less than 1/2 inch thick. Arrange the eggplant slices on a platter, sprinkle the coarse salt over them, and place another platter on top as a weight. Let rest for 1 hour.

Drain the eggplant slices, rinse them under cold running water to be sure all the salt is washed off, and dry them with paper towels.

Use a fork to lightly beat the eggs with fine salt and pepper to taste and the oregano in a small bowl. Heat the oil in a skillet over medium heat, and when it is hot, about 375°F, lightly flour the eggplant slices on both sides, dip them in the egg mixture, then in the bread crumbs, and fry them until lightly golden. Transfer to a serving platter lined with paper towels to absorb excess oil.

When all the eggplant is on the platter, remove the paper towels, sprinkle with fine salt, and serve hot with the lemon wedges.

VARIATION

Sometimes the bread crumbs are omitted.

pasta e piselli

PASTA AND PEAS

SERVES 4 TO 6

6 tablespoons extra-virgin olive oil

1/4 pound prosciutto or pancetta, coarsely ground or cut into very small pieces

20 very large sprigs Italian parsley, leaves only, coarsely chopped

12 small spring onions or scallions, white parts only, cleaned and coarsely chopped

Heat the oil in a large casserole over medium heat. When the oil is warm, add the prosciutto and lightly sauté it for 2 minutes. Add the parsley and spring onions and sauté for 2 minutes more, mixing constantly with a wooden spoon and adding the 1/2 cup broth as needed.

Season with salt and pepper. Add the peas and sauté for 2 minutes more.

Add the pasta and enough boiling water to cover it by 1 inch. Simmer, mixing every so often with a wooden spoon, for about 20 minutes.

1/2 cup completely defatted chicken broth, preferably homemade

Salt and freshly ground black pepper

1/2 pound shelled fresh peas or frozen "tiny tender" peas (see Note, below)

1/2 pound dried short pasta of different types (*pasta mischiata* or *munnezzaglia*), broken-up vermicelli or *perciatelli*, or whole *tubettini*, preferably imported Italian

TO SERVE

Italian parsley leaves

Taste for salt and pepper. Do not expect the pasta to cook al dente; it will be soft but not mushy, and the sauce will be completely absorbed by the pasta.

Serve hot, directly from the casserole, with several parsley leaves topping each serving.

piselli con "la ventresca"

PEAS WITH PANCETTA

SERVES 6

1 large yellow onion, cleaned and coarsely chopped

2 tablespoons (1 ounce) unsalted butter, instead of the traditional lard

2 tablespoons extra-virgin olive oil

1/4 pound pancetta, coarsely ground or cut into very small pieces

Salt and freshly ground black pepper

2 pounds shelled fresh peas or frozen "tiny tender" peas (see Note)

In the title of this recipe, ventresca *refers to pancetta, but the word can also refer to a specific cut of veal tripe.*

Place the onion, butter, and oil in a medium-sized casserole and set the casserole over medium heat. Sauté for 10 minutes or more, until the onion is translucent. Add the pancetta, season with salt and pepper, and sauté for 5 minutes more.

Add the peas and cook them until soft, about 15 minutes for fresh and 5 minutes for frozen, adding some lukewarm water as needed. The pea mixture should not be very wet. Serve hot.

NOTE: If using fresh peas, soak them in a bowl of cold water containing 1 tablespoon of flour, dissolved, for 30 minutes. This will tenderize their skin. If using frozen peas, do not defrost them before adding them to the sauce, or they will become too mushy.

VARIATION

Lightly beat two extra-large eggs with 3 tablespoons freshly grated local pecorino or Pecorino Romano cheese. Temper the egg mixture with 3 tablespoons hot water, then add this mixture to the peas just 2 minutes before they will be removed from the heat. Mix well and bring to a boil to finish. This version is a must for Easter, but it is also enjoyed by some year-round.

spaghetti di magro

PASTA WITH VEGETABLE SAUCE

SERVES 4 TO 6

1/2 cup extra-virgin olive oil

4 whole anchovies preserved in salt, boned, rinsed under cold running water, and cut into fourths; or 8 anchovy fillets packed in oil, drained and cut in half

3 large cloves garlic, peeled and finely chopped

4 heaping tablespoons capers preserved in wine vinegar, drained

1/4 pound Gaeta olives, pitted and cut into thirds

Salt and freshly ground black pepper

TO COOK THE PASTA

Coarse-grained salt

1 pound dried long pasta, such as spaghetti, vermicelli, or *perciatelli*, preferably imported Italian

TO SERVE

15 sprigs Italian parsley, leaves only, coarsely chopped

Pour the oil into a crockery or glass bowl and add the anchovies, garlic, capers, and olives. Season with salt and pepper and mix very well. Cover the bowl and refrigerate for at least 1 hour.

COOK THE PASTA: Bring a large pot of cold water to a boil over medium heat, add coarse salt to taste, then add the pasta and cook until al dente, 9 to 12 minutes depending on the brand.

Drain the pasta, transfer it to a large bowl, then pour the chilled sauce over it. Mix very well, transfer to a large serving platter, sprinkle the parsley over the pasta, and serve hot.

VARIATIONS

1. Use fresh or dried oregano instead of the parsley.
2. Add 1/2 pound fresh tomatoes, blanched (see page 263), skin and seeds removed, cut into pieces, along with the parsley or oregano.

OPPOSITE: *Gaeta olives are the olives most used by Neapolitans, in both uncooked and cooked dishes.*

peperoni al grattè

BAKED PEPPER CASSEROLE

SERVES 6

- 1/2 cup extra-virgin olive oil
- 6 bell peppers of different colors but not green
- 1/4 cup capers preserved in wine vinegar, drained
- 1/4 pound pitted Gaeta or Calamata olives, cut into small pieces
- 6 tablespoons very fine unseasoned bread crumbs, preferably homemade, lightly toasted
- Salt and freshly ground black pepper

Preheat the oven to 375°F, and use 1 tablespoon of the oil to coat the bottom and sides of a glass baking dish, preferably flameproof terra-cotta.

Clean the peppers, removing the stems, seeds, and all the filaments. Cut the peppers into 1/2-inch-wide strips and soak them in a bowl of cold water for 15 minutes.

Drain the peppers and arrange one-third of them in a layer on the bottom of the baking dish. Over the peppers, arrange one-third of the capers and one-third of the olives, then sprinkle with 2 tablespoons of the bread crumbs. Season with salt and pepper. Repeat for two more layers.

Drizzle the remaining 7 tablespoons oil over the top layer.

Bake for 35 minutes or more, until the peppers are cooked through and soft and golden on top. Serve directly from the baking dish.

peperoni in padella

SAUTÉED PEPPERS

SERVES 6

3 yellow bell peppers

3 red bell peppers

6 tablespoons extra-virgin olive oil

1 large clove garlic, peeled and left whole (optional)

Salt and freshly ground black pepper

1/4 cup red wine vinegar

TO SERVE

15 sprigs Italian parsley, leaves only, coarsely chopped

Rinse the bell peppers under cold running water, then pat them dry with paper towels. Roast them over hot ash or a burner according to the directions on page 57, removing and discarding the skins as instructed. Cut off the tops of the peppers, remove and discard all the seeds and filaments inside, then cut the peppers into 2-inch pieces.

Heat the oil in a large skillet over medium heat, and when the oil is warm, add the garlic if using. Sauté for a few seconds, then add the bell peppers, raise the heat, and sauté for about 5 minutes, stirring frequently with a wooden spoon. Season with salt and pepper to taste.

The bell peppers are ready when they are no longer completely soft, but still have some texture. Remove the garlic, if used, add the vinegar, and let it evaporate for 20 seconds. Serve hot, with the parsley.

peperoni in casseruola

PEPPER CASSEROLE

SERVES 4 TO 6

3 red bell peppers

3 yellow bell peppers

6 tablespoons extra-virgin olive oil

1 large clove garlic, peeled and left whole

Salt and freshly ground black pepper

1/4 cup capers preserved in wine vinegar, drained

3 tablespoons red wine vinegar, preferably homemade (page 17)

10 sprigs Italian parsley, leaves only, coarsely chopped

TO SERVE

Sprigs of fresh parsley

Clean the peppers, removing the stems, seeds, and all the filaments. Cut the peppers into strips 1 1/2 inches wide and soak them in a bowl of cold water for 30 minutes.

Heat the oil in a casserole over medium heat; when the oil is warm, add the garlic clove and sauté it for less than 20 seconds. Drain the peppers, add them to the casserole, increase the heat to high, and sauté for 3 to 4 minutes, seasoning with salt and pepper; the peppers should be cooked but still a little crunchy to the bite. Add the capers and the vinegar and cook for 1 minute more.

Discard the garlic and add the parsley. Mix very well, then transfer the peppers with all their juices to a large serving platter. Serve hot, with the parsley sprigs.

OPPOSITE: *This skillet contains* peperoncini, *cherry tomatoes, and an abundance of basil.*

Neapolitan *peperoncini* (also called *puparulillo*) are long, thin green peppers, not spicy like the smaller red ones used throughout Italy. In Naples, the red ones are called *cerasiello*. This dish may be used as a vegetable or as a sauce for pasta.

peperoncini e pomodorini

PEPERONCINI AND CHERRY TOMATOES

SERVES 6

2 pounds *peperoncini*, stems and the very tops removed, rinsed many times under cold running water to remove almost all the seeds

6 tablespoons extra-virgin olive oil

3 large cloves garlic, peeled and left whole

1 pound cherry tomatoes, sliced in half

Salt and freshly ground black pepper

10 fresh basil leaves

TO SERVE

Abundant fresh basil leaves

Once the peppers have been rinsed many times under cold running water, soak them in a bowl of cold water for 30 minutes.

Heat the oil in a large skillet over medium heat, and when the oil is warm, add the garlic and sauté until very light golden. Drain the peppers, add them to the skillet, and cook on high heat for 1 minute. Add the tomatoes, season with salt and pepper, lower the heat to medium, and cook 5 minutes longer, until the peppers are quite soft. The peppers and tomatoes should be cooked but keep their respective shapes.

Add the basil, mix very well, and serve hot, with more basil over each serving.

peperoni in insalata

SWEET BELL PEPPER SALAD

SERVES 4

2 yellow bell peppers, cleaned, seeded, all the filaments removed, cut into thin strips

2 red bell peppers, cleaned, seeded, all the filaments removed, cut into thin strips

3 cups cold water

2 cups red wine vinegar, preferably homemade (page 17)

Coarse-grained salt

Fine salt and freshly ground black pepper

1/4 cup extra-virgin olive oil

Soak the pepper strips in a bowl of cold water for 30 minutes. Bring the 3 cups of cold water and the vinegar to a boil in a large skillet. Add coarse salt to taste. Drain the peppers and add them to the skillet. Boil the peppers for 3 to 4 minutes, just long enough to remove the raw texture. (Do not overcook them or the skin will start detaching from the pulp, and it will be very unpleasant to the taste.)

Drain the peppers again and place them in a crockery or glass bowl. Season with fine salt and pepper, add the oil and the lemon juice, and mix very well.

2 tablespoons freshly squeezed lemon juice

2 large cloves garlic, peeled and cut into large slivers

10 fresh basil leaves, torn into thirds

10 sprigs Italian parsley, leaves only

Large pinch of dried oregano (optional)

TO SERVE

Sprigs of fresh basil or whole fresh basil leaves

1 lemon, cut into slices

Let the peppers rest for a few minutes before adding the garlic, basil, parsley, and oregano if using. Mix again, cover the bowl, and refrigerate for at least 2 hours.

Transfer the peppers and all their juices to a serving platter, and serve with the basil and lemon slices.

insalata di peperoni alla napoletana

PEPPER SALAD, NEAPOLITAN STYLE

SERVES 6 TO 8

3 large red bell peppers

3 large yellow bell peppers

6 whole anchovies preserved in salt, boned and rinsed under cold running water; or 12 anchovy fillets packed in oil, drained

Juice of 3 large lemons

1/4 cup extra-virgin olive oil

2 teaspoons fresh oregano leaves, or 1 large pinch of dried oregano

1 large red onion, preferably a Tropea onion, cleaned and thinly sliced

TO SERVE

6 tablespoons extra-virgin olive oil

Salt and freshly ground black pepper

Abundant fresh basil leaves, torn into thirds

Rinse the peppers under cold running water, then pat them dry with paper towels.

ROAST THE PEPPERS: Char the peppers over hot ash or a burner. Immediately transfer the charred peppers to a bowl, cover them with plastic wrap, and let rest for 30 minutes; the steam will cause the skins to detach completely. Hold the peppers under cold running water and remove and discard the loose skins.

Cut off the tops of the peppers and remove and discard the seeds and all the filaments inside. Cut the peppers into strips a little less than 1/2 inch wide, and place them in a crockery or glass bowl. Let rest, covered, in the refrigerator.

Cut the anchovy fillets into quarters and arrange them in a soup bowl. Pour the lemon juice and oil over them, season with the oregano, and top with the onion. Refrigerate, covered with plastic wrap, for at least 2 hours or, preferably, overnight.

When ready, transfer the peppers to a larger bowl. Drain the anchovies and onions, discarding the marinade, and add them to the bowl. Pour the 6 tablespoons oil over the salad and season with salt and pepper. Mix very well, transfer to a serving platter, distribute the basil on top, and serve.

OPPOSITE: Peperoni in Insalata *with lemon slices and sprigs of basil.*

peperoni e patate alla salernitana

PEPPERS AND POTATOES, SALERNO STYLE

SERVES 6

2 red bell peppers, cleaned, seeded, all the filaments removed, cut into 2-inch pieces

2 yellow bell peppers, cleaned, seeded, all the filaments removed, cut into 2-inch pieces

1/4 cup extra-virgin olive oil

Salt and freshly ground black pepper

2 tablespoons red wine vinegar

FOR THE POTATOES

1 pound all-purpose potatoes, peeled and cut into 1 1/2-inch pieces, left soaking in a bowl of cold water

1 cup vegetable oil (preferably a mixture of half sunflower oil, half corn oil)

2 large cloves garlic, peeled and left whole

TO SERVE

Fresh basil leaves (optional)

Soak the peppers in a bowl of cold water for 30 minutes. Place a skillet containing the olive oil over medium heat, and when the oil is lukewarm, drain the peppers and add them to the skillet. Season with salt and pepper and sauté for 5 minutes, stirring every so often with a wooden spoon.

Meanwhile, heat the vegetable oil in a skillet over medium heat, and when the oil is warm, about 200°F, drain the potatoes and dry them with paper towels. Add the potatoes to the skillet, raise the heat, and fry them until golden all over. Add the garlic cloves just before transferring the potatoes, using a strainer-skimmer, to a serving platter lined with paper towels to absorb excess oil.

When the peppers are ready, pour in the vinegar, mix very well, and let the vinegar evaporate for 1 minute. Add the potatoes, taste for salt and pepper, mix very well, and cook for 2 minutes more.

Transfer the potatoes and peppers to a serving platter, and serve hot with the basil, if using.

OPPOSITE: Peperoni e Patate alla Salernitana.

"puparuole 'mbuttunate"

PEPPERS STUFFED WITH EGGPLANT

SERVES 6

3 large red bell peppers

3 large yellow bell peppers

FOR THE STUFFING

2 medium-sized eggplants, about 8 ounces each

Coarse-grained salt

3 large cloves garlic, peeled and cut into slivers

1/2 cup extra-virgin olive oil

1/2 pound fresh tomatoes, blanched (see page 263), skin and seeds removed, cut into large pieces

ABOVE: *An assortment of bell peppers. Because they have a rather thick pulp and an extremely thin skin, in Neapolitan dishes, the skin is frequently left on.*

Preheat the oven to 375°F. Rinse the peppers under cold running water, then pat them dry with paper towels.

ROAST THE PEPPERS: Place a baking dish half full of cold water on the lower shelf of the oven. After a few minutes, put the whole peppers on the oven rack above the steaming water. Roast them for about 40 minutes, turning them three or four times; then remove them from the oven and put them in a plastic bag so the skin detaches from the peppers, about 15 minutes. Peel the peppers in a large bowl of cold water, removing and discarding all the skin. See Note, opposite.

Carefully cut off and reserve the tops of the peppers just 1 inch below the stem, leaving the stems attached. Remove all the seeds and filaments and let the peppers—shells and tops—rest on paper towels until needed.

PREPARE THE STUFFING: Peel the eggplants, cut them into 1-inch cubes, and place them on a serving platter. Sprinkle coarse salt on top and cover the eggplant with a second platter as a weight; let rest for 30 minutes. Drain the eggplant, rinse it under cold running water, and pat it dry with paper towels.

Place the garlic and 1/4 cup of the oil in a medium-sized casserole and set it over medium heat. Sauté the garlic for 1 minute, stirring every so often with a wooden spoon; the garlic should still be very light in color. Add the eggplant, sauté for a few minutes, then add the tomatoes and season with salt and pepper. Cook for 15 minutes. Add the parsley, basil, capers, olives, and anchovies, mix very well, and cook for 5 minutes more.

Transfer the contents of the casserole to a crockery or glass bowl and let cool for at least 30 minutes.

Preheat the oven to 375°F again and lightly oil a glass baking dish that will hold the peppers upright, one against the other.

Fill the peppers with the stuffing, cover them with their own tops, and arrange them, standing up, in the baking dish. Drizzle the remaining 1/4 cup oil over them, and pour the cold water into the pan. Bake for 40 minutes, until the peppers are still very juicy to the touch and the stuffing is completely amalgamated.

Salt and freshly ground black pepper

10 sprigs Italian parsley, leaves only

20 large fresh basil leaves, torn into thirds

2 tablespoons capers preserved in wine vinegar, drained

2 ounces Gaeta or Calamata olives, pitted and cut into small pieces

2 whole anchovies preserved in salt, boned, rinsed under cold running water, and cut into small pieces; or 4 anchovy fillets packed in oil, drained and cut into small pieces

PLUS

1/4 cup cold water

Remove the pan from the oven and let the peppers rest for at least 15 minutes before transferring them to a serving platter. The peppers may be eaten immediately, while still quite warm. But generally Neapolitans prefer to use them when they are at room temperature, after a few hours or even the following day.

NOTE: I use this technique for removing the skin so the peppers do not have the smoky taste they get when held over a flame. The smoky flavor is good when using peppers in other dishes, such as pepper salad (page 57).

patate al peperoni

POTATOES WITH SWEET PEPPER SAUCE

SERVES 6

1 large red bell pepper

1 large yellow bell pepper

1 large leek, cleaned, green part discarded

1/4 cup extra-virgin olive oil

Salt and freshly ground black pepper

1 1/2 cups very light and completely defatted chicken broth or vegetable broth, preferably homemade

1 1/2 pounds all-purpose potatoes, peeled, cut into 1 1/2-inch cubes, left soaking in a bowl of cold water

Hot red pepper flakes (optional)

2 medium-sized cloves garlic, peeled

15 sprigs Italian parsley, leaves only

TO SERVE

Sprigs of fresh basil

Clean the peppers, discarding the stems, seeds, and all the filaments. Cut the peppers into 1-inch pieces. Cut the leek into 1-inch disks. Place the peppers and leeks in a bowl of cold water and let stand for 30 minutes.

Set a heavy skillet containing the oil over medium heat, and when the oil is warm, drain the peppers and leeks, add them to the skillet, and sauté for 15 minutes, stirring occasionally with a wooden spoon. Season with salt and pepper, mix very well, and add 1 cup of the broth. Cover the skillet and cook for 20 minutes or longer, until the peppers and leeks are very soft.

Drain the potatoes and arrange them on top of the peppers and leeks. Season again with salt and pepper; add red pepper flakes to taste if using, then pour the remaining 1/2 cup broth into the skillet.

Cover the skillet and cook for 15 minutes more, shaking the pan several times to keep the potatoes from sticking on the bottom. By this time, the potatoes should be cooked and soft but still retain their shape. Let the vegetables rest, covered, for at least 5 minutes.

Finely chop the garlic and parsley together on a cutting board. When ready, transfer the contents of the skillet to a serving platter, sprinkle with the chopped mixture, and serve with the basil sprigs.

S*curilli*" are the zucchini blossoms that are eaten all over Italy, cooked in different ways, by themselves or as a condiment for pasta or rice. The name refers to both the full, yellow flowers and the still-green blossoms shown on the next page. I do not know of any other region that uses the blossoms when they are still very young and green, but they appear frequently in a variety of Neapolitan dishes, cooked in different ways such as deep-fried, served as an appetizer (page 179), and in the pasta sauce described here. This is one of many recipes to show the region's preference for vegetables that are not completely ripe, such as the still slightly green tomatoes loved for salad (page 110), over the completely sweet taste of ripe vegetables.

pasta con gli "scurilli"

PASTA WITH GREEN ZUCCHINI BLOSSOMS

SERVES 6

- 1 1/2 pounds "*scurilli*" (baby zucchini blossoms, still green in color), cleaned and all the stems removed
- 6 tablespoons extra-virgin olive oil
- 4 tablespoons (2 ounces) unsalted butter
- 1 large yellow onion, cleaned and finely chopped
- 3 large cloves garlic, peeled and left whole
- 10 sprigs Italian parsley, leaves only, finely chopped
- Salt and freshly ground black pepper
- 1 to 2 cups completely defatted chicken broth, preferably homemade
- 2 extra-large eggs
- 2 cups freshly grated local pecorino or Pecorino Romano cheese

TO COOK THE PASTA

- Coarse-grained salt
- 1 pound dried pasta such as vermicelli or *perciatelli*, preferably imported Italian

Soak the zucchini blossoms in a bowl of cold water for 30 minutes. Heat the oil and butter in a large casserole over medium heat, and when the butter is completely melted, add the onion, garlic, and parsley and sauté, stirring constantly with a wooden spoon, for about 5 minutes, or until the onion is translucent.

Drain the zucchini blossoms and add them to the casserole. Sauté for 5 minutes, season with salt and pepper, then add 1/2 cup of the broth. Simmer for 10 minutes or longer, until the blossoms are rather soft, adding more broth as needed.

COOK THE PASTA: Bring a large pot of cold water to a boil over medium heat, add coarse salt to taste, then add the pasta and cook until al dente, 9 to 12 minutes depending on the brand.

When the pasta is almost cooked, mix the eggs and the grated cheese in a crockery or glass bowl. Temper the eggs by adding 2 tablespoons of the boiling pasta water and mixing very well. Bring the zucchini blossom sauce back to a boil, add the egg mixture, and stir very well to be sure the eggs are cooked but not dry.

Drain the pasta, transfer it to a large bowl, and immediately add the sauce. Mix very well and serve hot.

OPPOSITE: *Still-green zucchini blossoms.*

zucchini "a scapece"

MARINATED ZUCCHINI

SERVES 6

- 6 medium-sized zucchini, about 4 ounces each
- Coarse-grained salt
- 1 cup extra-virgin olive oil
- 2 cups vegetable oil (preferably a mixture of half sunflower oil, half corn oil)
- Fine salt
- 2 cloves garlic, peeled and finely chopped
- 20 large fresh mint leaves
- 1/4 cup red wine vinegar, preferably homemade (page 17)

Cut off the ends of the zucchini and discard them. Place the zucchini in a bowl of cold water with coarse salt to taste; soak for 30 minutes. Drain the zucchini, pat them dry with paper towels, and cut them into disks less than 1/2 inch thick. Let the zucchini rest on paper towels to dry completely.

Heat 3/4 cup of the olive oil and all the vegetable oil in a large skillet over medium heat. When the oil is hot, about 375°F, add some of the zucchini slices and fry them until golden all over. Transfer them to a serving platter without draining them.

When all the zucchini are cooked and on the platter, sprinkle them with fine salt and the chopped garlic, then arrange the mint leaves over them. Drizzle on the vinegar and the remaining 1/4 cup olive oil. Let the zucchini rest until cool, about 1 hour.

Refrigerate, covered, for at least 2 hours before serving. This dish is always served cold.

LIRE 2400
LIRE
LIRE 4000
2200

the open-air markets

There are three main open-air markets in Naples: Mercatino Della Pignasecca, near Piazza Caritá; the Sant'Antonio; and the Porta Nolana, which sells fish and shellfish. Shopping in or just walking through these markets is a memorable experience. Here, as in most of the markets in southern Italy, the percentage of male customers is very high, and you will see them check each item with extreme care before they buy.

The call of the individual vendor is a tradition still very much alive in these markets, as is the language used to describe the different foods that are for sale. Lemons have the smell of the sea, figs are sweet like honey, but for seafood, the call usually describes the dish to be made with the specific fish. "*Che bella 'mpepatella*" ("what a beautiful *'mpepatella*") is what we would hear if mussels were being sold. Food is always described as "beautiful" rather than "good."

All of the stands remain in the same location year after year, and the vendors are like the main characters in a very lively, funny, and sometimes even poignant play. The *bannitore*—a boisterous performer who dances and plays musical instruments to advertise food products—is a frequent sight. On any given day, it is wonderful to watch the arrival

OPPOSITE: *Scenes from the markets of Naples.* **BELOW:** *The fruit vendor, or* il fruttaiuolo ambulante, *was once the most numerous type of vendor in the market.*

of the products early in the morning and the love and care that is taken to display them.

Traditionally perhaps the most numerous street vendors were *il fruttaiuolo ambulante*—the fruit sellers. As we read in Francesco de Boucard's famous essays about Naples, it was a business with a very small overhead that almost anyone could practice: "It is enough to have a basket, a scale (the so-called *bilancia*), a few coins (called *carlini* after King Charles I of Anjou), but mainly you need very strong shoulders and a voice like a tenor." So, even among these vendors there was a hierarchy.

The most respected fruit vendors were the ones selling strawberries. Early in the morning, they used to arrive at Via Toledo from the nearby countryside with baskets full of tiny wild strawberries that they had picked only a few hours before. Second to the strawberry vendors were the orange vendors, as even in the eighteenth century one of the most desired breakfasts was a bowl of fresh strawberries with freshly squeezed orange juice.

ABOVE: *Mussels and seaweed. Alghe fritters are prepared as part of the* gran fritto. *Seaweed is dipped in* pasta cresciuta *batter (page 180) then deep-fried.*
LEFT, TOP: *These unusual apples, called* mele annurche, *are grown mainly in the area of Melito di Napoli and in Miano, very close to Naples. Their skin is very red and the pulp white and very juicy, but not extremely sweet. They're picked from the tree when still completely unripe and kept under straw for a long time, until they become ripe and juicy.*

These apples are held very dear; they are the preferred fruit for children and the sick, and Neapolitans happily pay as much as twice the price for them as for apples from northern Italy.
LEFT, BELOW: *These "aguglie" fish are just one example of the bountiful fish and seafood found in the markets.*
BOTTOM, LEFT: *The best fresh figs are these so-called "troiani" from Statigliano, a town not far from Naples.*
BOTTOM, RIGHT: *A typical scene at the fish vendors.*

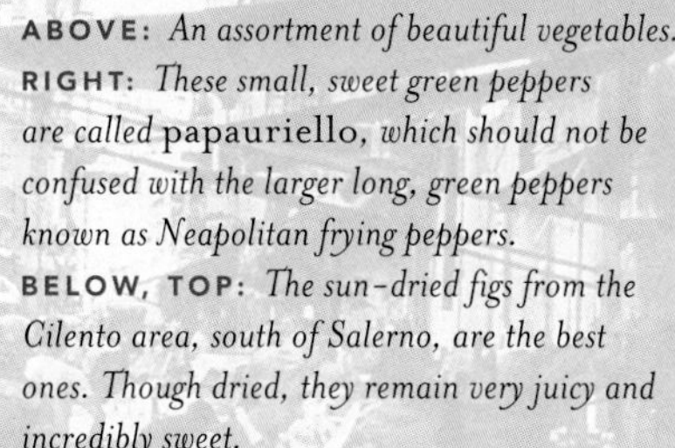

ABOVE: *An assortment of beautiful vegetables.*
RIGHT: *These small, sweet green peppers are called* papauriello, *which should not be confused with the larger long, green peppers known as Neapolitan frying peppers.*
BELOW, TOP: *The sun-dried figs from the Cilento area, south of Salerno, are the best ones. Though dried, they remain very juicy and incredibly sweet.*
BELOW, BOTTOM: *Hot peppers, known as* peperoncini *in Italian and* cerasiello *in Neapolitan.*

ABOVE: *Country-style bread* (pane cafone) *for sale at the Porta Nolana market. The word* cafone *is frequently used to refer to things—or people—that are not very refined. This is the only bread still baked in wood-burning ovens, and when it is delivered early in the morning, the aroma is still apparent, even when surrounded by the fragrance of the fresh fruits and vegetables.*

Today bread sold in open-air markets must be wrapped in plastic. This makes the shop owners unhappy because it causes the wonderful crusty bread to lose some of its crispness. So, most of the time, the shop owner "forgets" to wrap the bread.
LEFT: *Salamis in the Campania region require a very unusual preparation: The so-called Neapolitan salami is made with pork and veal meats and the seasonings are salt, black and hot pepper* (peperoncino), *and garlic that has been cooked in red wine.*
BELOW, RIGHT: *A typical scene at the fish vendor's stall.*

zuppe and *minestre*

Campania's regional cooking is full of zuppe *and* minestre *based on vegetables or legumes. Both are words meaning soup, but like so many foods typical of the region, dishes of the same name may vary greatly, or by one significant ingredient, depending on the town in which they are prepared. Campania serves pasta with a greater variety of vegetables than elsewhere in Italy. It is in these common dishes that the importance of vegetables in Neapolitan cooking becomes most apparent. Neapolitan cooking is also unique in its use of a remarkable variety of herbs and greens that grow wild in the fields; these are used to prepare wonderful soups that we cannot precisely reproduce anywhere else in the world.*

As they do all over Italy, legumes play a central role in Neapolitan cuisine. They function as a side course, vegetable course, in combination with pasta, and as the central ingredient in soups. The importance of beans is revealed by the names of two dishes included here: *Fagioli Assoluti* and *Fagioli e Pasta*—that's beans and pasta, not pasta and beans.

Given the frequency of their use, it is surprising that the variety of beans in the Campania region is limited when compared with the many types used in other parts of Italy. *Cannellini* (white kidney beans) are predominant, whereas *borlotti*, so-called Roman beans, are quite rare and *fagioli con l'occhio* (black-eyed peas) are rarer still. And yet both of these beans share the stage in most other parts of Italy.

Fava beans are popular in Campania and used mainly fresh, which means their season is limited. Dried fava beans are restricted primarily to soups. This is unlike nearby Puglia, where dried fava beans are used in many dishes. Although perhaps less frequently than in earlier times, *ceci* (chickpeas) are still used in Campania; recipes for pasta with chickpeas and a chickpea soup follow.

minestrone *or* zuppa di scarola e fagioli

ESCAROLE AND BEAN SOUP, NAPLES STYLE

SERVES 6 TO 8

FOR THE BEANS

2 cups dried *cannellini* (white kidney beans), picked over

1 large clove garlic, peeled and left whole

2 fresh basil leaves

3 sprigs Italian parsley, large stems removed

2 tablespoons extra-virgin olive oil

3 1/2 quarts cold water

FOR THE ESCAROLE AND OTHER VEGETABLES

2 pounds escarole, cleaned, large stems removed (yields about 1 1/2 pounds)

Coarse-grained salt

3 medium-sized stalks celery, cut into small pieces

10 sprigs Italian parsley, leaves only, coarsely chopped

2 large cloves garlic, peeled and finely chopped

4 small ripe tomatoes, blanched (see page 263), skin and seeds removed; or 4 canned tomatoes, preferably imported Italian, drained and seeded

1/4 cup extra-virgin olive oil

Salt and freshly ground black pepper

Soak the beans in a bowl of cold water overnight. The next morning, drain the beans, rinse them under cold running water, and put them in a medium-sized stockpot with the garlic, basil, parsley, and oil. Add the water and set the pot over medium heat. Simmer for 45 minutes, removing the foam that forms on the surface.

Meanwhile, soak the escarole in a bowl of cold water for 30 minutes. Bring a large pot of cold water to a boil over medium heat, add coarse salt to taste, then add the escarole and cook for 5 minutes. Drain the escarole very well and chop it coarsely.

Drain the beans (they will not yet be completely cooked), saving the cooking water. Discard the garlic, basil, and parsley. Reserve the beans in a crockery or glass bowl covered with a wet dish towel or wet paper towels.

Return the bean broth to the stockpot and add the escarole, along with the celery, parsley, garlic, tomatoes, and oil. Simmer for 20 minutes, then season with salt and pepper. Add the beans and simmer for 15 minutes more, or until the beans are very soft but still retain their shape. Taste again for salt and pepper.

Remove the pot from the heat and let the soup rest, covered, for 15 minutes before serving it.

minestra di patate

POTATO SOUP

SERVES 6

1 medium-sized carrot, scraped

1 stalk celery

1 small clove garlic, peeled

1 small red onion, cleaned

10 sprigs Italian parsley, leaves only

5 fresh basil leaves

2 ounces pancetta or prosciutto, coarsely ground or cut into very small pieces

1/4 cup extra-virgin olive oil

2 tablespoons (1 ounce) unsalted butter

Salt and freshly ground black pepper

Large pinch of hot red pepper flakes (optional)

1 pound all-purpose potatoes, peeled, cut into small cubes, and left soaking in a bowl of cold water

6 cups completely defatted chicken broth or vegetable broth, preferably homemade

TO SERVE

6 thick slices country-style bread, lightly toasted

Sprigs of fresh basil

Finely chop the carrot, celery, garlic, onion, parsley, and basil all together on a cutting board. Mix the ground pancetta with the chopped vegetables.

Place a medium-sized casserole containing the oil and butter over medium heat. When the butter is almost melted, add the vegetable mixture and sauté until the onion is translucent, about 5 minutes. Season with salt, pepper, and the red pepper flakes if using. Then drain the potatoes and add them to the casserole. Sauté for 5 minutes, stirring every so often with a wooden spoon.

Add 1 cup of the broth and simmer for 5 minutes. Add the remaining broth and simmer until the potatoes are almost mashed, about 25 minutes. Taste for salt and pepper.

When ready to serve, place the toasted bread in individual soup bowls, ladle potato soup on top, and let the soup rest for a few minutes before serving it with a basil sprig in each bowl.

RIGHT: *Another day at the market.*

minestra *or* menesta di patate e carciofi

POTATO AND ARTICHOKE SOUP

SERVES 6

2 large artichokes

1 lemon, cut in half

1 medium-sized yellow onion, cleaned and coarsely chopped or thinly sliced

2 ounces pancetta or prosciutto, coarsely ground or cut into very small pieces

1/4 cup extra-virgin olive oil

1 pound all-purpose potatoes, peeled, cut into small pieces, and left soaking in a bowl of cold water

Salt and freshly ground black pepper

Pinch of hot red pepper flakes (optional)

5 cups completely defatted chicken broth, preferably homemade

10 fresh basil leaves

Medium-sized pinch of dried oregano

TO SERVE

Fresh basil leaves

Soak the artichokes for 30 minutes in a bowl of cold water containing the squeezed lemon halves. Clean the artichokes (see page 263), removing the outer green leaves and the choke, and cut them into eighths. Return the artichokes to the acidulated water until needed.

Place a medium-sized casserole containing the onion, pancetta, and oil over medium heat and sauté for 3 to 4 minutes, stirring constantly with a wooden spoon. Drain the potatoes and add them to the casserole. Mix very well and sauté for 5 minutes, stirring every so often with a wooden spoon. Season with salt, pepper, and the red pepper flakes if using.

Add 1 cup of the broth along with the basil and oregano, mix very well, and cook for 20 minutes more, stirring every so often with a wooden spoon. Drain the artichokes and add them to the casserole along with another cup of the broth. Add the remaining broth, 1 cup at a time, as needed.

The soup is ready when the potatoes are almost all dissolved and the artichokes are very soft, about 30 minutes. The consistency of the soup should be rather thick, like a very uneven potato "cream" with pieces of artichoke.

Taste for seasoning, then let the soup rest for a few minutes before serving. It may be served hot or at room temperature, with fresh basil leaves on each serving.

minestra di zucchini

ZUCCHINI SOUP WITH EGGS AND CHEESE

SERVES 6

2½ pounds small zucchini, but not the miniature kind, cleaned

1 tablespoon coarse-grained salt

4 tablespoons (2 ounces) unsalted butter

2 tablespoons extra-virgin olive oil

15 scallions, cleaned, white part only, coarsely chopped; or 1 large white onion, cleaned and coarsely chopped

2 cups completely defatted chicken or meat broth, preferably homemade

Salt and freshly ground black pepper

1 cup whole milk

3 extra-large eggs

6 tablespoons freshly grated Parmigiano

20 large fresh basil leaves, torn into thirds

TO SERVE

Several *crostini* (small squares of country-style bread, lightly toasted)

6 tablespoons freshly grated Parmigiano

Abundant fresh basil leaves

Soak the zucchini for 30 minutes in a bowl of cold water containing the coarse salt. Drain the zucchini, rinse them under cold running water, then cut them into disks less than ½ inch thick.

Place the butter and oil in a medium-sized casserole over low heat. When the butter is almost melted, add the scallions and sauté for 15 minutes. The scallions should still be very light in color. Add the zucchini, mix very well, cover the casserole, and raise the heat to medium. Cook for 2 minutes, then add the broth and season with salt and pepper. Simmer for 10 minutes more. By this time, the zucchini should be cooked and rather soft.

Bring the milk to a boil over medium heat, then remove it from the heat and immediately add the eggs, one at a time, mixing very well after each addition. (In this way you temper the eggs.) Add the cheese and the basil, mix again, and pour everything into the casserole containing the simmering zucchini mixture. Stir constantly until the soup reaches a boil and the broth has thickened.

Pour the hot soup over the *crostini* placed in individual soup bowls, then sprinkle with the Parmigiano and basil leaves, and serve.

OPPOSITE: *In the Piazza Pignasecca, which is the heart of the market,* "il convive col profano" *(the sacred lives together with the profane). Here, the tabernacle is shown in the midst of watermelons for sale.*

eria
1
del

"cianfotta"

MIXED VEGETABLE STEW

SERVES 8

3 medium-sized eggplants, about 2 pounds total, peeled and cut into 2-inch cubes

2 tablespoons coarse-grained salt

1/2 cup extra-virgin olive oil

2 large yellow onions, cleaned and coarsely chopped

2 small cloves garlic, peeled and finely chopped

1 1/2 pounds all-purpose potatoes, peeled, cut into 1-inch cubes, and left soaking in a bowl of cold water

4 red or yellow bell peppers, cleaned, seeded, all filaments removed, cut into large pieces

1 1/2 pounds ripe tomatoes, blanched (see page 263), skin and seeds removed, cut into 2-inch pieces

Salt and freshly ground black pepper

15 sprigs Italian parsley, leaves only, coarsely chopped

10 large fresh basil leaves, torn into thirds

This dish probably originated in Calabria, where it is called "Ciambrotta," *meaning "a mixture of ingredients." The Neapolitan version is very similar to the original. In the Cosenza area,* fare "ciambrotta" *(to make* "ciambrotta"*) means to have a big party with your friends.*

Place the eggplant cubes on a tray, sprinkle them with the coarse salt, and put a serving platter over them as a weight. Let rest for 1 hour.

Heat the oil in a large casserole over medium heat. When the oil is warm, add the onions and garlic and sauté for 5 minutes, or until the onions are translucent. Drain the eggplant cubes and rinse them well under cold running water to remove all the salt. Drain the potatoes. Raise the heat to medium, then add the eggplant, peppers, potatoes, and tomatoes. Season with salt and pepper.

Cover the casserole and cook for 30 minutes, mixing every so often with a wooden spoon. At this point, a rather large amount of liquid will have been released from the vegetables. Raise the heat to high, uncover the casserole, and let all the liquid evaporate. Some of the vegetables will be completely cooked and others overcooked; that is the correct texture for this dish.

Sprinkle the parsley and basil over the vegetables and mix very well. Remove the casserole from the heat, cover it, and let it rest until cool. This vegetable dish is most often eaten at room temperature. You may refrigerate it; just bring it back to room temperature before serving.

VARIATIONS

1. Leave the garlic whole.
2. Add 1 tablespoon tomato paste, preferably homemade (page 23), with the tomatoes.
3. Add 1/2 pound peas with the other vegetables.
4. Lightly sauté all the vegetables, one after the other, in a little olive oil; then mix them together and finish cooking in the casserole.

"menesta maritata" *or* "pignato maritato" *or* "pignato grasso"

MIXED VEGETABLE SOUP

SERVES 8 TO 10

4 pounds mixed meats and poultry, such as veal, beef, hen, sausages, and some veal bones with marrow

1 piece (about 6 ounces) prosciutto bone

4 quarts cold water

Coarse-grained salt

6 pounds mixed leafy vegetables, such as spinach, Swiss chard, chicory, savoy cabbage, escarole, and basil leaves

1/4 pound spicy *caciocavallo* or provolone cheese, in one piece

Hot red pepper flakes

Place all the meats and bones in a stockpot, add the water, and set over medium heat. Simmer for 1 1/2 hours, constantly removing the foam that forms on top of the broth, and season with a little coarse salt. Strain the broth and let cool for 1 hour; then refrigerate, covered, overnight.

The next morning, soak all the vegetables in a bowl of cold water for 30 minutes. Remove all the fat from the top of the broth and transfer the broth to a new stockpot. Set the pot over medium heat and when this very rich broth reaches a boil, add all the vegetables.

Simmer for 25 minutes, adding the *caciocavallo* just 5 minutes before removing the pot from the heat. Season with red pepper flakes, cover, and let the soup rest for 15 minutes before serving.

fagioli "alla maruzzara"

BEANS COOKED LIKE SNAILS

SERVES 6

2 cups dried *cannellini* (white kidney beans), picked over

1/4 cup extra-virgin olive oil

1 large ripe tomato, about 8 ounces, cut into large pieces; or 8 ounces drained canned tomatoes, preferably imported Italian, cut into large pieces

10 sprigs Italian parsley, leaves only, coarsely chopped

2 large cloves garlic, peeled and coarsely chopped

Freshly ground black pepper

Abundant hot red pepper flakes

Coarse-grained salt

Soak the beans in a bowl of cold water overnight. The next morning, drain the beans, rinse them under cold running water, and place them in a medium-sized casserole.

Add 6 cups cold water, the olive oil, tomato, parsley, and garlic and season with black pepper and a lot of red pepper flakes. Set the casserole over medium heat and simmer, adding lukewarm water if needed, until the beans are cooked and soft but retain their shape, about 1 hour.

Season with coarse salt, simmer for 1 minute more, then transfer everything to a bowl, and serve hot.

In Neapolitan dialect, "*maruzza*" means snail. The most popular dish prepared with snails is a casserole made of sautéed snails with lots of hot pepper. Therefore, "*alla maruzzara*" (in the style of snails) means cooked with a lot of hot pepper.

zuppa "alla maruzzara"

BEAN SOUP, COOKED LIKE SNAILS

SERVES 6

2 cups fresh *cannellini* (white kidney beans), or 1 cup dried *cannellini*, picked over

2 ounces pancetta or prosciutto, in 1 piece

6 tablespoons extra-virgin olive oil

2 large ripe tomatoes, about 1½ pounds total, blanched (see page 263), skin and seeds removed; or 1½ pounds drained canned tomatoes, preferably imported Italian, seeded

4 large cloves garlic, peeled and cut into thin slivers

4 large stalks celery, cut into small pieces

Freshly ground black pepper

Hot red pepper flakes to taste

Abundant fresh oregano leaves, or a large pinch of dried oregano

Salt

TO SERVE

6 thick slices country-style bread, toasted on both sides

If you are using dried *cannellini*, soak them in a bowl of cold water overnight. The next morning, drain the beans and rinse them under cold running water. Place the drained (or fresh) beans in a medium-sized casserole. Add the pancetta to the casserole, along with 2 tablespoons of the oil and the tomatoes, garlic, and celery. Season with black pepper and red pepper flakes.

Add enough cold water to cover the beans by 1½ inches. Set the casserole over medium heat and simmer for 1 hour or longer, until the beans are completely cooked but still retain their shape. Add the oregano and salt to taste, and simmer for 1 minute more. The soup should be rather spicy and peppery.

Place the toasted bread in individual soup bowls and ladle the soup over it. Drizzle the remaining 4 tablespoons oil over the servings, and serve hot.

fagioli assoluti

"STRICTLY" BEANS

SERVES 6 TO 8

- 2 cups dried *cannellini* (white kidney beans), picked over
- 2 tablespoons extra-virgin olive oil
- 8 cups cold water
- Coarse-grained salt
- 15 sprigs Italian parsley, leaves only, coarsely chopped
- 3 large cloves garlic, peeled and finely chopped
- Large pinch of hot red pepper flakes

TO SERVE

- 3 tablespoons extra-virgin olive oil
- 20 fresh oregano leaves, or a large pinch of dried oregano

Here, assoluti *means that the beans are eaten without pasta, but with different sauces. The phrase* vino assoluto *reflects the same idea: wine drunk without adding water.*

Soak the beans in a bowl of cold water overnight. The next morning, drain the beans, rinse them under cold running water, and place them in a medium-sized casserole. Add the oil and cold water. Set the pot over medium heat and simmer until the beans are completely cooked but retain their shape, about 1 hour. Add salt to taste, mix very well, and simmer for 1 minute more.

Transfer the beans and a little of their liquid to a serving platter, sprinkle the parsley, garlic, and red pepper flakes on top, and mix gently. Drizzle with a little of the oil and serve hot, with some oregano on each serving.

RIGHT: *Handfuls of dried legumes.*

zuppa di ceci alla napoletana

CHICKPEA SOUP, NEAPOLITAN STYLE

SERVES 8 TO 10

2 cups dried chickpeas, picked over

1 teaspoon baking soda

4 fresh sage leaves

2 large cloves garlic, peeled and left whole

2 pig's feet, about 1 1/2 pounds total, or 1/2 pound prosciutto or pancetta in one piece, cut into small cakes

FOR THE SAUCE

1 small yellow onion, cleaned

2 medium-sized stalks celery

1 carrot, scraped

10 sprigs fresh Italian parsley, leaves only

1 small clove garlic, peeled

6 tablespoons extra-virgin olive oil

Salt and freshly ground black pepper

Hot red pepper flakes (optional)

TO SERVE

8 to 10 thick slices country-style bread, toasted on both sides; or thick slices of stale bread (at least 3 days old), untoasted

Soak the chickpeas with the baking soda in a bowl of cold water overnight. The next morning, place a medium-sized casserole containing 4 quarts cold water over medium heat. Drain the chickpeas, rinse them under cold running water, and add them to the casserole along with the sage, garlic, and pig's feet. Simmer for about 1 hour or until the chickpeas are completely cooked and rather soft.

PREPARE THE SAUCE: Finely chop the onion, celery, carrot, parsley, and garlic all together on a cutting board. Heat the oil in a medium-sized skillet over medium heat, and when the oil is warm, add the chopped ingredients and sauté for 2 minutes. Season with salt, black pepper, and red pepper flakes if using. Mix very well and keep sautéing, adding a little lukewarm water if needed, until the onion is translucent, about 15 minutes.

Remove and discard the sage leaves and the two garlic cloves from the chickpeas. Transfer the sautéed vegetable mixture from the skillet to the casserole containing the chickpeas, and simmer for 5 minutes more. At this point, some of the chickpeas will be almost puréed, giving the *zuppa* the correct, almost creamy texture.

Remove the pig's feet. You may either discard them or bone them, cut the meat into small pieces, and return it to the *zuppa*. If prosciutto or pancetta is used, do not remove it.

Place the toasted bread in individual soup bowls, and pour some of the broth and some of the chickpeas over each. Serve hot.

The regional cooking of Campania is full of *zuppe* based on vegetables or legumes. I want to mention two more that are worth knowing: *Zuppa di Cardoni* (Cardoon Soup) and *Zuppa di Lenticchie e Boraggine* (Lentil Soup with Borage Leaves). The first soup is very interesting: Stalks of cardoon (a vegetable resembling large bunches of flat, wide celery) are parboiled in salted water, then cooked in chicken broth with added chicken meat, sausages, and meatballs, served with a generous addition of cubed fresh mozzarella. Borage is an herb and, like cardoon, it is quite popular in Campania. For the *zuppa*, borage leaves are cooked together with lentils, tomatoes, and garlic, then served with some extra-virgin olive oil poured on top. The addition of the oil on top is more typical of Tuscany and Umbria and quite rarely seen in Campania.

zuppa di zucchini

ZUCCHINI SOUP

SERVES 4 TO 6

2 1/2 pounds small zucchini, cleaned

Coarse-grained salt

4 tablespoons (2 ounces) unsalted butter, instead of the traditional lard

2 tablespoons extra-virgin olive oil

Salt and freshly ground black pepper

6 cups completely defatted chicken or meat broth, preferably homemade, or lukewarm water

4 extra-large eggs

6 tablespoons freshly grated aged local pecorino or Pecorino Romano cheese

Abundant fresh basil leaves

TO SERVE

4 to 6 thick slices country-style bread, toasted on both sides, or *friselle* (Neapolitan toasted half rolls)

Fresh basil leaves

Cut the zucchini into 1-inch pieces, put the pieces in a bowl of cold water, add coarse salt to taste, and soak for 30 minutes.

Drain the zucchini pieces, rinse them under cold running water, and pat them dry with paper towels.

Place a stockpot containing the butter and oil over medium heat, and when the butter is melted, add the zucchini and lightly sauté for 10 minutes. Season with salt and pepper. Add 5 cups of the broth or water, bring to a simmer, and cook for 15 minutes.

ABOVE: Friselle *are classic Neapolitan toasted rolls shaped like half a ring. They are used to absorb the broth of many dishes, such as fish soups. They are also used as the base for* caponata *(page 146), but first they are soaked in water and sprinkled with some red wine vinegar.*

Heat the remaining 1 cup broth, then lightly mix it with the eggs and cheese, then add them to the stockpot. Mix very well and cook for 2 minutes more.

To serve, place the toasted bread or *frisella* in individual soup bowls. Add the basil to the soup, mix thoroughly, and pour the soup over the toast, topping each serving with more basil leaves. Serve immediately.

AL FRUTTETO D'ORO
BIBITE
FREDDE
2.000
2.500
2.000

zuppa di fagioli alla napoletana

BEAN SOUP, NEAPOLITAN STYLE

SERVES 4 TO 6

- 1 1/2 cups dried *cannellini* (white kidney beans), picked over
- 3 quarts cold water or completely defatted chicken broth, preferably homemade
- 6 tablespoons extra-virgin olive oil
- Coarse-grained salt
- 2 large cloves garlic, peeled and cut into small slivers
- 2 large stalks celery, cut into small pieces
- 1 pound fresh tomatoes, blanched (see page 263), skin and seeds removed, cut into small pieces; or 1 pound drained canned tomatoes, preferably imported Italian, seeded
- Salt and freshly ground black pepper

TO SERVE

- 4 to 6 thick slices country-style bread, toasted on both sides; or 4 to 6 thick slices stale bread (at least 3 days old), untoasted

Soak the beans in a bowl of cold water overnight. The next morning, drain the beans and rinse them under cold running water. Place the beans in a medium-sized casserole, add the cold water or broth and 2 tablespoons of the oil, and set the pot over medium heat. Cook the beans until they are rather soft, about 1 hour. When the beans are almost cooked, add coarse salt to taste and simmer for 2 minutes more.

Meanwhile, place a small saucepan containing the remaining 4 tablespoons oil over medium heat, and when the oil is warm, add the garlic and celery and sauté for 1 minute, being careful that the garlic does not become more than golden. Add the tomatoes and season with salt and pepper (keep in mind that the beans will be very mild in taste if you are using water rather than broth). Cook for about 15 minutes, stirring every so often with a wooden spoon and adding some of the bean broth if needed.

When the *zuppa* is done, the amount of bean broth still in the casserole should be about 6 cups; if there is more, remove and discard the extra. Transfer the tomato sauce from the saucepan to the beans, mix very well, and simmer for 2 minutes more. Taste for salt and pepper.

Place the toasted bread in individual soup bowls, then ladle some of the beans with broth over them. Grind more black pepper over each serving, and serve hot.

VARIATION

Add 1/2 pound cleaned, chopped chicory to the beans when they are half cooked.

OPPOSITE: *A produce stand specializing in fruit.*

zuppa di fagioli alla carrettiera

PEPPERY BEAN SOUP, CASERTA STYLE

SERVES 4 TO 6

- 1 1/2 cups dried *cannellini* (white kidney beans), picked over
- 3 cloves garlic, peeled and finely chopped
- 3 stalks celery, cut into small pieces
- 1 pound fresh tomatoes, blanched (see page 263), skin and seeds removed, cut into large pieces; or 1 pound drained canned tomatoes, preferably imported Italian, seeded
- 5 tablespoons extra-virgin olive oil
- Very large pinch of hot red pepper flakes
- Freshly ground black pepper
- Large pinch of dried oregano
- Coarse-grained salt

TO SERVE

- 4 to 6 thick slices country-style bread, toasted on both sides; or 4 to 6 thick slices stale bread (at least 3 days old), untoasted
- Extra-virgin olive oil

Soak the beans in a bowl of cold water overnight. The next morning, place a pot containing 4 quarts cold water over medium heat, and when the water reaches a boil, drain the beans and add them to the pot. Simmer for 20 minutes.

Add the garlic, celery, tomatoes, oil, red pepper flakes, and black pepper to taste. Simmer for 40 minutes more, or until the beans are completely cooked but still retain their shape. Season with the oregano and coarse salt to taste, mix very well, and simmer for 1 minute more. The soup should be quite peppery and thick, without a large amount of broth.

Place the toasted bread in individual soup bowls, then ladle the soup over them. Drizzle some olive oil over each serving, and serve hot.

fagioli e pasta *or* "'e fasule c'a pasta"

ANTIQUE BEANS AND PASTA

SERVES 6 TO 8

2 cups dried *cannellini* (white kidney beans), picked over

8 cherry tomatoes

2 large cloves garlic, peeled and left whole

2 large stalks celery, cut into pieces

1/2 flat tablespoon coarse-grained salt

PLUS

3 large cloves garlic, peeled

3 large stalks celery

1/2 cup extra-virgin olive oil

Salt and freshly ground black pepper

1/2 pound dried short pasta of different types (*pasta mischiata* or *munnezzaglia*), or broken-up vermicelli or *perciatelli*, preferably imported Italian

Soak the beans in a bowl of cold water overnight. The next morning, drain the beans, rinse them under cold running water, and put them in a medium-sized casserole along with the tomatoes, garlic, celery, and coarse salt. Add enough water to cover everything by 2 inches. Set the casserole over medium heat and simmer until the beans are completely cooked and soft, about 1 hour, adding lukewarm water as needed.

Remove 1/2 cup of the beans and save them for later use. Let the remaining beans and other ingredients rest in the casserole for 30 minutes.

Transfer the contents of the casserole to a blender or food processor and blend into a paste. Finely chop the garlic and celery together on a cutting board. Heat the olive oil in a skillet over medium heat, and when the oil is warm, add the chopped ingredients and sauté for 10 minutes, stirring every so often with a wooden spoon. Season with salt and pepper.

Transfer the bean purée to a clean casserole, along with the reserved whole beans, and set the casserole over medium heat. When it reaches a boil, transfer the sautéed vegetables and all their juices from the skillet to the casserole. Mix very well and simmer for 5 minutes more.

Add the pasta and cook it until rather soft. (The cooking time varies a lot, depending on which pasta you use. Just keep in mind that it will be 3 to 4 minutes longer than normal, since the pasta is being cooked in much less liquid.) As the pasta cooks, be careful that nothing is sticking to the bottom of casserole. The consistency of this soup should be rather thick, but add some lukewarm water if necessary. Taste for salt and pepper and serve hot.

Someone cooked this dish for me, proudly announcing that it was from Vietri, a city famous for its ceramics. When I tried to confirm the origin of this version of *pasta e fagioli* with Tony May, a real Neapolitan, he was most upset: He corrected me with the information that the birthplace of this dish was also his own birthplace, Torre del Greco, a town just outside of Naples.

pasta e fagioli con le vongole

PASTA AND BEANS WITH CLAMS

SERVES 6 TO 8

1 recipe *Pasta e Fagioli alla Napoletana*, prepared according to the directions on page 86

PLUS

1 pound small clams

Coarse-grained salt

1/3 cup cold water

1 tablespoon extra-virgin olive oil

Salt and freshly ground black pepper

While you prepare the Neapolitan pasta and beans, soak the clams for 30 minutes in a bowl of cold water containing a little coarse salt.

While the pasta is cooking in the soup, drain the clams, rinse them under cold running water, and place them in a skillet with the cold water and oil. Set the skillet, covered, over high heat and cook the clams for about 8 minutes, seasoning them with salt and pepper. Discard any clams that have not opened.

Transfer the clams to a plate and strain the juices from the skillet through paper towels directly into the soup.

When the pasta is rather soft, add the clams, mix the soup very well, and serve hot.

pasta e fagioli con le "croste"

PASTA AND BEANS WITH CHEESE RIND

SERVES 6 TO 8

1 recipe *Pasta e Fagioli alla Napoletana*, prepared according to the directions on page 86

PLUS

2 pieces Parmigiano cheese rind, about 3 inches square; or 1 piece Parmigiano cheese rind and 1 piece local pecorino or Pecorino Romano rind, each about 3 inches square

Soak the beans as described on page 86. Add the two pieces of cheese rind when you place the beans in the casserole, along with the other ingredients, including the cold water.

Remove the rinds when you add the pasta. When the pasta is rather soft, mix the soup very well, and serve hot.

pasta e ceci alla napoletana

PASTA AND CHICKPEAS, NEAPOLITAN STYLE

SERVES 6 TO 8

2 cups dried chickpeas, picked over

1 teaspoon baking soda

1/2 cup extra-virgin olive oil

Coarse-grained salt

3 large cloves garlic, peeled and finely chopped

10 sprigs Italian parsley, leaves only, coarsely chopped

Freshly ground black pepper

Large pinch of dried oregano

1 pound dried short pasta of different types (*pasta mischiata* or *munnezzaglia*), or broken-up vermicelli or *perciatelli*, preferably imported Italian

Soak the chickpeas with the baking soda in a bowl of cold water overnight. The next morning, drain the chickpeas, rinse them under cold running water, and place them in a casserole with enough water to cover them by 2 inches. Add 1 tablespoon of the oil and set the casserole over medium heat. Simmer, covered, adding more lukewarm water as needed, until the chickpeas are cooked, about 1 1/2 hours. Add coarse salt to taste, the remaining 7 tablespoons oil, and the garlic, parsley, pepper, and oregano.

Add the pasta and cook it until rather soft. (The cooking time varies a lot, depending on which pasta you use. Just keep in mind that it will be 3 to 4 minutes longer than normal, since the pasta is being cooked in much less liquid.) As the pasta cooks, be careful that nothing is sticking to the bottom of casserole. The consistency of this soup should be rather thick, but add some lukewarm water if necessary. Before serving, taste for salt and pepper. Do not be concerned if some of the chickpeas are overcooked or even falling apart—this is the correct texture for the dish.

Serve hot, with more black pepper ground onto each serving.

From its name, *pasta e fagioli*, this would appear to be an ordinary bean soup, the classic pasta and bean soup that is eaten all over Italy. But Neapolitans go beyond the basics. First of all, they typically change the name, calling it "*i fagioli con la pasta*." This gives us a sense that the pasta is no longer the shining star of the dish, and that the beans themselves and their preparation follow a kind of ritual, or at least that there is a deference to ingredients and preparation that does not accommodate inventive or fashionable ideas. I do not expect that a lot of people will prepare this recipe, although the taste is absolutely superb. Its long cooking time and combination of ingredients are so far removed from the latest fashions of presentation, texture, and—most unfortunately—taste that it is not a dish that most of the "in" restaurants are comfortable serving.

pasta e fagioli alla napoletana

PASTA AND BEANS, NEAPOLITAN STYLE

SERVES 6 TO 8

2 cups dried *cannellini* (white kidney beans), picked over

1 large clove garlic, peeled and left whole

1 medium-sized stalk celery, cut into large pieces

6 cherry tomatoes

1/2 cup extra-virgin olive oil

Coarse-grained salt

Freshly ground black pepper

Large pinch of dried oregano

1/2 pound dried short pasta of different types (*pasta mischiata* or *munnezzaglia*), or broken-up vermicelli or *perciatelli*, preferably imported Italian

TO SERVE

Sprigs of fresh oregano

Soak the beans in a bowl of cold water overnight. The next morning, drain the beans, rinse them under cold running water, and put them in a medium-sized casserole along with the garlic, celery, cherry tomatoes, 1 tablespoon of the oil, and enough cold water to cover by 2 inches. Set the casserole over medium heat and simmer, covered, adding more lukewarm water as needed, until the beans are cooked and very soft, about 1 1/2 hours.

Remove one quarter of the beans, place them in a crockery or glass bowl, and let rest, covered, until needed. Transfer the remaining contents of the casserole to the bowl of a blender or food processor, and blend until a very creamy paste forms. Pour this cream back into the casserole, add salt, pepper, oregano, and the remaining 7 tablespoons oil, and bring to a boil over medium heat.

Add the pasta and cook it until rather soft. (The cooking time varies a lot, depending on which pasta you use. Just keep in mind that it will be 3 to 4 minutes longer than normal, since the pasta is being cooked in much less liquid.) As the pasta cooks, be careful that nothing is sticking to the bottom of casserole. The consistency of this soup should be rather thick, but add some lukewarm water if necessary. Just 2 minutes before the pasta is ready, add the reserved whole beans. Serve hot, with sprigs of oregano.

VARIATIONS

1. Add one small yellow onion, cleaned and cut into large pieces, along with the other vegetables.
2. Use chicken or vegetable broth instead of the water.
3. Fresh basil leaves may be used for serving instead of the oregano.

OPPOSITE: *Whether you call this* Pasta e Fagioli *or* I Fagioli con la Pasta, *this is your basic Neapolitan pasta and bean dish.*

pasta e fave alla napoletana

PASTA AND FAVA BEANS, NEAPOLITAN STYLE

SERVES 6 TO 8

$1\frac{1}{2}$ pounds unshelled dried fava beans, picked over, or 2 pounds fresh fava beans

$\frac{1}{2}$ cup extra-virgin olive oil

1 large yellow onion, cleaned and coarsely chopped

1 medium-sized clove garlic, peeled and finely chopped

$\frac{1}{4}$ pound pancetta, coarsely ground or cut into very small pieces

Salt and freshly ground black pepper

Coarse-grained salt

$\frac{1}{2}$ pound dried short pasta of different types (*pasta mischiata* or *munnezzaglia*), or broken-up vermicelli or *perciatelli*, preferably imported Italian

10 sprigs Italian parsley, leaves only, coarsely chopped

ABOVE: *Surrounded by fresh produce at an open-air market.*

If you are using dried fava beans, soak them in a bowl of cold water overnight. The next morning, shell them, rinse under cold running water, and let rest in a bowl of cold water until needed. If you are using small fresh fava beans, soak them in a bowl of cold water for 30 minutes; you do not need to shell them.

Heat the oil in a medium-sized casserole over medium heat, and when the oil is warm, add the onion and garlic and sauté for 2 minutes, stirring with a wooden spoon. Add the pancetta, mix very well, and cook for 5 minutes more.

Drain the fava beans and add them to the casserole. Mix very well and cook for 2 minutes. Add enough water to cover the beans by 1 inch, cover the casserole, and simmer until the beans are cooked and soft (for dried beans about 35 minutes, and for fresh ones, if they are very fresh and small, about 20 minutes). Season with salt and pepper 10 minutes after you have added the water.

When the beans are almost ready, bring a medium-sized pot of cold water to a boil, add coarse salt to taste, then add the pasta and cook for about 8 minutes (several minutes less than for al dente). Drain the pasta, add it to the casserole containing the beans, and simmer until the pasta is rather soft, about 5 minutes, adding lukewarm water as needed.

Just before removing the casserole from the heat, add the parsley and mix very well. Let the soup rest for a few minutes before serving it.

pasta e fave alla salernitana

PASTA AND FAVA BEANS, SALERNO STYLE

SERVES 4 TO 6

1 pound unshelled dried fava beans, picked over

6 tablespoons extra-virgin olive oil

3 large cloves garlic, peeled and coarsely chopped

6 cherry tomatoes

7 cups cold water

Coarse-grained salt

Freshly ground black pepper

5 sprigs Italian parsley, leaves only

Large pinch of hot red pepper flakes

1/2 pound dried short pasta of different types (*pasta mischiata* or *munnezzaglia*), or broken-up vermicelli or *perciatelli*, preferably imported Italian

TO SERVE

Extra-virgin olive oil

Soak the beans in a bowl of cold water overnight. The next morning, shell them, rinse under cold running water, and let rest in a bowl of cold water until needed.

Pour the oil into a stockpot and set the pot over medium heat. When the oil is lukewarm, add the garlic and lightly sauté for less than 1 minute; the garlic should still be very light in color. Add the fava beans, cherry tomatoes, and the cold water. Season with coarse salt and pepper.

Bring the mixture to a simmer and cook until the beans are almost completely dissolved, about 1 hour. Add the parsley and cook for 5 minutes more. Stir every so often with a wooden spoon because the dissolved fava beans have a tendency to stick to the bottom of the pan.

Remove the stockpot from the heat and let the fava mixture rest until it is lukewarm, about 30 minutes.

Transfer the contents of the stockpot to the bowl of a blender or food processor, and blend very well. Return the bean purée to the stockpot and set the pot over medium heat. Taste for salt and pepper, and add the red pepper flakes.

When the purée reaches a boil, put in the pasta and cook it until rather soft, adding a little boiling water as needed. (This is the classic way to cook the pasta. A shortcut not loved at all by the people of Campania is to parboil the pasta in salted water, drain it, and add it to the purée.)

Mix the soup very well and serve hot or at room temperature after no longer than 1 hour. In Salerno, some olive oil is drizzled over each serving.

pasta e cavolo

PASTA AND CABBAGE

SERVES 6

1 medium-sized cabbage (*cavolo "cappuccio,"* or plain cabbage, not savoy) about 2 pounds, cleaned, all large veins removed and all leaves cut into 2-inch-wide strips

Coarse-grained salt

1 tablespoon unsalted butter

3 tablespoons extra-virgin olive oil

1/4 pound pancetta or prosciutto, thinly sliced

2 stalks celery, cut into large pieces

2 carrots, scraped and cut into large pieces

1 large yellow onion, cleaned and cut into large pieces

5 cups completely defatted chicken broth, preferably homemade, lukewarm

5 cherry tomatoes

Salt and freshly ground black pepper

TO COOK THE PASTA

Coarse-grained salt

1/2 pound dried short pasta of different types (*pasta mischiata* or *munnezzaglia*), or broken-up vermicelli or *perciatelli*, preferably imported Italian

TO SERVE

10 sprigs Italian parsley, leaves only, coarsely chopped

Soak the cabbage strips in a bowl of cold water for 30 minutes. Bring a large pot of cold water to a boil over medium heat, adding coarse salt to taste. Drain the cabbage and blanch it for 1 minute in the boiling water. Drain the cabbage again and rinse it under cold running water.

Put the butter and oil in a medium-sized casserole and set the casserole over low heat. When the butter has melted, arrange the pancetta, covering the bottom of the casserole with the slices. Then place the celery, carrots, and onions over the pancetta and, finally, add the parboiled cabbage on top.

Raise the heat to medium and cook for 5 minutes without stirring; rather, shake the casserole two or three times. Add the broth and the cherry tomatoes, season with salt and pepper, cover, and cook for 1 1/2 hours, mixing every so often with a wooden spoon. By this time, the cabbage and all the vegetables will be completely cooked and very soft.

Let the mixture rest in the casserole for about 30 minutes before transferring it to a blender or food processor. Blend very well to get a smooth cream. Return the cream to the casserole and place the casserole over low heat. Taste for salt and pepper and simmer for 15 minutes, stirring every so often with a wooden spoon.

Meanwhile, bring a medium-sized pot of cold water to a boil over medium heat, adding coarse salt to taste; add the pasta and cook it for 5 minutes. Drain the pasta, transfer it to the casserole containing the cabbage cream, and simmer for about 5 minutes more, until the pasta is completely cooked but not mushy. The consistency of this soup should be rather thick.

Serve hot, with the parsley.

pasta e zucca

PASTA WITH SQUASH

SERVES 6

3 large cloves garlic, peeled

3 stalks celery, cut into large pieces

6 cherry tomatoes

1 butternut or acorn squash, about 3 pounds, peeled, all the seeds and filaments removed, cut into large pieces

Large pinch of coarse-grained salt

1/2 cup extra-virgin olive oil

About 4 cups cold water, cold chicken broth, or cold vegetable broth

10 sprigs Italian parsley, leaves only, coarsely chopped

Salt and freshly ground black pepper

Large pinch of hot red pepper flakes

1/2 pound dried short pasta of different types (*pasta mischiata* or *munnezzaglia*) or broken-up vermicelli or *perciatelli*, preferably imported Italian

Finely chop the garlic and celery together on a cutting board. Cut the cherry tomatoes in half. Place the squash pieces in a bowl of cold water with the coarse-grained salt, and let soak for 15 minutes.

Heat 5 tablespoons of the oil in a medium-sized casserole over medium heat, and when the oil is warm, add the celery mixture and sauté for 5 minutes, stirring every so often with a wooden spoon.

Drain the squash and rinse under cold running water, then add it to the casserole. Sauté for 2 minutes, then add enough cold water to cover by 1 inch. Simmer, covered, for 10 minutes. Add the cherry tomatoes and parsley. Season with salt, pepper, and red pepper flakes. Cook the squash, covered, until it falls apart, about 1 hour, adding more liquid as needed.

Transfer the contents of the casserole to a crockery or glass bowl and let rest until cool, about 30 minutes. Pour the mixture into a blender or food processor, and process until a very creamy paste forms.

Pour the cream back into the casserole and place it over medium heat. Taste for salt, pepper, and the red pepper flakes; the cream should be rather spicy, not sweet at all. Add the remaining 3 tablespoons oil, mix very well, and bring the soup to a boil.

Add the pasta and cook until soft. (The cooking time varies a lot depending on which pasta you use. Just keep in mind that it will take 3 to 4 minutes longer than normal, since the pasta is cooked in much less liquid.) As the pasta cooks, be careful that nothing is sticking to the bottom of the casserole; if necessary, add some lukewarm water, but remember that the consistency of this soup should be rather thick. Serve hot.

NOTE: Cheese is never served with this soup.

CHAPTER THREE

naples: the home of dried pasta and tomatoes like no others in the world

1600
4.000 KILO
3200 KILO
1600
Frutta

Naples is responsible for popularizing the ripe, red tomato, not only for its own cuisine but for the entire world. In the sixteenth century, when tomatoes first arrived in Italy from the New World, they were small and yellowish. Fried green tomatoes, a Florentine dish made from the unripe fruit, was the initial documented use. In his first Neapolitan cookbook, *Il Cuoco Galante* (*The Galant Cook*), published in 1773, the author, Vincenzo Corrado, included only one tomato dish—a green tomato baked in a crust.

By the early years of the nineteenth century, Neapolitans had revolutionized the tomato, allowing it to become red and juicy before cooking with it. An entire cuisine was transformed by the sauces made from these flavorful, ripe tomatoes, which were added to meat, fish, and vegetable dishes, but most notably to pasta. The signature dish of modern Naples, pasta with tomato sauce, was born. Around 1840, it became known internationally as "pasta in the latest Neapolitan style."

San Marzano tomatoes, or *pomidori di San Marzano*, are considered the best tomatoes for preparing all the different Neapolitan tomato sauces—in Naples and beyond. These plum tomatoes are cultivated in Salerno, in the area between Sarno and Nocera Inferiore. They are oval shaped with a shiny red color and few seeds. As Neapolitans prefer, they are not extremely sweet and have no aftertaste.

Authentic San Marzano tomatoes are extremely fragile and have only a short shelf life. They are difficult to can because they break easily, but they are available and imported to the United States in canned form. Unfortunately, a new, supposedly improved variety of San Marzano tomatoes is being grown and exported today. Labeled "rectified San Marzano tomatoes," they last longer and do not require the special care required by authentic San Marzano tomatoes, which must be protected by tents and harvested at night. Although the so-called rectified tomatoes are cheaper and retain their shape when canned, the unique taste and texture of the true San Marzano is sacrificed.

Fresh San Marzano-type tomatoes are also being sold under the name San Marzano in the United States, even if they are grown in California. To combat this masquerade, cans of genuine San Marzano tomatoes have begun to carry the official seals of the Italian government and the consortium of growers. Look for them at Italian markets or specialty food shops.

Like most non-Neapolitans (and even many natives), I have not had the opportunity to taste the Corbarino, a rare tomato from Corbara, which is near the Amalfi coast. Those who have tell me that this tomato captures the flavors of the sea near which it's grown—it's a little sour with a slight taste of fish—while retaining the natural sweetness of tomatoes. When a pasta dish is prepared with Corbarino tomatoes, it is said that "the clams have just escaped."

PRECEDING PAGES AND ABOVE: *Fresh tomatoes are front and center at these Neapolitan vegetable stands.*

"pommarola" alla napoletana

THE CLASSIC NEAPOLITAN TOMATO SAUCE

MAKES ABOUT 3 CUPS (ENOUGH FOR 1 POUND OF VERMICELLI)

- 3 pounds ripe tomatoes, preferably San Marzano-type plum tomatoes, cut into large pieces
- 2 medium-sized carrots, scraped and cut into small pieces or coarsely chopped
- 2 large red onions, peeled
- 2 stalks celery, cut into small pieces
- 4 tablespoons (2 ounces) unsalted butter, instead of the traditional lard
- 1/4 cup extra-virgin olive oil
- Salt and abundant freshly ground black pepper
- 16 fresh basil leaves, torn into thirds

Place the tomatoes, carrots, one of the onions, coarsely chopped, and the celery in a nonreactive casserole, preferably flameproof terra-cotta, over medium heat. Cover the casserole and cook for 25 minutes, mixing every so often with a wooden spoon to be sure nothing is sticking on the bottom.

Pass the contents of the casserole through a food mill into a crockery or glass bowl, using the disk with the smallest holes.

Finely chop the remaining onion and transfer the onion to the same casserole. Add the butter and olive oil. Set the casserole over medium heat and lightly sauté until the onion becomes translucent, about 5 minutes. Add the strained tomato mixture, season with salt and abundant pepper, then add the basil and simmer for at least 25 minutes more. The tomato sauce is now ready to be used.

sugo di pomodoro all'aglio alla salernitana

GARLIC TOMATO SAUCE, SALERNO STYLE

MAKES ABOUT 3 CUPS (ENOUGH FOR 1 POUND OF VERMICELLI)

- 2 large cloves garlic, peeled and cut into slivers
- 1/2 cup extra-virgin olive oil
- 2 pounds ripe but not overripe tomatoes, preferably San Marzano-type plum tomatoes, blanched (see page 263), skin and seeds removed, and cut into "fillets"
- Salt and freshly ground black pepper
- 10 fresh basil leaves

Place a medium-sized nonreactive casserole, preferably flameproof terra-cotta, containing the garlic and oil over medium heat, and sauté until the garlic is very light golden.

Add the tomato fillets and cook them for a few minutes over medium heat. The fillets should still retain their shape and be barely cooked.

Season with salt and pepper, add the basil, and cook for 30 seconds more, stirring constantly. The sauce is now ready; serve while still very hot.

vermicelli *or* perciatelli al sugo di pomodoro alla salernitana

VERMICELLI OR *PERCIATELLI* AND TOMATO SAUCE FROM SALERNO

SERVES 4 TO 6

- 2 pounds ripe but not overripe tomatoes, left whole
- 1/4 cup extra-virgin olive oil
- 1 clove garlic, peeled and left whole
- Salt and freshly ground black pepper
- Coarse-grained salt
- 1 pound dried vermicelli or *perciatelli*, preferably imported Italian
- 4 large fresh basil leaves

Wash the tomatoes very well, removing the stems. Place the whole tomatoes in a medium-sized nonreactive casserole, preferably flameproof terra-cotta, and press them gently with the palms of your hands to flatten them slightly. Place the casserole, covered, over low heat and cook for 15 minutes, shaking the casserole several times to be sure nothing sticks to the bottom. Remove the casserole from the heat and pass the contents through a food mill into a crockery or glass bowl, using the disk with the smallest holes.

Heat the oil in the same casserole over low heat, and when the oil is warm, add the garlic and lightly sauté for 30 seconds. Discard the garlic and add the strained tomatoes. Simmer for 30 minutes, adding salt and pepper to taste after 15 minutes.

Add the pasta and cook it until rather soft. (The cooking time varies a lot, depending on which pasta you use. Just keep in mind that it will be 3 to 4 minutes longer than normal, since the pasta is being cooked in much less liquid.) As the pasta cooks, be careful that nothing is sticking to the bottom of casserole. The consistency of this soup should be rather thick, but add some lukewarm water if necessary.

Just a few minutes before the sauce is ready, add the basil leaves. Drain the pasta, transfer it to a large bowl, pour the sauce over it, and mix.

sugo di pomodoro alla salernitana

TOMATO SAUCE, SALERNO STYLE

MAKES ABOUT 3 CUPS (ENOUGH FOR 1 POUND OF VERMICELLI)

- 1 yellow onion, cleaned and coarsely chopped
- 1/2 cup extra-virgin olive oil
- 2 pounds ripe tomatoes, blanched (see page 263), skin and seeds removed; or 2 pounds drained canned tomatoes, preferably imported Italian, seeded
- Salt and freshly ground black pepper
- 10 fresh basil leaves, torn into thirds

Place the onion and oil in a medium-sized nonreactive casserole, preferably flameproof terra-cotta, over medium heat and sauté for 2 minutes, mixing constantly to be sure the onion does not brown. Pour the contents of the casserole through a strainer into a bowl and return the strained oil to the casserole; discard the onion.

Place the casserole over low heat, add the tomatoes, and cook for about 25 minutes, until a rather dense sauce has formed.

Taste for salt and pepper, add the basil, and cook for 1 minute more. The sauce is now ready to be used.

vermicelli al pomodoro alla napoletana

VERMICELLI WITH NEAPOLITAN TOMATO SAUCE

SERVES 4 TO 6

2 pounds ripe tomatoes, blanched (see page 263), skin and seeds removed; or 2 pounds drained canned tomatoes, preferably imported Italian, seeded

6 tablespoons extra-virgin olive oil

Salt and freshly ground black pepper

20 large fresh basil leaves

Coarse-grained salt

1 pound dried vermicelli, preferably imported Italian

6 heaping tablespoons freshly grated Parmigiano

2 large cloves garlic, peeled and finely chopped

From this sauce arose the famous dish Spaghetti with Tomato Sauce, which in Neapolitan dialect is called "Spaghetti e'l Pummarele 'Ncoppe."

If you are using fresh tomatoes, cut them into large pieces. Place the fresh or canned tomatoes in a large skillet, add the oil, and set the skillet over medium heat. Sauté for 10 minutes, stirring every so often with a wooden spoon. Season with salt and pepper. The tomatoes should be barely cooked—not completely mushy. Tear ten basil leaves into thirds, add them, mix very well, and cook for 2 to 3 minutes more. The sauce should be rather thick.

Bring a large pot of cold water to a boil over medium heat, add coarse salt to taste, then add the pasta and cook until al dente, 9 to 12 minutes depending on the brand.

Drain the pasta, transfer it to a large bowl, add the cheese, and mix very well. Then transfer it to a warmed serving platter. Pour the tomato sauce over the pasta and sprinkle it with the chopped garlic and the remaining basil leaves, left whole. Serve hot.

sugo di pomodoro con la pancetta

TOMATO SAUCE WITH PANCETTA

MAKES ABOUT 3 CUPS (ENOUGH FOR 1 POUND OF VERMICELLI)

6 tablespoons extra-virgin olive oil

1/4 pound pancetta or prosciutto, finely ground or cut into tiny pieces

3 pounds ripe tomatoes, preferably San Marzano-type plum tomatoes, cut into small pieces; or 3 pounds drained canned San Marzano-type plum tomatoes, preferably imported Italian, cut into small pieces

1 large yellow onion, cleaned and coarsely chopped

3 medium-sized cloves garlic, peeled and finely chopped

Salt and freshly ground black pepper

Heat the oil in a medium-sized nonreactive casserole, preferably flameproof terra-cotta, over medium heat, add the pancetta, and sauté for 5 minutes, stirring constantly with a wooden spoon. Add the tomatoes, onion, and garlic, cover the casserole, and simmer for at least 40 minutes, stirring every so often with the wooden spoon.

Pass the contents of the casserole through a food mill into a crockery or glass bowl, using the disk with the smallest holes. Then place the sauce back in the casserole, season with salt and pepper, and simmer to the consistency of a light paste, about 20 minutes. The sauce is now ready to be used.

2 CHILI
2000

vermicelli o perciatelli alla puttanesca

VERMICELLI OR *PERCIATELLI* IN SAVORY TOMATO SAUCE

SERVES 4 TO 6

6 tablespoons extra-virgin olive oil

4 large cloves garlic, peeled and left whole

$1^{1}/_{2}$ pounds ripe tomatoes, blanched (see page 263), skin and seeds removed; or $1^{1}/_{2}$ pounds drained canned tomatoes, preferably imported Italian, seeded

3 tablespoons capers preserved in wine vinegar, drained

3 ounces Gaeta olives, pitted

Coarse-grained salt

1 pound dried vermicelli, *perciatelli*, or spaghetti, preferably imported Italian

20 sprigs Italian parsley, leaves only

4 whole anchovies preserved in salt, boned and rinsed under cold running water; or 8 anchovy fillets packed in oil, drained

Salt and freshly ground black pepper

TO SERVE

Fresh basil leaves

Place the oil in a medium-sized nonreactive casserole, preferably flameproof terra-cotta, over medium heat, and when the oil is warm, add the garlic and lightly sauté until very light golden.

Remove and discard the garlic, add the tomatoes, and cook for 10 minutes. Add the capers and olives, and cook for 2 minutes more.

Meanwhile, place a large pot of cold water over medium heat, and when it reaches a boil, add coarse salt to taste, then add the pasta, and cook until al dente, 9 to 12 minutes depending on the brand.

To finish the sauce, finely chop the parsley and cut the anchovies into small pieces. When the sauce is ready, lower the heat and add the parsley and the anchovies. Mix well, cook for 2 minutes more, and season with salt and pepper.

Drain the pasta, transfer it to a large bowl, pour the sauce over it, and mix. Place the pasta on a large serving platter and serve topped with fresh basil leaves.

VARIATIONS

1. The garlic may be cut into small slivers, sautéed, and left in the tomato sauce.
2. Add hot red pepper flakes to taste with the seasoning.

OPPOSITE: *The famed San Marzano tomatoes.*

As we see in many nineteenth-century drawings, pasta was originally sold on the streets, already cooked, with grated cheese clinging to the long, wet strands that were held in the hand. Later, a little tomato was sometimes added as a patriotic tribute to the red-shirted Garibaldi and his role in the 1861 unification of Italy.

vermicelli "o' garibaldi"

VERMICELLI AND TOMATO SAUCE

SERVES 4 TO 6

2 1/2 pounds ripe tomatoes, blanched (see page 263), skin and seeds removed; or 2 1/2 pounds drained canned tomatoes, preferably imported Italian, seeded

Coarse-grained salt

1 pound dried vermicelli or spaghetti, preferably imported Italian

TO SERVE

Abundant fresh basil leaves

Freshly ground black pepper

6 heaping tablespoons freshly grated aged local pecorino or Pecorino Romano cheese

Place the fresh or canned tomatoes in a medium-sized nonreactive casserole, preferably flameproof terra-cotta, over medium heat. Season with salt and cook, stirring every so often with a wooden spoon, for 45 minutes.

Meanwhile, bring a large pot of cold water to a boil over medium heat and add coarse salt to taste. Add the pasta and cook until al dente, 9 to 12 minutes depending on the brand.

Drain the pasta, put it in a large bowl, and add the still very warm tomato sauce. Mix well and transfer to a serving platter. Serve hot, with abundant fresh basil leaves, pepper, and the cheese.

vermicelli *or* perciatelli al pomodoro alla marinara

VERMICELLI OR *PERCIATELLI* WITH TOMATO SAUCE, SAILOR'S STYLE

SERVES 4 TO 6

6 tablespoons extra-virgin olive oil

1 1/2 pounds fresh tomatoes, blanched (see page 263), skin and seeds removed, cut into large pieces

2 cloves garlic, peeled and cut into thin slivers

1/4 cup capers preserved in wine vinegar, drained

3 ounces pitted Gaeta olives, cut into thirds

Salt and freshly ground black pepper

Coarse-grained salt

1 pound dried vermicelli or *perciatelli*, preferably imported Italian

10 sprigs Italian parsley, leaves only, coarsely chopped

2 whole anchovies preserved in salt, boned, rinsed under cold running water, and cut into small pieces; or 4 anchovy fillets packed in oil, drained and cut into small pieces

Heat the oil in a medium-sized nonreactive casserole, preferably flameproof terra-cotta, over medium heat, and when the oil is warm, add the tomatoes and cook for 2 minutes. Then add the garlic and lightly sauté for 5 minutes, stirring every so often with a wooden spoon.

Add the capers and olives and season with salt and pepper, keeping in mind that the anchovies will be salty.

Meanwhile, place a large pot of cold water over medium heat, and when it reaches a boil, add coarse salt to taste, then add the pasta, and cook until al dente, 9 to 12 minutes depending on the brand.

When the tomatoes are barely cooked, add the parsley and anchovies, mix very well, and cook for 1 minute more. Drain the pasta, transfer it to a large bowl, pour the sauce over it, and mix.

maccheroni alla marinara

PASTA WITH TOMATO SAUCE, SAILOR'S STYLE

SERVES 4 TO 6

10 large sprigs Italian parsley, leaves only

2 large cloves garlic, peeled and finely chopped or left whole

6 tablespoons extra-virgin olive oil

2 pounds ripe tomatoes, blanched (see page 263), skin and seeds removed, cut into large pieces

Salt and freshly ground black pepper

Coarse-grained salt

1 pound dried *perciatelli* or spaghetti, preferably imported Italian

1/4 cup capers preserved in wine vinegar, drained

3 ounces pitted Gaeta olives, cut into pieces

TO SERVE

Abundant fresh basil leaves

Place the parsley, garlic, oil, and tomatoes in a crockery or glass bowl, season with salt and pepper, and mix very well. Cover the bowl and refrigerate for at least 2 hours.

Bring a large pot of cold water to a boil over medium heat and add coarse salt to taste. Add the pasta and cook until al dente, 9 to 12 minutes depending on the brand.

Drain the pasta, transfer it to a large bowl, add the cold tomato sauce, and stir in the capers and olives. Mix very well and serve topped with abundant fresh basil.

VARIATION

Finely chop the parsley and garlic together on a cutting board. Heat the olive oil in a medium saucepan over medium heat. When the oil is warm, add the chopped ingredients and sauté for less than 20 seconds. Add the tomatoes and cook for a few minutes: The tomatoes should remain in pieces, not break down into a sauce. Season with salt and pepper.

Meanwhile, bring a large pot of cold water to a boil over medium heat, add coarse salt to taste, add the pasta, and cook until al dente, 9 to 12 minutes depending on the brand.

When the pasta is almost ready, add the capers and olives to the sauce and mix very well. Drain the pasta, transfer it to a large bowl, pour in all the sauce, and mix very well. Transfer to a large serving platter and serve hot, topped with abundant basil.

OPPOSITE: *Ripe tomatoes on the vine.*

This dish, from the volcanic Isle of Procida, is traditionally made from grilled tomatoes that are cooked one by one, using the same old-fashioned method that was used for toasting coffee beans at home. The coffee beans were placed in a perforated cylindrical container that was rotated over hot ash. In the same way, the tomatoes for this sauce are grilled until their skins are lightly burned. After grilling, the tomato pulp is much sweeter than when cooked on the stovetop. This sweetness, plus the bitter taste of the skins and the completely uncooked olive oil, makes for some surprising contrasts.

la carrettiera di procida

PASTA FROM PROCIDA

SERVES 4 TO 6

$1^1/_2$ pounds ripe but not overripe tomatoes, preferably San Marzano-type plum tomatoes

$^3/_4$ cup extra-virgin olive oil

3 medium-sized cloves garlic, peeled and finely chopped

Salt and freshly ground black pepper

Large pinch of hot red pepper flakes

20 fresh oregano leaves, or a large pinch of dried oregano

Coarse-grained salt

1 pound dried *perciatelli* or spaghetti, preferably imported Italian

TO SERVE

Fresh basil or oregano leaves

All the carrietierre *are peppery and based on cooked tomatoes with aromatic herbs that differ from one region to another. This version lives up to its peppery name, but differs in that it is not really a sauce. The tomatoes are cooked over charcoal, but do not dissolve.*

If you are using a grill, have the hot ashes ready; if you are using an oven, preheat it to 450°F.

Wash the tomatoes well and dry them. Use a fork to prick the tomatoes in two or three places. Place them on a grill rack over the hot ashes and roast them, turning them twice, until charred all over. If you are using the oven, very lightly oil a jelly-roll pan, arrange the tomatoes on it, and bake them for 40 minutes, turning the tomatoes twice; by this time, the skin of the tomatoes should be almost as burnt as if you had cooked them over ash.

Transfer the roasted tomatoes to a plate and carefully skin them. Cut them into large pieces and put them in a large crockery or glass bowl. Add the oil, garlic, salt and pepper to taste, large pinch of red pepper flakes (or less, to your taste), and the oregano. Mix well with a wooden spoon.

Bring a large pot of cold water to a boil, add coarse salt to taste, then add the pasta and cook until al dente, 9 to 12 minutes depending on the brand.

Drain the pasta and transfer it to the bowl of sauce. Mix well, place on a warm serving platter, sprinkle with the basil or oregano, and serve hot.

maccheroni con i pomodori alla salernitana

PASTA WITH STUFFED TOMATOES, SALERNO STYLE

SERVES 6

6 large round tomatoes, ripe but not overripe

Fine salt

FOR THE STUFFING

2 large white stalks celery, all strings removed

10 sprigs Italian parsley, leaves only

1 large clove garlic, peeled

2 heaping tablespoons capers preserved in wine vinegar, drained

2 whole anchovies preserved in salt, boned and rinsed under cold running water; or 4 anchovy fillets packed in oil, drained

4 large fresh basil leaves

Salt and freshly ground black pepper

2 tablespoons extra-virgin olive oil

TO COOK THE TOMATOES

1/2 cup extra-virgin olive oil

Salt and freshly ground black pepper

FOR THE PASTA

Coarse-grained salt

1 pound dried *maccheroni*, preferably imported Italian

10 sprigs Italian parsley, leaves only, coarsely chopped

TO SERVE

Abundant fresh basil leaves

In this dish from Salerno, pasta is paired with vegetables yet again. The stuffed tomatoes seem like they could be a complete dish, but not to the locals. Here they are the main ingredient of an unusual sauce that is always eaten along with pasta.

Wash the tomatoes very well and cut them in half horizontally. Remove all the seeds, sprinkle a little fine salt inside each of the tomato halves, and place them upside down over paper towels. Let rest for 30 minutes.

PREPARE THE STUFFING: Finely chop the celery, parsley, garlic, capers, anchovies, and basil all together on a cutting board. Transfer the mixture to a crockery or glass bowl, add salt and pepper to taste, then add the oil and mix very well. Spoon some of the stuffing into each tomato half.

COOK THE TOMATOES: Heat the 1/2 cup oil in a large skillet over medium heat, and when the oil is warm, arrange the stuffed tomatoes in one layer in the skillet. Season with salt and pepper, sprinkling not only the tomatoes but also the oil in the skillet. Gently cook for 20 minutes or more, until the tomatoes are very soft but still whole.

COOK THE PASTA: Bring a large pot of cold water to a boil over medium heat, add coarse salt to taste, then add the pasta and cook until al dente, 9 to 12 minutes depending on the brand.

When it is ready, drain the pasta and add the parsley and enough oil from the tomatoes to coat the pasta completely. Mix very well, then transfer the pasta to a serving platter. Place the tomatoes over the pasta, scatter the basil leaves over all, and serve immediately. Each serving will consist of a portion of pasta with two stuffed tomato halves arranged on top.

VARIATION

Instead of sautéing the tomatoes in a skillet, place them with the oil in a baking dish and bake in a preheated 400°F oven for 25 minutes.

pasta con pomodori ripieni al forno

PASTA WITH BAKED STUFFED TOMATOES

SERVES 6

6 medium-sized round tomatoes, ripe but not overripe

Fine salt

FOR THE STUFFING

2 large cloves garlic, peeled

10 large sprigs Italian parsley, leaves only

6 large fresh basil leaves

4 heaping tablespoons freshly grated aged local pecorino or Pecorino Romano cheese

4 heaping tablespoons very fine unseasoned bread crumbs, preferably homemade, lightly toasted

Salt and freshly ground black pepper

6 tablespoons extra-virgin olive oil, or more if needed to make a smooth stuffing

PLUS

3 tablespoons extra-virgin olive oil

3/4 cup cold water

Salt and freshly ground black pepper

Large pinch of hot red pepper flakes

FOR THE PASTA

Coarse-grained salt

1 large clove garlic, peeled and cut into thin slivers

1 pound dried long pasta, such as *perciatelli* or spaghetti, preferably imported Italian

Abundant fresh basil leaves

Wash the tomatoes very well and cut them in half horizontally. Remove all the seeds, sprinkle a little fine salt inside each of the halves, and place them upside down on paper towels. Let rest for 10 minutes.

PREPARE THE STUFFING: Finely chop the garlic, parsley, and basil all together on a cutting board, then mix them with the grated pecorino and bread crumbs. Transfer all these ingredients to a bowl, season with salt and pepper, and add the oil. Mix very well, adding more oil if the stuffing is not very smooth.

Preheat the oven to 375°F.

Spoon the stuffing into the tomato halves and place them all in a glass baking dish. Mix the oil and the water together, seasoning with salt and pepper and the red pepper flakes. Pour this mixture into the baking dish and bake for 25 minutes, or until the tomatoes are very soft.

COOK THE PASTA: Bring a large pot of cold water to a boil over medium heat and add coarse salt to taste and the garlic slivers. Add the pasta and cook until al dente, 9 to 12 minutes depending on the brand.

Meanwhile, transfer the tomatoes to a serving platter and cover them with aluminum foil to keep them very warm, leaving all the juices in the baking dish.

When the pasta is ready, drain it, and add it to the baking dish with the still-hot juices in the pan. Add the basil, mix very well, and serve immediately. Each serving will consist of a portion of pasta with two stuffed tomato halves.

OPPOSITE: *Pasta with Baked Stuffed Tomatoes, foreground, with Mount Vesuvius in the background.*

Neapolitan *caponata*, also known as *panzella alla marinara*, is generally much more elaborate than the *caponata* from other parts of Campania. It may be composed of anchovies, onions, tomatoes, garlic, green peppers, and olives seasoned with salt and pepper, olive oil, and red wine vinegar. These ingredients are mixed with some lightly soaked sea biscuits, or *friselle*.

caponata alla napoletana

NEAPOLITAN "CAPONATA" SALAD

SERVES 4

1 1/2 pounds ripe but not overripe tomatoes, preferably San Marzano–type plum tomatoes

1/3 cup extra-virgin olive oil

Salt

2 large red onions, preferably Tropea type, cleaned and very thinly sliced, soaking in a bowl of very cold water

4 *friselle* (Neapolitan toasted half rolls)

2 tablespoons red wine vinegar

Abundant fresh basil leaves

Cut the tomatoes into 1 1/2-inch pieces and place them in a crockery or glass bowl. Season the tomatoes with the oil and salt to taste. Drain the onions, leaving the slices whole, and add them to the tomatoes.

Briefly soak the *friselle* in cold water and place one on each serving plate. Drizzle 1/2 tablespoon of the vinegar on top of each *frisella*.

Add the basil to the tomatoes and mix very well. Arrange some of the tomato mixture over each *frisella* and serve.

VARIATIONS

1. Add one yellow or red bell pepper, cleaned and cut into thin strips.
2. With or without the peppers in the first variation, add 4 ounces canned tuna, packed in olive oil, and drained.

RIGHT: *A vendor proudly displays his special "Perini" Tomatoes in this hand.*

pasta in insalata alla napoletana

PASTA WITH TOMATO SALAD, NEAPOLITAN STYLE

SERVES 4 TO 6

1 pound ripe tomatoes, blanched (see page 263), skin and seeds removed, cut into 1-inch-wide strips

1/4 pound pitted Gaeta olives, cut in half

3 heaping tablespoons capers preserved in wine vinegar, drained

Salt and abundant freshly ground black pepper

1/2 cup extra-virgin olive oil

Coarse-grained salt

1 pound dried *mostaccioli*, preferably imported Italian

TO SERVE

Abundant fresh basil leaves

Do not confuse this dish with the typical American cold pasta salad. Here, the pasta is just cooked, and while still very hot, quickly but thoroughly tossed with the cut-up and dressed tomatoes. The combination is served immediately, so the pasta remains warm.

Place the tomatoes in a crockery or glass bowl along with the olives and capers. Season with salt and abundant black pepper. Add the oil, mix very well, and let rest, covered, in the refrigerator for at least 1 hour.

Bring a large pot of cold water to a boil over medium heat, add coarse salt to taste, then add the pasta and cook until al dente, 9 to 12 minutes depending on the brand.

Drain the pasta. Remove the tomato mixture from the refrigerator and combine it with the pasta. Sprinkle the basil leaves all over, mix well, and serve immediately. The pasta should still be very warm.

insalate di pomodoro alla napoletana

NEAPOLITAN TOMATO SALADS

EACH SERVES 4

USING NOT COMPLETELY RIPE TOMATOES

- $1\frac{1}{2}$ pounds tomatoes (not plum tomatoes), very light green or slightly reddish in color, cleaned, washed very well, and cut into $\frac{3}{4}$-inch-thick slices
- 5 tablespoons extra-virgin olive oil
- Fine salt and freshly ground black pepper
- 2 medium-sized cloves garlic, peeled and finely chopped
- $\frac{1}{2}$ tablespoon fresh oregano leaves, or a very large pinch of dried oregano

USING VERY RIPE TOMATOES

- $1\frac{1}{2}$ pounds ripe San Marzano-type plum tomatoes, trimmed, washed very well, and cut in half vertically
- $\frac{1}{4}$ cup extra-virgin olive oil
- Coarse-grained salt
- Freshly ground black pepper
- 10 large fresh basil leaves, torn into thirds
- Several ice cubes

USING NOT COMPLETELY RIPE TOMATOES: Arrange the tomato slices on a serving platter. Drizzle the oil over them, and season with fine salt and pepper. At the very last moment before serving, sprinkle the garlic and oregano over the tomatoes.

USING VERY RIPE TOMATOES: Arrange the tomato halves, cut sides up, on a serving platter. Drizzle the oil over them, season with coarse salt and pepper, and arrange the basil on top.

Place the ice cubes among the tomato halves and serve immediately. The tomatoes should be very cold.

ABOVE: *The first of these salads features tomatoes that are "vierdi, vierdi"—not completely ripe.*

timballo di maccheroni e pomodori

TIMBALE OF PASTA AND TOMATOES

SERVES 8 TO 10

1 pound dried short pasta, such as *maccheroncini*, *pennette*, or *tubetti*, preferably imported Italian

1 1/4 cups extra-virgin olive oil

4 pounds ripe but not overripe tomatoes (choose medium-sized, round vine tomatoes), cut in half

Salt and freshly ground black pepper

Dried oregano leaves

3/4 pound *fiordilatte* (mozzarella made from cow's milk), cut into thin slices

Abundant fresh basil leaves

2 whole anchovies preserved in salt, boned, rinsed under cold running water, and cut into small pieces; or 4 anchovy fillets packed in oil, drained and cut into small pieces

1/4 cup unseasoned bread crumbs, preferably homemade, lightly toasted

TO SERVE

Fresh basil sprigs

Pasta timbales are very popular throughout southern Italy. They may have a crust, usually made of a sweetened pastry, or they can be baked in a mold or any kind of deep, drum-shaped pan.

Soak the pasta in 1/2 cup of the oil for 30 minutes. Preheat the oven to 375°F.

Lightly oil the bottom and sides of a medium-sized nonreactive casserole, preferably flameproof terra-cotta or enamel. Use a fourth of the tomato halves to make a layer on the bottom of the casserole, arranging them with the cut sides down. Make a second layer of tomatoes, this time with the cut sides facing up. Season with salt, pepper, and oregano, then layer half of the mozzarella on top. Sprinkle some of the basil leaves over the mozzarella and season again with salt, pepper, and oregano.

From this point on, when you make the different layers, include two or three pieces of anchovy in each and season with salt, pepper, and oregano.

Arrange half of the pasta, with half of its unabsorbed oil, over the mozzarella. Make another layer, using half of the remaining tomatoes, then a layer of the remaining pasta; layer on the remaining mozzarella, basil, and, finally, the remaining tomatoes, cut sides down. Pour the remaining 3/4 cup of oil over the top and sprinkle with bread crumbs.

Cover the casserole and bake for 40 minutes. By this time, the pasta should be cooked and soft. Gently mix everything together and serve hot, topped with fresh basil sprigs.

RIGHT: *Notice how the tomatoes, mozzarella, and pasta are layered in this timbale.*

dried pasta

LEFT: *Shopkeepers used to combine the broken-up pieces of pasta from different boxes to create* pasta mischiata *(mixed pasta). Actually, the Neapolitan word for such a mixture,* munnezzaglia, *better describes the idea of all the broken pieces mixed together. Today, such a mixture has become the "official" pasta in Naples, to be used for almost all the pasta dishes with vegetables or legumes.*

Until the unification of Italy in 1860, northern Italians called Neapolitans mangiamaccheroni *(macaroni eaters). This was not meant as a compliment. By this time, pasta had become almost a staple of the Neapolitan diet, but that was not the case elsewhere in Italy. Soon after unification, however, the rest of the country followed suit, and pasta factories began to appear in the Liguria region. But there is no doubt that Naples remains the capital of dried commercial pasta available under the generic name* maccheroni.

Italians have been making fresh pasta for hundreds, if not thousands, of years (long before Marco Polo ever traveled to China). In the early days of the Roman Empire, wheat was imported into Italy from Egypt and the northwestern African coast. By the fall of the empire, Sicily had become the granary of the Mediterranean world, and most authorities now feel that pasta originated there. Milled wheat was mixed with water and then dried in the sun and sea air to preserve it, not only for long-term storage but for sea voyages.

Originally, pasta was eaten mixed with honey, sugar, and cinnamon—this was, after all, before the sixteenth-century arrival of tomatoes from the New World. Mixed and shaped by hand, both dried and fresh egg pastas were being eaten all over Italy by the Middle Ages.

The great medieval writer and poet Giovanni Boccaccio (1313–1375) includes a famous description of homemade pasta in his celebrated collection of stories, *The Decameron*. In the third story, told on the eighth day, he writes of pasta made in the shape of *tortelli* and *maccheroni* and cooked in a capon broth. Although *The Decameron* was written in and takes place near Florence, Boccaccio loved Naples, having spent his formative years there, and some of his stories were inspired by his Neapolitan memories.

Amalfi, Gragnano, Torre del Greco, and Torre Annunziata—all small towns not far from Naples—became the primary production centers for commercial pasta. As when pressing grapes for wine, the first step of making pasta—mixing flour and water—was done by people standing barefoot in very large containers. The dough was then shaped using a rustic wooden machine, and often still allowed to dry in the sun. But even this primitive process allowed for a much larger production of pasta than the small batches made by hand.

Between the fourteenth and fifteenth centuries, a number of guilds arose across Italy to regulate the making of specific kinds of pasta. These included the Guild of Vermicellari (vermicelli-makers), formed in Naples in 1579.

The advantage that Naples had, and still has, was the availability of durum wheat from the nearby Tavoliere delle Puglie, as it is now called, which produces what is possibly the finest wheat in Italy. By law, Italian pasta must be made with durum wheat. It is the hardest of all wheats, and its density, high protein, and gluten content make the semolina flour it produces perfectly suited to pasta-making. Durum wheat is also the only wheat with a yellow endosperm, which gives the pasta its golden color. It is said that prior to the twentieth century, durum wheat was also imported from the Russian Ukraine, at that time the wheat belt of Europe.

There were few changes in the production of dried pasta until the late nineteenth century, at which time the kneading and extrusion processes became mechanized. However, it was not until the first half of the twentieth century that the drying process became dependent on electricity rather than sea air.

The cuts of dried pasta are divided into two general categories: long pasta and short pasta. The long, round pasta cuts begin with *zitoni*, *zita*, *mezzani*, and *maccaroncelli*, and extend to the even longer *perciatelli*, *bucatini*, *vermicelloni*, *vermicelli* (or spaghetti), the thinner *vermicellini* (or spaghettini), and

RIGHT, TOP: *The Venetians gave the world the fork many centuries ago, but we have a Neapolitan to thank for the addition of the fourth tine. A certain Gennaro Spadaccini (Gennaro being a very common name in Naples, after the patron saint of the city), a member of one of the Bourbon courts, saw the necessity of this when eating the long pasta. It must be twisted several times all around the fork, classically without the help of a soupspoon, until a small ball forms.* **RIGHT, BOTTOM:** *Here in the Voiello Pasta Factory, we see the old style of vermicelli or spaghetti, which is very long and curved at the end. In the old days, the top round part sometimes was detached and in particular used for some of the thicker soups, like those with pasta and beans. This round part was called* archetti.

the thinnest of all, *capellini*. Almost all the long pastas, especially vermicelli and spaghetti, have drastically changed over the years, becoming much shorter to accommodate shelf space. In the old days, pasta in the shops was kept in large wooden or straw boxes, and customers were able to buy exactly the quantity they needed, from 2 ounces up.

Long, flat, very wide pasta is called lasagna. In Naples, lasagne, the familiar layered-pasta dish of the same name, is usually prepared with dried commercial pasta rather than the fresh pasta that is used in central and northern Italy. Then there is *lasagnette*, *fettucce*, *fresine*, and *passarelle* (or linguine), and the smallest, *linguettine*.

Among the many cuts of short pasta are *paccheri*, *rigatoni*, *maltagliati*, and *penne*. The very small pastas that are generally eaten in soup, such as *stelline*,

acini di pepe, and *anellini*, are not popular among Neapolitans because Neapolitan cuisine generally does not favor broths.

Today these traditional pasta names have become part of history. Some have fallen out of fashion or, although the shapes have not changed, they have been given a new name by the pasta manufacturer.

No matter what the name, there are some very strict rules in Naples about when certain cuts of pasta should be used, and in what dishes. With *ragù* sauce, only *ziti*, *paccheri*, or *schiaffoni* must be used. Once the pasta is cooked, it must be completely coated with melted butter and the appropriate cheese—preferably the local pecorino—before the sauce is added. The only pastas that "team" with *Salsa alla Genovese* (page 123) are *penne*, *mezzani*, and *maltagliati*; the only cheese to be used is the northern Parmigiano.

But when we talk about fresh tomato sauce, fragrant with basil, only spaghetti or vermicelli is to be used. The Neapolitans say *"C'a pummarola 'ncoppa"* ("the tomato sauce sits on the pasta"), meaning that the pasta and the sauce are more than perfectly matched, they are united.

In and around Naples, long pastas like vermicelli and spaghetti are cooked until *vierde, vierde*, or "green and not ripe at all"—that is, not quite to the *al dente* stage that is preferred in the rest of Italy. Short pastas (and rice), on the other hand, are cooked to just past the *al dente* stage, until they are what northern Italians would consider overcooked. Pasta is always cooked in so much boiling water that the water is said to have "the power of the sea, abundant, so the pasta is able to swim in it."

Finally, pasta dishes in Naples are not strictly served as first courses as in other areas of Italy. There are several pasta preparations, for example, such as *Frittata di "Scamarro"* (page 116), that are specifically meant to be served as appetizers.

LEFT: *A beautifully illustrated antique dried pasta label of the Voiello company.*

Unlike the normal frittata that is usually part of a meal, this eggless frittata is eaten only as a snack. The world *"scammaro"* means that the omelet pan is so well cleaned the pasta will not stick to its surface. *Frittata di "Scammaro"* is mainly a street food sold by the numerous *"friggitorie"* that specialize in all kinds of fried foods, from vegetables to meat and even fruit. It was also in these shops that *Zitoni Ripieni* (stuffed *zitoni*; see *Bugialli on Pasta*, pages 338–339) were sold.

frittata di "scammaro"

PASTA OMELET WITHOUT EGGS

SERVES 4 TO 6

Coarse-grained salt

1/2 pound dried long pasta such as vermicelli, preferably imported Italian

4 tablespoons (2 ounces) unsalted butter or lard

Salt and freshly ground black pepper

TO COOK

1 teaspoon extra-virgin olive oil

Bring a large pot of cold water to a boil over medium heat, add coarse salt to taste, then add the pasta and cook it for 8 to 11 minutes (1 minute less than for normal al dente).

Drain the pasta and place it in a bowl. Add the butter and season with salt and pepper. Mix very well and let rest, covered, until cool, at least 30 minutes. (You may cook the pasta a day ahead.)

Very lightly oil an 8-inch nonstick omelet pan and place it over the lowest heat you can. When the pan is warm, in about 5 minutes, transfer the pasta to the pan. Use a spatula to gently press down on the pasta to level it. Cook it for 15 minutes on each side, shaking the pan every so often.

The omelet is ready when both sides are lightly golden and quite crisp, but still chewy.

RIGHT: Frittata di "Scammaro" *is an eggless frittata.*

vermicelli "aglio e oglio"

VERMICELLI WITH GARLIC, OLIVE OIL, AND PARSLEY

SERVES 4 TO 6

Coarse-grained salt

1 pound dried vermicelli, preferably imported Italian

3/4 cup extra-virgin olive oil

4 very large cloves garlic, peeled and left whole

4 whole hot red peppers *(peperoncini)*, or more according to taste

Salt and freshly ground black pepper

20 large sprigs Italian parsley, leaves only, coarsely chopped

ABOVE: *A dried pasta store hangs its wares above and around the entrance.*

"Oglio" *is the Neapolitan word for olive oil* (olio).

Bring a large pot of cold water to a boil over medium heat, add coarse salt to taste, then add the pasta and cook until al dente, for 9 to 12 minutes depending on the brand.

Meanwhile, heat the oil and the garlic in a small saucepan over medium heat. Sauté until the garlic is very lightly colored. Discard the garlic, add the *peperoncini,* and gently sauté until lightly crisp; season with salt and pepper.

At this moment, the pasta should be ready. Drain the pasta, transfer it to a large bowl, add the hot oil and sautéed peppers and the parsley, and mix very well. Serve hot.

CHAPTER FOUR

neapolitan meat sauces and other meat dishes

GALLERIA UMBERTO I

When we think of the foods from Naples and the Campania region, the first things that come to mind are commercial dried pastas, naturally, as well as fresh vegetables and a variety of rich desserts. Fish is also central to the regional diet, primarily seafood such as calamari, cuttlefish, and octopus. The emphasis on fish is understandable—the Mediterranean, which supplies an abundant variety of seafood, borders the length of Campania.

Meat and poultry are eaten in Campania, inland more so than by the sea, but they are not a staple of the region's gastronomy. Because of this, it is surprising, but perhaps a compensation, that Naples has the two most celebrated meat sauces in Italy. One, probably of local origin, is the great *ragù*. "*La Genovese*," the other great sauce, is clearly an imported sauce; however, the story of how it came to Naples has been obscured by time. The Neapolitan *Ragù di Carne* (page 122) is without doubt the most complex and intriguing meat sauce in Italy. Like the very popular *Salsa alla Genovese* (page 123), it plays a central role in the Neapolitan cuisine.

There are a number of historical references to the *ragù*, the most important being the one that appears in the classic cookbook by Ippolito Cavalcanti (*Cucina Teorico-Practica*, 1837), who is considered one of the founders of modern Neapolitan cuisine. In his book, we also find precise step-by-step instructions for his recipe *Maccheroni con Parmigiano e Sugo* (Macaroni with Parmesan and Sauce).

Even today, when everyone is (unfortunately) looking for shortcuts, if you ask a Neapolitan how to prepare a *ragù*, before you hear about the meat—the main ingredient, after all—you will be edified on the "musts" for best results:

- *Flameproof terra-cotta pot*
- *Wooden spoon*
- *Homemade tomato paste*
- *Wonderful wine from a vineyard near Mount Vesuvius*
- *Local pecorino, which is not to be confused with other sheep's milk cheese*
- *Other ingredients such as basil and cinnamon*

And then you will be warned that you must have a lot of patience, because it takes many hours to prepare this sauce in the proper manner. In the old days, it was believed that the best *ragù* was made by people whose jobs required that they sit still for long periods, such as *guardaporta* (doormen) or *solachianiello* (shoemakers), for it was thought that they had the most patience. Sunday is the traditional day to make the sauce, as the cook is able to fully concentrate on keeping the sauce below a simmer, or "*pippiare*," as it is called in Neapolitan slang, for many hours.

There are many different opinions about the origin of the other famous meat sauce of Naples: *Salsa alla Genovese*, or simply "*la Genovese*." Was a family with the last name of Genovesi the inventor of this sauce? Or was the sauce prepared by people who had come from Genoa, perhaps living in a section of Naples (like a "little Genoa"), holding on to their traditions and still cooking in the style of their city? In Cavalcanti's cookbook, we find many recipes for different dishes—not just sauces—described as "in the style of Genoa" or other regions of Italy, and even other countries. Since the origin is often associated with the title of the dish, I am of the opinion that

Salsa alla Genovese originated in Genoa, where a very similar sauce of the same name is still made.

Ragù di Carne and "*la Genovese*" have many subtle differences. For example, pecorino cheese is used with the *ragù* sauce, while the northern Parmigiano is a must for the *Genovese* sauce. Even the sequence is a component. For example, when preparing "*la Genovese*," the cooked pasta must first be tossed with butter and Parmigiano before the sauce is added.

Even the cut of the pastas has evolved into two different shapes. Pasta used with the *ragù* include the tubular, short pastas *paccheri* and *ziti*, and for the *Genovese* sauce, smaller tubular pastas such as penne, *mezzani*, and *maltagliati*, and gnocchi are preferred.

Neapolitans love sausages as a main dish ("*Sacicce e Friarelli*," page 141), but they are also often used to flavor savory dishes. There are different types of sausages, but the best known is the spicy Neapolitan sausage, which is the ancestor of the United States' beloved pepperoni.

Another popular sausage is the so-called *cervellatine*, which is prepared with pork meat, mixed together with some lard, salt, and black pepper to season, as well as red wine. Often these sausages are eaten in combination with vegetables, as in "*Sacicce e Friarelli*," or added in pieces to meat sauces such as the famous *Ragù di Carne*. For the "*Menesta Maritata*," a thick soup, a sausage called *penzetelle* is preferred. Made from leftover pieces of pork, this sausage is quite utilitarian; however, any peppery pork sausage would be appropriate.

A type of sausage almost forgotten, to my knowledge, is the one prepared with water buffalo meat, and turkey meat, and mixed with pork fat and seasoned with a lot of hot pepper, fennel, and anise seeds. It was a specialty of Caserta called *salsiccia di bufala* (buffalo meat sausages). I have not tasted these sausages, but I have tasted the buffalo meat. I had the same reaction when I ate kangaroo meat in Australia: It is not bad, but lamb is much better!

RIGHT, TOP: *These spicy Neapolitan sausages are just one of a variety of sausages used in Neapolitan cooking.*
RIGHT, BOTTOM: *Prepared* braciole *or* bracioline involtate *in a butcher shop. For Pasta with "Braciola" Sauce, see page 127.*
PRECEDING PAGES: *The Palazzo Reale (Royal Palace) and the Piazza del Plebiscito.*

A multitude of dishes can be prepared with the pair of sauces that follow. After the first course of a pasta served with the sauce, it is customary to serve the meat that has been taken from the sauce. In this way, the pasta and meat courses are distinct. Sometimes (and more frequently in the case of the *Ragù di Carne*) the whole piece of meat is replaced with a large *braciola*, or *brasciola* (a large beef or veal cutlet) that is stuffed with parsley, grated cheese, perhaps some garlic, raisins, and pine nuts, and then rolled and tied before cooking (*Braciola Involtata*). Sometimes *Polpettone al Ragù* (meat loaf) is used instead. Among the other dishes that feature these sauces are *Gnocchi di Patate con Ragù* (page 125), *Braciola al Ragù*, and *Lasagne di Carnevale* (see *Bugialli on Pasta*, pages 186–187).

ragù di carne

THE CLASSIC NEAPOLITAN MEAT SAUCE

MAKES ABOUT 6 CUPS

FOR THE MEAT

2 pounds beef rump roast or top round, in 1 piece

10 sprigs Italian parsley, leaves only, finely chopped

1/4 pound pancetta or prosciutto, coarsely ground or cut into very small pieces

Freshly ground black pepper

FOR THE *RAGÙ*

1/2 cup extra-virgin olive oil

4 tablespoons (2 ounces) unsalted butter

2 large yellow onions, about 12 ounces total, cleaned and chopped

1 small clove garlic, peeled and finely chopped

3 fresh basil leaves, torn into thirds

1/2 pound pancetta or prosciutto, coarsely ground or cut into very small pieces

1/4 pound prosciutto, coarsely ground or cut into very small pieces

Salt and freshly ground black pepper

Pinch of ground cinnamon

2 cups dry red wine

6 heaping tablespoons tomato paste, preferably homemade (page 23) or imported Italian, mixed with 1/4 cup lukewarm water

Tie the meat with string like a salami (see page 263). Mix the parsley with the pancetta and season with pepper. Use a paring knife to make several holes in the meat and fill the holes with the parsley-pancetta mixture. Place a medium-sized casserole, preferably flameproof terra-cotta or enamel, containing the oil and butter over low heat. When the oil is lukewarm, add the onions, garlic, basil, pancetta, and prosciutto. When the butter is completely melted, put in the meat and slowly sauté it until lightly golden all over, about 30 minutes.

Season with salt, pepper, and the cinnamon. Add 1 tablespoon of the red wine along with 1 tablespoon of the diluted tomato paste, and cook until the tomato paste is absorbed and the wine has evaporated. Continue this process, adding wine and tomato paste in small quantities, until they are used up, about 1 1/2 hours. During this time, stir frequently with a wooden spoon and turn the meat several times.

When all the wine and tomato paste have been used, add enough water to completely cover the meat. Cover the casserole and let the sauce barely simmer (in Neapolitan this is called *pippiare*, "like a pipe"), until the meat is completely cooked and a very rich sauce has formed, about 2 hours. Transfer the meat to a serving platter and cover the platter to keep it from drying out. Simmer the sauce for about 1 hour longer, until it is very smooth, rather thick, quite dark in color.

Classically, the sauce is ready to be used at this point for different dishes such as pasta or gnocchi, or to accompany the meat, cut into slices. Nowadays, if less fat is preferred, the sauce is allowed to cool, then placed in the refrigerator overnight so the congealed fat may be removed the next day before reheating and using the sauce.

salsa alla genovese *or* "la genovese"

GENOVESE SAUCE

MAKES ABOUT 8 CUPS

2 pounds beef rump roast or top round, in 1 piece

1/2 pound pancetta, thinly sliced

10 slices prosciutto, or 14 additional thin slices pancetta (the pancetta slices are smaller)

3 medium-sized carrots, scraped

2 large stalks celery

3 pounds yellow onions, cleaned

10 sprigs Italian parsley, leaves only

5 fresh basil leaves

4 fresh sage leaves

1 small clove garlic, peeled

1 tablespoon fresh rosemary leaves

6 tablespoons extra-virgin olive oil

6 tablespoons (3 ounces) unsalted butter, cut into large pats

3 bay leaves

Salt and freshly ground black pepper

Large pinch of freshly grated nutmeg, or 1 whole clove, or a pinch of ground cinnamon

3 cups dry white wine

About 4 cups completely defatted chicken or beef broth, preferably homemade, lukewarm

Wrap the meat with six slices of the pancetta and tie it with string like a salami (see page 263). Cut the remaining pancetta into very small pieces or grind it with a meat grinder. Use the prosciutto slices (or the additional pancetta slices) to line the inside of a heavy casserole, preferably flameproof terra-cotta or enamel, covering the bottom and halfway up the sides.

Finely chop the carrots, celery, onions, parsley, basil, sage, garlic, and rosemary all together on a cutting board. Place half of the chopped ingredients in the casserole, together with the pancetta, oil, and butter. Arrange the meat on top, then arrange the remaining chopped vegetables, herbs, and the bay leaves over the meat, and set the casserole over medium heat. Sauté for 20 minutes or longer, stirring every so often with wooden spoon, until all the vegetables and herbs are dark golden.

Season with salt and pepper and add the nutmeg, clove, or cinnamon, as desired. Add the wine 1 cup at a time, covering the casserole after each addition and cooking for 30 minutes, stirring every so often with a wooden spoon. Then start adding the broth, 1/2 cup or more at a time, so the meat remains almost covered, and cook until the sauce is quite homogenous and rather thick and the meat is completely cooked and very soft, about 1 1/2 hours.

Transfer the meat to a separate dish. Taste the sauce for salt and pepper and cook, uncovered, over medium heat for 15 minutes or more. Discard the bay leaves and the clove if used.

The sauce is now ready to be used as it is for different dishes such as *Penne o Mezzani con "la Genovese"* or *Gnocchi di Patate con "la Genovese"* (page 124), or it can be passed through a food mill, using the disk with smallest holes, and reduced for 10 minutes more over medium heat to a very homogenous sauce. It can also accompany the slices of meat, a dish known as *Carne con Sugo alla Genovese*.

Potato gnocchi must be very light, a texture achieved by omitting the eggs and grated cheese and adding only some seasoning—such as salt and pepper—to the riced potatoes. The dish known as *"strangulaprieve"* is similar to the potato gnocchi, but much heavier because a lot of flour is added to the potato dough and then served with a *ragù* sauce. It has long been assumed that the dish got the name "strangle the priest" by the legendary capacity of some priests to eat large quantities of these gnocchi so quickly as to be almost "strangled" by them. But now a more refined explanation comes out: Some scholars today feel that this Neapolitan word comes directly from the Greek words *stroggulo* and *preptos*, meaning a round, spherical body.

gnocchi di patate con "la genovese"

POTATO GNOCCHI WITH *GENOVESE* SAUCE

SERVES 6 TO 8

FOR THE GNOCCHI

3 pounds all-purpose potatoes

Coarse-grained salt

1/2 cup freshly grated Parmigiano

1 1/4 cups unbleached all-purpose flour

Salt and freshly ground black pepper

FOR THE SAUCE

1/2 recipe *Genovese* sauce (page 123)

TO COOK AND SERVE THE GNOCCHI

6 tablespoons (3 ounces) unsalted butter

Coarse-grained salt

1/2 cup freshly grated Parmigiano, or more to taste

PREPARE THE GNOCCHI: Place the potatoes in a stockpot, add coarse salt to taste, and add enough cold water to cover the potatoes by 3 inches. Set the pot, uncovered, over medium heat and cook the potatoes until very soft, about 35 minutes, depending on their size. Drain, then peel the potatoes while they are still very hot. Pass them through a potato ricer onto a cutting board, using the disk with the smallest holes. Let them rest until cool.

When the potatoes are cool, knead the grated Parmigiano and 1 cup of the flour into them, and season with salt and pepper. Keep kneading until a potato dough forms. Cut the potato dough into several pieces, and using your fingers and the heavily floured palms of your hands, roll them out into "ropes" about 1 inch in diameter. Cut each rope into 1/2-inch pieces.

HEAT THE SAUCE AND COOK THE GNOCCHI: Place a wide pot of cold water over medium heat. Reheat the *Genovese* sauce. Warm a serving platter containing the butter so that the butter melts on it. When the water in the pot reaches a boil, add coarse salt to taste, then add the gnocchi, ten to fifteen at a time. When the gnocchi float to the surface of the water, immediately transfer them to the warmed platter using a skimmer.

When all the gnocchi are on the serving platter, sprinkle half of the Parmigiano over them. Serve with a generous amount of the meat sauce and more cheese.

VARIATIONS

1. Shape the gnocchi like a "C" by pressing each one into the tines of a fork or the concave part of a cheese grater.
2. Add one whole egg to the potatoes along with the cheese and flour.

If a dish has the added description "*alla Sorrentina,*" it is to be cooked in the style of Sorrento: Most often, some mozzarella is cut into pieces and added to the dish, which is then baked. The only time a basic ingredient is changed is in *Cannelloni alla Sorrentina*; here, the stuffing is wrapped with a crepe rather than a pasta square (manicotti). To make either the *Gnocchi di Patate con "la Genovese" alla Sorrentina* or the *Gnocchi di Patate con Ragù alla Sorrentina*, cut 1/4 pound buffalo-milk mozzarella into 1/2-inch cubes and arrange the cheese over the top of the dish before baking.

gnocchi di patate con ragù

POTATO GNOCCHI WITH *RAGÙ*

FOR THE GNOCCHI

1 recipe *Gnocchi di Patate* (page 124), made with 1/2 cup freshly grated local pecorino or Pecorino Romano cheese instead of Parmigiano

FOR THE SAUCE

1/2 recipe *Ragù di Carne* (page 122)

TO FINISH

1/2 cup freshly grated local pecorino or Pecorino Romano cheese

Prepare the potato gnocchi following the instructions on page 124, substituting the percorino for the Parmigiano when kneading the cheese, potatoes, and flour, and substituting *ragù di carne* for the *Genovese* sauce.

Preheat the oven to 375°F.

Once the gnocchi are cooked, sauced, and sprinkled twice with the pecorino (before and after saucing), transfer the gnocchi and the sauce from the serving dish to a large baking dish. Bake for 15 minutes.

Serve hot, directly from the baking dish.

OSPEDALE
delle
BAMBOLE
RESTAURI SACRI

pennette al sugo di braciola

PENNETTE WITH "BRACIOLA" SAUCE

SERVES 8

1 pound top round of beef, in 1 piece, butterflied

FOR THE PASTE

3 cloves garlic, peeled

15 sprigs Italian parsley, leaves only

1/4 cup freshly grated Parmigiano

2 tablespoons unsalted butter

Salt and freshly ground black pepper

About 1/4 cup unbleached all-purpose flour

FOR THE SAUCE

2 medium-sized yellow onions, cleaned

20 sprigs Italian parsley, leaves only

1 stalk celery

2 cloves garlic, peeled

6 tablespoons extra-virgin olive oil

4 tablespoons unsalted butter

3 tablespoons red wine vinegar

Salt and freshly ground pepper

1 1/2 pounds ripe but not overripe tomatoes, blanched (see page 263), skin and seeds removed; or 1 1/2 pounds drained canned tomatoes, preferably imported Italian, seeded

About 2 cups completely defatted meat or chicken broth, preferably homemade

PLUS

Coarse-grained salt

1 1/2 pounds dried short tubular pasta, such as *pennette* (which is shorter than normal penne pasta), preferably imported Italian

TO SERVE

Freshly grated Parmigiano

OPPOSITE: "Ospedale delle Bambole" *(Hospital for Dolls) is one of the most amusing shops in Naples.*

Pound the meat between two pieces of parchment paper. Place the garlic, parsley, Parmigiano, and 2 tablespoons of the butter in a blender or food processor and grind until a paste forms. Season with salt and pepper and mix well. Spread this paste all over the meat, then roll up the meat and tie it like a salami (see page 263). Lightly flour the rolled-up meat.

Finely chop the onions, parsley, celery, and garlic all together on a cutting board, or process all these ingredients in a blender or food processor until they are completely integrated.

Heat the oil and butter in a medium-sized nonreactive casserole over medium heat, and when the butter is completely melted, place the meat in the casserole and sauté until very light golden all over. Pour the vinegar over the meat and let it evaporate for 30 seconds; arrange the chopped vegetables on top of the meat and sauté for 5 minutes more, turning the meat over several times. Season again with salt and pepper to taste, then add the tomatoes.

Cover the casserole, reduce the heat to low, and simmer for 40 minutes, turning the meat over twice. Add 1 cup of the broth and simmer, covered, for at least 1 hour, adding more broth if needed. The sauce is ready when it becomes rather thick, very uniform, and almost translucent. Remove the meat and transfer it to a warm serving platter. The meat should be quite soft at this point and, with the string removed, it can be sliced and served with some of the sauce. This dish is called *Braciole al Sugo*. Taste the sauce for salt and pepper, mix very well, and simmer for a few more minutes, uncovered.

When the sauce is nearly done, bring a pot of cold water to a boil over medium heat and add coarse salt to taste. Add the pasta and cook for 8 to 11 minutes, depending on the brand, 1 minute less than for normal al dente. Drain the pasta, transfer it to a large casserole, pour the sauce over, and set the casserole over medium heat. Mix very well and sauté for 1 minute.

Serve hot, with freshly grated Parmigiano.

"cazuncelli 'mbuttunati"

STUFFED HALF-MOON *TORTELLI* OR *PANZAROTTI*

SERVES 6 TO 8

FOR THE SPONGE

1/2 cup plus 1 tablespoon unbleached all-purpose flour

1 tablespoon semolina flour

1/2 ounce fresh compressed yeast, or 1 envelope active dry yeast

1/2 cup lukewarm water for fresh yeast or warm water for dry

Pinch of salt

FOR THE STUFFING

1/4 pound prosciutto, coarsely ground or cut into very small pieces

1/4 pound Neapolitan salami, coarsely ground or cut into very small pieces

15 large sprigs Italian parsley, leaves only

15 fresh basil leaves

Salt and freshly ground black pepper

2 extra-large eggs

FOR THE DOUGH

1 1/2 cups unbleached all-purpose flour

1 tablespoon semolina flour

1 tablespoon extra-virgin olive oil

1/3 cup lukewarm water

Large pinch of salt

TO FRY THE *CAZUNCELLI*

1/4 cup extra-virgin olive oil

2 cups vegetable oil (preferably a mixture of half sunflower oil, half corn oil)

TO SERVE

1 recipe *"Pommarola" alla Napoletana* (page 96)

Fresh basil leaves

MAKE THE SPONGE: Mix together the 1/2 cup unbleached all-purpose flour and the semolina flour in a small bowl. Make a well in the center. In a separate bowl, dissolve the yeast in the lukewarm or warm water, then pour it into the well along with the salt. Use a wooden spoon to gradually incorporate all the flour. Sprinkle the remaining tablespoon of flour over the top, cover the bowl with a cotton dish towel, and let it rest in a warm place away from drafts until the sponge has doubled in size, about 1 hour.

PREPARE THE STUFFING: Place the prosciutto and salami in a crockery or glass bowl, and finely chop the parsley and basil together on a cutting board. Transfer the chopped herbs to the bowl containing the prosciutto mixture, season with salt and pepper, and add the eggs. Mix very well with a wooden spoon to combine all the ingredients. Cover and refrigerate until needed.

PREPARE THE DOUGH: When the sponge is ready, combine the 1 1/2 cups all-purpose flour and the semolina flour, arrange the mixture in a mound on a pastry board, and then make a well in the center. Pour the sponge into the well along with the oil, water, and salt. Using a wooden spoon, mix together the ingredients in the well, then gradually begin incorporating flour from the rim of the well. Start mixing with your hands, working the flour into the dough little by little, until almost all the flour is incorporated.

Start kneading in a folding motion and continue until all the remaining flour is incorporated and the dough is elastic and smooth. Using a rolling pin, roll out the dough on a lightly floured surface until it is less than 1/2 inch thick. Use a cookie cutter 4 inches in diameter to cut out six to eight disks.

Place a heaping teaspoon of the stuffing in the center of each disk, fold the pastry over, and carefully pinch the edges to seal them around the stuffing. Let the *cazuncelli* rest, covered with parchment paper on a floured towel, for at least 30 minutes.

FRY THE *CAZUNCELLI*: Heat the olive oil and vegetable oil in a skillet over medium heat. When the oil mixture is hot, about 375°F, start frying the *cazuncelli*, a few at a time, until lightly golden all over, about 1 minute. Transfer the *cazuncelli* to a serving platter lined with paper towels, and when they are all cooked and on the platter, remove the towels. Serve hot, topped with the warmed tomato sauce and fresh basil leaves.

VARIATION

Serve the *cazuncelli* plain, sprinkled with a little salt.

bistecca *or* filetti alla pizzaiola

STEAK OR FILLETS, *PIZZAIOLA* STYLE

SERVES 4

- 1 large T-bone steak, or 4 slices fillet about $1^1/2$ inches thick
- $^1/4$ cup extra-virgin olive oil
- 4 large cloves garlic, peeled and cut into large slivers
- Salt and freshly ground black pepper
- $1^1/2$ pounds ripe tomatoes, blanched (see page 263), skin and seeds removed, and cut into large pieces; or $1^1/2$ pounds drained canned tomatoes, preferably imported Italian, seeded
- Large pinch of dried oregano
- 2 ounces prosciutto, cut into thin strips (optional)

When a dish is prepared "alla pizzaiola," *it means that the recipe is an old one, that in the past it was prepared in the same oven as the pizza.*

Trim most of the extra fat from the meat, but do not remove all of it. Place a skillet containing the oil over medium heat, and when the oil is rather hot, about 300°F, add the garlic and the meat. Sear the meat on both sides until lightly golden. Season with salt and pepper. Using a slotted spoon, transfer the meat before it is cooked to your taste—rare, medium rare, or well done—to a serving platter and cover the meat to keep it warm.

Immediately add the tomatoes to the skillet containing the meat juices and the garlic pieces. Cook for a maximum of 3 minutes, stirring with a wooden spoon, and season with salt and pepper. The tomato sauce will not be evenly smooth.

Return the meat to the skillet, sprinkle the oregano over it, and cook for 1 to 3 minutes, depending on the size of the meat and the desired doneness.

Serve hot, with the sauce spooned over the meat. If using the prosciutto strips, arrange them on top.

costata alla pizzaiola

T-BONE STEAK, *PIZZAIOLA* STYLE

SERVES 4

1/2 cup extra-virgin olive oil

3 large cloves garlic, peeled and left whole

1 T-Bone steak, about 1 1/2 pounds

Salt and freshly ground black pepper

1 1/2 pounds ripe but not overripe tomatoes, with skin and seeds, cut into 1/2-inch slices; or 1 1/2 pounds drained canned tomatoes, preferably imported Italian, cut into 1/2-inch slices

Large pinch of dried oregano leaves

Pinch of hot red pepper flakes

1 cup dry white wine

Heat the oil in a medium-sized casserole or a skillet with a lid over medium heat. When the oil is warm, about 250°F, add the garlic and the meat, season with salt and pepper, and sauté for 2 minutes or until lightly golden. Turn the meat over, season with salt and pepper, and cook for 2 more minutes.

Transfer the meat to a serving platter and add the tomatoes to the casserole. Season the tomatoes with salt, pepper, the oregano, and the red pepper flakes. Sauté, stirring every so often with a wooden spoon, for 3 to 4 minutes, then add the wine and let evaporate for 15 minutes.

Return the meat to the casserole, spoon some of the sauce over it, cover, and cook for 2 minutes on each side for medium rare, or longer if you prefer it more well done. Serve hot, with the sauce.

trippa alla napoletana

TRIPE, NEAPOLITAN STYLE

SERVES 4

1 pound veal tripe

1 large fresh tomato, about 1/2 pound, cleaned and left whole

Coarse-grained salt

5 tablespoons extra-virgin olive oil

2 large cloves garlic, peeled

1 small red onion, cleaned

10 sprigs Italian parsley, leaves only

1/2 cup dry white wine

Salt and freshly ground black pepper

2 tablespoons tomato paste, preferably homemade (see page 23)

1 cup lukewarm water

3 extra-large eggs

3/4 cup freshly grated Parmigiano

TO SERVE

5 sprigs Italian parsley, leaves only, coarsely chopped

Parboil the tripe with the tomato and coarse salt according to the directions on page 273. Cut the tripe into strips less than 1/2 inch wide.

Heat the oil in a medium-sized casserole over very low heat as you finely chop the garlic, onion, and parsley together on a cutting board. When the oil is warm, raise the heat and add the chopped ingredients. Sauté for 2 minutes, then add the tripe, mix very well, and cook for a few minutes more. Add the wine and let evaporate for 2 to 3 minutes.

Season the tripe with salt and pepper, then dissolve the tomato paste in the cup of lukewarm water and add it to the casserole. Cover and cook for 15 minutes more. By this time, the tripe should be completely cooked and rather soft.

Lightly beat the eggs together with the grated Parmigiano, and add the mixture to the casserole. Mix well and keep stirring until the eggs are cooked but quite soft, about 2 minutes.

Sprinkle the parsley over the tripe and serve hot.

bollito e fagioli

BOILED MEAT AND BEANS

SERVES 4 TO 6

1 cup dried *cannellini* (white kidney beans), picked over

Coarse-grained salt

1 whole anchovy preserved in salt, boned and rinsed under cold running water; or 2 anchovy fillets packed in oil, drained

10 sprigs Italian parsley, leaves only, finely chopped

Salt and freshly ground black pepper

6 tablespoons extra-virgin olive oil

FOR THE MEAT

$1^1/_2$ pounds boneless beef for boiling, or enough short ribs to yield $1^1/_2$ pounds meat

Coarse-grained salt

1 red onion, cleaned

1 stalk celery

2 medium-sized carrots, scraped

5 sprigs Italian parsley, leaves only

TO SERVE

2 extra-large eggs, hard-boiled, shelled, and cut into small pieces

2 large lemons, thinly sliced

5 whole anchovies preserved in salt, or 10 anchovy fillets, boned and rinsed under cold running water and cut into thirds; packed in oil, drained

15 sprigs Italian parsley, leaves only

3 tablespoons capers preserved in wine vinegar, drained

$^1/_2$ cup extra-virgin olive oil

Salt and freshly ground black pepper

Soak the beans in a bowl of cold water overnight. The next morning, drain the beans and rinse them under cold running water. Place a pot of cold water over medium heat, and when the water reaches a boil, add the beans and simmer for about 1 hour. By this time, the beans should be soft but still retain their shape. Add coarse salt to taste and simmer for 1 minute more. Drain the beans, transfer to a crockery or glass bowl, and place a piece of paper towel dampened in cold water over the beans.

COOK THE MEAT: Cook the beef or short ribs in boiling water seasoned with coarse salt, along with the onion, celery, carrots, and parsley for $1^1/_2$ hours or more. The meat should be soft and very juicy.

Just before the meat is finished, coarsely chop the anchovies and parsley together on a cutting board and transfer the mixture to a crockery or glass bowl. Season with salt and pepper, add the oil, and mix very well. Add the parsley sauce to the beans and mix very well.

Arrange the meat in the center of a large platter—if using boneless beef, cut it into rather thick slices. Spoon the beans all around the meat, and arrange the hard-boiled eggs, lemon slices, anchovies, parsley, and the capers around the beans. Drizzle with the oil and season with salt and pepper. Serve hot.

PREVIOUS PAGE: *In Naples, the sacred and profane go hand in hand.*

I was very surprised to find this recipe in Cavalcanti's book. Today, *farro* (or spelt, as it is sometimes called in English) has been all but forgotten in the everyday menu of Campagna. But we should remember that *farro* was the type of wheat used by the ancient Romans to prepare the famous *pulis,* which was the predecessor of polenta. Cavalcanti not only knew of the main ingredient, *farro,* but he was even aware of its step-brother, *farretto*. In Italian, the word *farretto* is a diminutive and implies something small and cute. But in gastronomy, *farretto* refers to *farro* cultivated in the mountains. It is not of the best quality, and so is used most of the time in thick soups or minestrone, or in a type of polenta. The *farretto* that Cavalcanti used would have come from the Abruzzi region, which at that time was part of the Kingdom of Naples.

farretto alla cavalcanti

CAVALCANTI'S *FARRETTO*

SERVES 6

- 1 1/2 cups raw *farretto* (spelt from the mountains)
- 6 cups completely defatted chicken or beef broth, preferably homemade
- 1 small carrot, scraped and cut into small pieces
- 1 small yellow onion, cleaned and cut into small pieces
- 1 stalk celery, cut into small pieces
- 1/2 pound beef such as sirloin, in 1 piece
- 2 extra-large eggs
- 3/4 cup freshly grated Parmigiano
- Salt and freshly ground black pepper

TO SERVE

- Freshly grated Parmigiano
- 6 sprigs fresh basil

Soak the *farretto* in a bowl of cold water overnight. The next morning, drain the *farretto* and rinse it many times under cold running water. Place a medium-sized casserole containing 4 cups of the broth over medium heat, and when it reaches a boil, add the soaked *farretto* along with the vegetables and the meat. Add enough lukewarm water to cover everything by 4 inches. Simmer for 1 to 1 1/2 hours, adding more lukewarm water as needed. The *farretto* should be really overcooked, with most of the liquid absorbed.

Remove the casserole from the heat and let it rest, covered, until completely cool, about 1 hour. Use a food processor or blender to finely blend the contents of the casserole, then transfer everything to a clean casserole.

Start tempering the eggs by mixing them together with the Parmigiano, then with the remaining 2 cups of broth, heated. Combine thoroughly, then pour the egg mixture into the casserole containing the ground *farretto*. Stirring constantly with a wooden spoon, bring the mixture to a boil over medium heat. Season with salt and pepper and continue stirring until a rather thick "cream" forms, about 5 minutes. Ladle this cream into individual bowls and let rest for at least 5 minutes.

Before serving, sprinkle with more Parmigiano and add a sprig of fresh basil.

zuppa di soffritto

NEAPOLITAN WINTER SOUP

SERVES 6 TO 8

2 pounds, in total, chicken or turkey gizzards and chicken or turkey hearts, all cut into 1/2-inch pieces

Coarse-grained salt

4 tablespoons (2 ounces) unsalted butter

1/4 cup extra-virgin olive oil

1/2 cup dry red wine or 1/4 cup red wine vinegar, preferably homemade (page 17)

2 ounces Sweet Bell Pepper Paste (page 24)

2 ounces tomato paste, preferably homemade (page 23) or imported Italian

2 bay leaves

1 flat tablespoon fresh rosemary leaves

2 pounds ripe tomatoes, or 2 pounds drained canned tomatoes, preferably imported Italian

1/2 to 1 teaspoon hot red pepper flakes

4 chicken livers, cleaned and quartered

TO SERVE

6 to 8 *friselle* (Neapolitan toasted half rolls) or *crostini* (small squares of toasted country-style bread)

Carefully wash the gizzards and hearts under cold running water. Set a pot of cold water over medium heat, and when the water reaches a boil, add coarse salt to taste. Add the gizzards and hearts and boil for 1 minute. Drain the meat and discard the water.

Place a large casserole containing the butter and oil over medium heat, and when the butter is almost melted, add the gizzards and hearts and sauté for 5 minutes. Pour in the wine or the vinegar and let evaporate for 2 minutes, or until reduced by half. Add the pepper paste, tomato paste, bay leaves, and the rosemary and sauté for 5 minutes more.

If using fresh tomatoes, cut them into pieces. Pass the fresh or canned tomatoes through a food mill into a crockery or glass bowl, using the disk with the smallest holes. Add the tomatoes to the casserole along with the red pepper flakes. Let simmer for 1 hour, stirring every so often with a wooden spoon and adding lukewarm water, 1/2 cup at a time, if the *zuppa* becomes too thick.

By this time, all the meat should be very soft. Carefully wash the chicken livers under cold running water, add the livers, and simmer for 5 minutes more.

Discard the bay leaves, and serve the soup over *friselle* or some *crostini*.

spiedini di polpette

MEATBALLS ON A SKEWER

SERVES 4 TO 6

1/2 pound ground sirloin

1 tablespoon extra-virgin olive oil

1 medium-sized clove garlic, peeled and finely chopped

3 tablespoons freshly grated Parmigiano

1 extra-large egg

5 sprigs Italian parsley, leaves only, finely chopped

Salt and freshly ground black pepper

12 slices country-style bread, crusts removed, about 3 inches square and 1/2 inch thick

8 thin slices pancetta or prosciutto, cut in half

16 large fresh sage leaves

TO COOK

4 tablespoons (2 ounces) unsalted butter

1/4 cup extra-virgin olive oil

TO SERVE

1 lemon, cut into thin slices

Place the meat in a crockery or glass bowl along with the oil, garlic, Parmigiano, egg, and parsley. Season with salt and pepper and mix very well with a wooden spoon.

Divide the mixture into eight portions and shape each portion to the size of the bread slices. If possible, choose four strong branches of sage to use as skewers. Otherwise, use four small wooden skewers.

Place a slice of bread on a cutting board, and top it with a piece of pancetta, then a sage leaf, one portion of the meat, another sage leaf, a pancetta piece, and one more slice of bread. Repeat this process once more, beginning with the pancetta and continuing to pile the ingredients one on top of the other, finishing with the bread. To thread all these ingredients onto a skewer, insert the pointed end of the skewer down through the piled-up ingredients. Repeat this entire procedure with the remaining three skewers.

Preheat the oven to 375°F.

COOK THE MEATBALLS: Place an ovenproof skillet containing the butter and oil over medium heat. When the butter is just melted, place the four skewers of meatballs in the skillet and sauté, basting, until golden on all sides, about 4 minutes. Transfer the skillet from the burner to the oven for about 10 minutes, or until the meat is cooked but still pinkish.

Serve with the lemon slices.

Polpettone di Carne, or Neapolitan meat loaf, is not always made with ground meat that is shaped like a loaf of bread. Sometimes even a large pounded *braciola* (a large, boneless veal or beef cutlet) that has been stuffed and rolled up is referred to as "*polpettone*." The following recipe is a combination of two dishes: The ground meat, mixed with different seasonings, is spread out like a cutlet, stuffed, and then rolled. An egg-white wash is brushed over the rolled-up meat to keep it together and prevent the juices from escaping.

polpettone di carne

STUFFED MEAT LOAF

SERVES 6 TO 8

2 slices (3 ounces) white bread, crusts removed

1/2 cup milk

20 sprigs Italian parsley, leaves only

2 cloves garlic, peeled

This is very good served with some Peppers Preserved in Red Wine Vinegar (page 18) or some preserved papacelle.

Soak the bread in the milk in a crockery or glass bowl for 30 minutes. Then transfer the soaked bread with all the milk to a small saucepan, and set the pan over low heat. Cook the bread, breaking it up in the milk and mixing constantly with a wooden spoon until a very smooth paste forms,

$1^1/_2$ pounds ground beef

4 heaping tablespoons freshly grated Parmigiano

Salt and freshly ground black pepper

2 extra-large eggs

6 ounces cow's milk mozzarella *(fiordilatte)*, cut into less than $^1/_2$-inch cubes

$^1/_4$ pound boiled ham, sliced about $^1/_2$ inch thick, then cut into thin strips

About 6 tablespoons unbleached all-purpose flour

4 tablespoons (2 ounces) unsalted butter, at room temperature

$^1/_4$ cup extra-virgin olive oil

1 extra-large egg white

about 10 minutes. Let it rest until cold, about 30 minutes. (Making a paste from the bread, instead of adding the bread when it is just soaked, makes the meat loaf much lighter.)

Finely chop the parsley and garlic together on a cutting board. Put the meat, parsley mixture, Parmigiano, and the bread paste in a large bowl and mix very well. Season with salt and pepper and add the eggs. Mix again to be sure all the ingredients are well amalgamated.

Transfer the mixture to a piece of parchment paper, then shape it into a rectangle about $^3/_4$ inch thick. Distribute the mozzarella cubes over the mixture, then scatter the ham on top. Holding the parchment paper on the narrow side, use it to roll the meat into the shape of a salami around the cheese and ham stuffing. Lay the parchment paper flat again, and sprinkle the flour all over it. Roll the loaf in the flour to coat it evenly.

Preheat the oven to 375°F. Spread the butter in an ovenproof glass baking dish, then pour in the oil. Carefully transfer the meat loaf to the baking dish. Use a fork to lightly beat the egg white. Then, with a brush, coat the meat loaf with the egg white. Bake for 20 minutes for medium-rare, basting the meat with its juices two or three times.

Remove the dish from the oven, transfer the meat loaf to a cutting board, and cut it into 1-inch-thick slices. Serve hot.

pollo alla cacciatora alla napoletana

NEAPOLITAN CHICKEN, HUNTER'S STYLE

SERVES 4 TO 6

1 chicken, about $3^1/_2$ pounds, cut into 12 pieces

$^1/_4$ cup extra-virgin olive oil

2 tablespoons (1 ounce) unsalted butter

1 medium-sized red onion, cleaned and coarsely chopped or thinly sliced

1 small clove garlic, peeled and left whole

2 medium-sized sprigs rosemary

Salt and freshly ground black pepper

1 pound cherry tomatoes, cut in half

OPPOSITE: Polpettone di Carne, *sliced and served hot.*

Rinse the chicken under cold running water, then pat it dry with paper towels.

Place a medium-sized nonreactive casserole containing the oil, butter, onion, garlic, and one sprig of the rosemary over medium heat. When the oil and butter start sizzling, arrange the chicken pieces in the casserole and raise the temperature to high. Sauté the chicken for 10 minutes, turning it over several times. Season with salt and pepper.

Remove the garlic clove and add the tomatoes. Mix very well and lower the heat to medium. Cook, covered, for about 20 minutes, turning the chicken several times.

By this time, the chicken should be almost cooked and a rather thick sauce will have formed. Add the remaining rosemary sprig, increase the heat to high again, and reduce, uncovered, for 5 minutes more. Transfer the chicken and the sauce to a warmed serving platter, and serve hot.

coniglio alla cacciatora in bianco

RABBIT, HUNTER'S STYLE, FROM ISCHIA

SERVES 4

1 rabbit, about 3 pounds, cleaned, head and liver removed and discarded, cut into 12 pieces

4 cups cold water

3 tablespoons red wine vinegar

1/2 cup extra-virgin olive oil

Salt and freshly ground black pepper

4 large cloves garlic, peeled

1 tablespoon fresh rosemary leaves

1 cup dry white wine

1 to 1 1/2 cups very light chicken or vegetable broth, preferably homemade, lukewarm; or lukewarm water

TO SERVE

20 sprigs Italian parsley, leaves only

2 medium-sized cloves garlic, peeled

Rinse the rabbit under cold running water, then soak it for 1 hour in a bowl containing the cold water mixed with the vinegar. Drain the rabbit, rinse it again under cold running water, and dry it with paper towels.

Place a medium-sized casserole containing the oil over medium heat, and when the oil is rather hot, about 300°F, add the rabbit. Lightly sauté it, turning the pieces occasionally, for 15 minutes. Season with salt and pepper.

Finely chop the garlic and rosemary together on a cutting board and add the mixture to the casserole. Mix very well.

Add 1/2 cup of the wine and cook for 5 minutes. Add the remaining wine, cover the casserole, and cook until the rabbit is very golden in color and soft, adding broth as needed, about 45 minutes. The rabbit should be golden in color and very tender but not dry.

Finely chop the parsley and garlic together on a cutting board. Serve the rabbit with a little bit of the juices and the parsley mixture.

coniglio in padella con le olive

RABBIT WITH OLIVES

SERVES 4 TO 6

1 rabbit, about 2 pounds, cleaned, head and liver removed and discarded

4 cups cold water

1/2 cup red wine vinegar

FOR THE PESTO

3 large cloves garlic, peeled

10 large fresh sage leaves, all stems removed

1 heaping tablespoon fresh rosemary leaves

1 small potato, about 3 ounces, peeled and cut into small pieces

Rinse the rabbit under cold running water, then soak it for 1 hour in a bowl containing the cold water mixed with the vinegar.

PREPARE THE PESTO: Using a knife, blender, or food processor, finely chop the garlic, sage, rosemary, potato, fine salt, pepper, and red pepper flakes all together on a cutting board.

Drain the rabbit, rinse it again under cold running water, and pat it dry with paper towels. Cut the rabbit into ten pieces and dry again.

COOK THE RABBIT: In a skillet large enough to hold the rabbit pieces in one layer, heat the oil over medium heat. When the oil is warm, add the rabbit pieces and lightly sauté them until lightly golden on all sides. Season with salt and pepper.

1 teaspoon fine salt

1/2 teaspoon freshly ground black pepper

Very large pinch of hot red pepper flakes

TO COOK THE RABBIT

6 tablespoons extra-virgin olive oil

Salt and freshly ground black pepper

1 cup dry white wine

2 tablespoons tomato paste, preferably homemade (page 23)

1 1/2 to 2 cups completely defatted chicken broth, preferably homemade

TO SERVE

1/2 cup Gaeta olives, left whole

10 sprigs Italian parsley, leaves only

Add the wine 1/2 cup at a time; when the wine is reduced by half, add the pesto and mix well. Cook for 2 minutes more, stirring to make sure that nothing is sticking to the bottom of the skillet.

Add the tomato paste, mix well, then add the broth, 1/2 cup at a time, and cook, covered, until the rabbit is very soft but still juicy, about 35 minutes. Taste again for salt and pepper and cook uncovered for a few minutes longer, until a rather thick sauce forms.

Add the olives, mix very well, and transfer everything to a large serving platter. Sprinkle the parsley over all and serve hot.

agnello al pomodoro

LAMB WITH TOMATO SAUCE

SERVES 4 TO 6

1 1/2 pounds ripe but not overripe tomatoes

2 very large cloves garlic, peeled

20 large sprigs Italian parsley, leaves only

Salt and freshly ground black pepper

Several pinches of hot red pepper flakes

3 pounds very young lamb, with bones, cut into large pieces

1 1/2 pounds baking potatoes, peeled and cut into 1 1/2-inch cubes, left soaking in a bowl of cold water

1/4 cup extra-virgin olive oil

1 cup cold water

2 tablespoons very fine unseasoned bread crumbs, preferably homemade, lightly toasted

Preheat the oven to 375°F. Meanwhile, cut the tomatoes into slices 3/4 inch thick. Line the bottom of a heavy medium-sized nonreactive casserole, preferably flameproof terra-cotta or enamel, with the tomato slices.

Finely chop the garlic and parsley together on a cutting board. Season the tomatoes with salt, pepper, and red pepper flakes, sprinkle the garlic mixture over the tomatoes, and season again with a little salt, pepper, and red pepper flakes.

Arrange the lamb over the tomatoes in the casserole, then place the potato cubes in the spaces between the pieces of meat. Season again with salt, pepper, and red pepper flakes. Pour the oil over the lamb, add the water, and sprinkle the bread crumbs over the top.

Cover the casserole and cook it for 2 hours, without mixing or turning the meat.

Remove the casserole from the oven and let the meat rest, covered, for 10 minutes before serving it directly from the casserole: Each serving should include lamb, potatoes, and the juices from the almost-dissolved tomatoes.

agnello con le papacelle

LAMB SHANKS WITH PEPPER SAUCE

SERVES 6

5 tablespoons extra-virgin olive oil

6 very small lamb shanks, about 4 pounds total

2 large cloves garlic, peeled and left whole

3 tablespoons red wine vinegar

Salt and freshly ground black pepper

1 cup dry white wine

2 to 3 cups completely defatted chicken broth, preferably homemade

About 10 ounces red and yellow peppers preserved in wine vinegar (page 18), drained and sliced into thin strips

TO SERVE

15 sprigs Italian parsley, leaves only

2 small cloves garlic, peeled

Papacelle, *a variety of peppers (see photo, pages 28–29), are not available outside Naples and the surrounding area, so I use bell peppers preserved in wine vinegar as a substitution.*

Heat the oil over medium heat in a skillet that has a lid. When the oil is warm, add the lamb and sauté for 5 minutes or longer, until the meat is lightly colored all over. Add the garlic and vinegar, raise the heat to high, and cook, uncovered, until the vinegar evaporates completely, about 1 minute. Season with salt and pepper, add the wine, and cook for 10 minutes more. Lower the heat to medium and add 1 to 2 cups of the broth, 1/2 cup at a time, cooking between additions.

Cover the skillet and cook for 1 hour or more, until the meat is almost well done and very soft, adding broth as needed and turning the meat over several times. The cooking time depends on the size of the lamb shanks and whether spring lamb or older lamb is used. Stop cooking the meat when it is almost well done and very soft.

Use a slotted spoon to transfer the meat to a plate, retaining the juices in the skillet, then cover the meat with aluminum foil to keep it warm. Add the peppers to the skillet and sauté for 2 minutes, then season with salt and pepper. Discard the garlic cloves, then add the remaining 1 cup broth and simmer for 10 minutes.

Return the meat to the skillet, mix very well, and cook for 10 minutes more, or until the meat is completely cooked and soft and the peppers almost dissolve into a sauce.

Chop the parsley and garlic together on a cutting board. Transfer the lamb, pepper sauce, and all the juices from the skillet to a warmed serving dish. Sprinkle with the parsley mixture, and serve hot.

VARIATION

This dish may be prepared with pork chops, in which case the cooking time is much shorter.

"sacicce e friarelli"

SAUSAGES AND BROCCOLI RAAB

SERVES 6

3 pounds broccoli raab

Coarse-grained salt

6 sweet Italian sausages, about 4 ounces each

2 tablespoons extra-virgin olive oil

1 cup cold water

Salt and freshly ground black pepper

Abundant hot red pepper flakes

Sausages sautéed with broccoli raab is a very popular and beloved dish. Broccoli raab is called "friarelli" *because the most common way to cook this vegetable is to sauté it.* "Friare" *means to sauté or fry in Neapolitan dialect.*

Clean the broccoli raab, discarding the large tough stems, and soak it in a bowl of cold water for 30 minutes.

Bring a large pot of cold water to a boil over medium heat, add coarse salt to taste, then drain the broccoli raab and add it to the pot. Cook until it is soft, not crunchy. In Italy, we always boil it until it's tender, not only for the texture but also to remove the bitter taste.

Drain the broccoli raab, rinse it under cold running water, and lightly squeeze it to remove excess moisture, then coarsely chop it on a cutting board.

Using a fork, prick the sausages in several places. Pour the oil into a medium-sized casserole and set it over medium heat. When the oil is warm, add the sausages and lightly sauté for 2 minutes. Add the cold water and simmer for about 15 minutes, turning the sausages several times. By this time, they will be cooked through.

Add the broccoli raab, season with salt, pepper, and red pepper flakes, and sauté for 10 minutes more, stirring constantly with a wooden spoon. Serve hot.

RIGHT: *Fresh broccoli raab, or* "friarelli," *in the marketplace.*

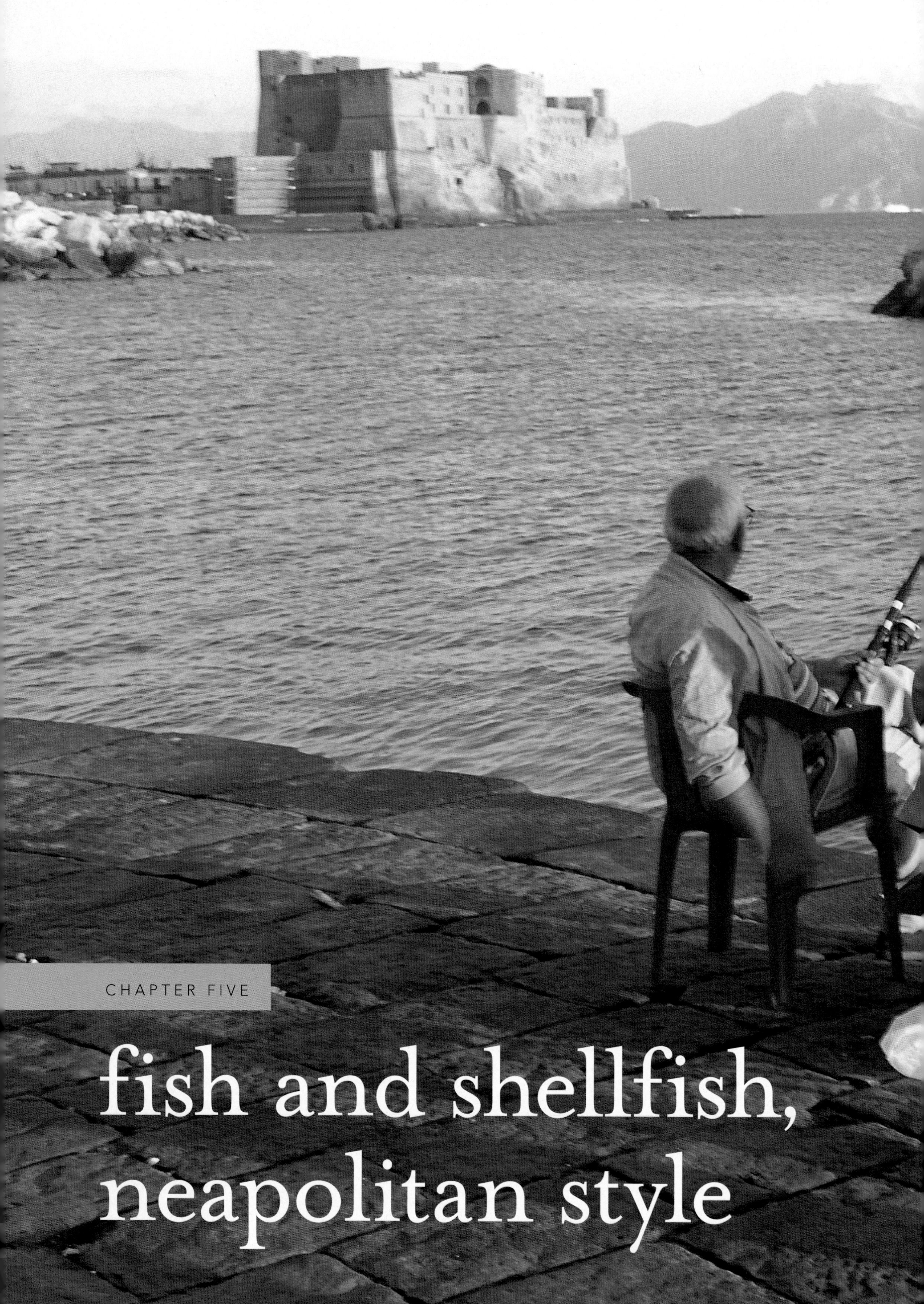

CHAPTER FIVE

fish and shellfish, neapolitan style

Many writers, in fact, some of the great names of literature, have written about Naples over the centuries. They were captivated not only by its Roman and Greek ruins and beautiful baroque architecture, but also by the unique charm of its everyday life: the humor, the theatricality, and more often than not, the food.

Much of what has been written about the city and its colorful inhabitants is contained in collections of essays, and more information about Neapolitan food is offered in these books than in any recipe book. So as we reconstruct the history of Neapolitan cooking we rely heavily on these literary sources.

Characteristically, Naples is known for its wonderful bay, the shining sun, and its many traditional songs expressing themes of love and friendship or hatred and enmity. Orlando di Lasso (1532–1594), the greatest composer of the Renaissance, wrote several sets of wonderful songs in the local Neapolitan language that are full of the ribald humor and fun of the city. He knew Naples extremely well because, when he was a child famous for his beautiful voice, he worked as a singer for the vice king of Sicily (who at that time ruled Naples).

And so it is not such a surprise that for an almost complete list of the different types of fish used in Naples, we can refer to the "*Canzone del Guarracino*," a song by an anonymous poet of the eighteenth century that, in a tarantella dance rhythm, describes the fight between the *guarracino* and the *alletterato* fish. The latter fish is very similar to tuna, with a lot of spots on its skin resembling letters of the alphabet; hence its name, which comes from the Italian word for letters. In the song, the two fish fight to gain the favor of a *sardella*, and throughout, almost all of the other Neapolitan fish are named, making it the most exhaustive list of fish that are available in the markets even today.

Neapolitans love fish, which makes sense, given their proximity to the Tyrrhenian Sea. And they prefer to cook it whole, leaving on the head and tail so that it retains the taste of the sea. When the whole fish is baked, some lemon juice or vinegar is added, as many feel this reinforces the sea's aroma. What Neapolitans don't like is the *trancia*—or slice—so popular in northern Italy. They say "Fish cooked without its bone is tasteless." Because of this, waiters in every restaurant are trained to bone the fish for you at the table.

The variety of fish and shellfish you see in the Neapolitan markets is incredible: tiny clams, mussels, *calamari*, and *seppie* (cuttlefish or ink squid), fresh anchovies and sardines, *dorade*, grouper, and swordfish (more often than tuna). There are boxes of mixed fish ready to be used for frying, known as the *fritto di paranza* (small fish from the net), and mixtures of larger fish for making Naples' celebrated *zuppa di pesce* (fish soup). Among these fish is the Mediterranean *scorfano*,

which has very little meat but imparts a great deal of flavor; it is also used in the French bouillabaisse.

Without a doubt, the favorite seafood of Naples is the octopus. Whether cooking baby octopuses or larger ones, Neapolitan cooks are masters of its tender preparation. In winter, until not so many years ago, one could find stands in the markets with huge cauldrons from which completely cooked *purpo* or *polpo* (octopus) was sold. The octopus was served with a piece of bread dipped in its broth and lots of black pepper.

The cry of the fish vendor still heard today is *polpi veraci*, meaning "real" octopus, which refers to the octopuses that have two lines of suckers on their tentacles to attach themselves to the rocks. Those with only one line of suckers, called *sinischi*, must lie in the sand on the bottom of the sea. They are considered to be of a much lower quality and are less in demand.

In the past, octopuses were caught in the Bay of Naples, not far from the Santa Lucia quarter. The fishermen trapped small octopuses in old and half-broken terra-cotta amphoras (the same kind of jugs that were used, to serve water on the streets, called *mommara* or *mummara*). They would attach a row of the small amphoras to a thin rope, placing some stones inside to weigh them down as they lay in the sea overnight. By the following morning, the octopuses would have removed all the stones and hidden themselves inside the amphoras, thinking they had found a safe place to rest. For the fishermen, it was very easy to pull up the containers and remove the naïve octopuses.

TOP AND BOTTOM: *Scenes from the fish market.*
OPPOSITE: La venditrice di acqua solfura *carries water in her amphoras, which are known as* "mommara."
PRECEDING PAGES: *These fisherman have a good view of Castel Dell'ovo in the Borgo Marinari, once a fishing village, just opposite the district of Santa Lucia. In Roman times, the villa of Lucius Licinius Lucullus was in this location, next an order of monks took over, and finally the fortress was built.*

crostini alla napoletana

CANAPÉS, NEAPOLITAN STYLE

SERVES 4 TO 6

3/4 cup plus 4 teaspoons extra-virgin olive oil

12 slices country-style bread, each about 3 by 2 inches and 3/4 inch thick

1 mozzarella (about 1/2 pound), preferably buffalo-milk mozzarella imported from Italy, cut into 12 slices

6 whole anchovies preserved in salt, boned, rinsed under cold running water, each fillet cut into thirds; or 12 anchovy fillets, packed in oil, drained and cut into thirds

1 very large or 2 medium-sized tomatoes, ripe but not overripe, cut into small pieces

Dried oregano

Salt and freshly ground black pepper

In preparing this dish, the slices of bread are fried on one side only, as when making Chinese shrimp toasts. Then the rest of the ingredients are placed on the fried side and the crostini *are baked. Although no longer so popular in Naples, a variant of this canapé is served in Rome, where it is known as* Spiedini alla Romana. *Several slices of bread are alternated with slices of mozzarella on a skewer, then baked and served with anchovies.*

Heat the 3/4 cup oil in a small skillet over medium heat, and when the oil is rather hot, about 300°F, use a pair of tongs to hold each piece of bread—the *crostino*—while you lightly fry one side in the oil for about 25 seconds. The bread should be barely golden on the cooked side. Repeat until all the bread slices have been fried on one side only.

Preheat the oven to 375°F.

Lightly oil a baking dish and arrange all the *crostini*, fried side facing up, in the dish. Over each piece of bread place first a slice of mozzarella, then three pieces of anchovy, then some of the tomato pieces. Season with oregano, salt, and pepper to taste. Drizzle 1 teaspoon of oil over each *crostino*.

Bake for 15 minutes and serve hot.

sarde ripiene *or* sarde "'mbuttunate"

STUFFED SARDINES

SERVES 3 AS A MAIN COURSE
OR 6 AS AN APPETIZER

12 fresh sardines, about 1½ pounds total, cleaned, boned, heads and tails removed

Coarse-grained salt

1 lemon, cut in half

10 sprigs Italian parsley, leaves only

1 fresh basil leaf

1 large clove garlic, peeled

10 Gaeta olives, pitted

1 heaping tablespoon capers preserved in wine vinegar, drained

2 heaping tablespoons very fine unseasoned bread crumbs, preferably homemade, lightly toasted

6 tablespoons extra-virgin olive oil

Salt and freshly ground black pepper

TO SERVE

Sprigs of Italian parsley

1 lemon, cut into thin slices

Soak the sardines for 10 minutes in a bowl of cold water containing a large pinch of coarse salt and the squeezed lemon halves. Drain and rinse the sardines, and pat them dry with paper towels.

Finely chop the parsley, basil, garlic, olives, and capers together on a cutting board. Transfer the chopped ingredients to a bowl, add 1 heaping tablespoon of the bread crumbs, 2 tablespoons of the oil, and salt and pepper to taste. Mix very well.

Preheat the oven to 400°F and lightly oil a glass baking dish.

Place a portion of the stuffing on each sardine, then fold the sardine together as if you are closing a book. Arrange the stuffed sardines in the baking dish, pour the remaining 4 tablespoons oil over them, and sprinkle with the remaining heaping tablespoon of bread crumbs. Bake for 10 minutes, until the sardines are completely cooked and a very light crust has formed on top.

Transfer the sardines to a serving platter, and serve with the parsley sprigs and lemon slices.

pesce spada ripieno

STUFFED SWORDFISH STEAKS

SERVES 4

2 swordfish steaks, about 3/4 pound each and 1 1/2 inches thick, without bones

Coarse-grained salt

1 lemon, cut in half

15 sprigs Italian parsley, leaves only

4 fresh basil leaves

3 large cloves garlic, peeled

20 Gaeta olives, pitted

3 heaping tablespoons capers preserved in wine vinegar, drained

6 heaping tablespoons very fine unseasoned bread crumbs, preferably homemade, lightly toasted

1/2 cup extra-virgin olive oil

Salt and freshly ground black pepper

TO SERVE

Sprigs of Italian parsley

Fresh basil leaves

Several Gaeta olives

1 lemon, cut into thin slices

This is a modern adaptation of Sarde Ripiene *(page 147), but even though it is made with swordfish rather than sardines, this is an authentic preparation.*

Soak the fish for 30 minutes in a bowl of cold water containing a large pinch of coarse salt and the squeezed lemon halves. Then drain and rinse the swordfish, and pat it dry with paper towels. Gently remove the skin from the fish and cut each steak into two pieces. Butterfly each piece, making sure not to slice them all the way through.

Use a knife, a blender, or a food processor to finely chop the parsley, basil, garlic, olives, and capers. Transfer the chopped ingredients to a crockery or glass bowl, add 3 heaping tablespoons of the bread crumbs and 4 tablespoons of the olive oil, and season with salt and pepper. Mix very well.

Preheat the oven to 400°F and lightly oil a glass baking dish.

Place 2 tablespoons of the stuffing inside each butterflied piece of fish, fold the fish together, and transfer it to one of the oiled baking dishes. Arrange some of the remaining stuffing over each piece, then drizzle the remaining 4 tablespoons oil over the top. Finish by sprinkling the remaining 3 heaping tablespoons bread crumbs over all.

Bake the swordfish for about 10 minutes; it should be completely cooked, no longer pinkish, and very soft to the touch. Remove from the oven, let the fish rest for a few minutes, and then serve with the parsley, basil, olives, and lemon slices.

OPPOSITE: Pesce Spada Ripieno *are made with butterflied swordfish steaks.*

In the past, before the appearance of rubber pacifiers, babies in and around Naples would suck on a piece of bread that had been soaked in sugar water and wrapped in a piece of cheesecloth. This was called *"pupatella."* The very adult *"pupatella"* used for this recipe uses cheesecloth to wrap crabs, which are then crushed and cooked along with the other ingredients of the sauce. The use of this word to describe a cooking technique is very typical of Neapolitan humor, and Neapolitans prepare many types of *"pupatelle"* made from a variety of ingredients for different sauces or dishes.

"la pupatella"

PERCIATELLI WITH CRAB SAUCE

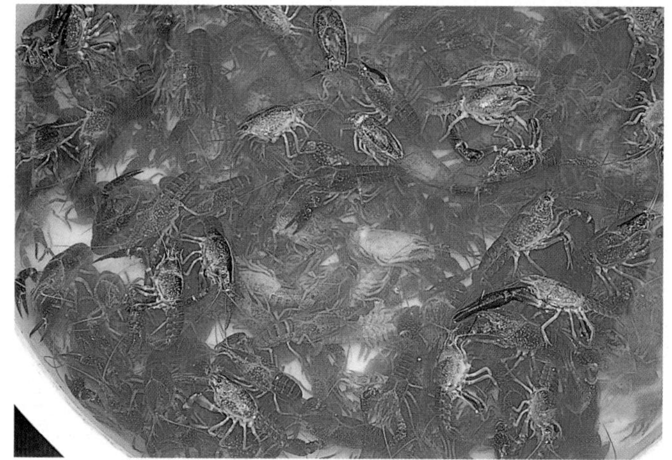

SERVES 4 TO 6

4 medium-sized crabs, cleaned

Coarse-grained salt

1 large lemon, cut in half

2 pounds ripe tomatoes, cut into large pieces; or 2 pounds undrained canned tomatoes, preferably imported Italian

1/3 cup extra-virgin olive oil

3 large cloves garlic, peeled and left whole

3 cups cold water

Salt and freshly ground black pepper

Large pinch of hot red pepper flakes

PLUS

Coarse-grained salt

1 pound dried long pasta, such as spaghetti or *perciatelli*, preferably imported Italian

15 sprigs Italian parsley, leaves only, coarsely chopped

5 fresh basil leaves, torn into thirds

Soak the crabs for 30 minutes in a bowl of cold water containing a large pinch of coarse salt and the lemon halves.

Drain the crabs and tie them in a cheesecloth bag. If you have a large marble mortar, place the wrapped crabs in it, and use the pestle to completely crack the crab shells. Transfer the cheesecloth with the crabs and all the juices from the mortar to a nonreactive casserole, preferably flameproof terra-cotta or enamel.

If you do not have a marble mortar, place the crabs, wrapped in cheesecloth, in the casserole and crack their shells with a heavy meat pounder.

Add the tomatoes, oil, garlic, and 1 cup of the water to the casserole and place it over medium heat. Simmer for 1 hour, turning the bag with the crabs several times.

Transfer the cheesecloth bag to a small pot, and set the casserole aside. Add 2 cups of the cold water to the pot and simmer for 1 hour over medium heat.

Discard the cheesecloth with the crabs, and transfer the cooking water to the casserole containing the sauce. Simmer until the sauce becomes rather thick, about 30 minutes. Taste for salt and pepper and add the red pepper flakes.

Meanwhile, bring a large pot of cold water to a boil, add coarse salt to taste, then add the pasta and cook for 8 to 11 minutes, depending on the brand (1 minute less than for normal al dente).

Drain the pasta, transfer it to the casserole with the sauce, and stir constantly until the sauce is completely incorporated, about 1 minute.

Sprinkle with the parsley and basil, mix, then transfer to a large warmed serving platter and serve hot.

cozze gratinate

BAKED STUFFED MUSSELS

SERVES 4 TO 6

1 1/2 pounds mussels in the shell, scrubbed very well

1 large lemon, cut in half

Coarse-grained salt

1/2 cup extra-virgin olive oil

2 tablespoons cold water

2 large cloves garlic, peeled

10 large sprigs Italian parsley, leaves only

3 flat tablespoons very fine unseasoned bread crumbs, preferably homemade, lightly toasted

Freshly ground black pepper

TO SERVE

Juice of 1 large lemon

OPPOSITE: *Fresh crabs for sale. Several regions of southern Italy prepare a soup or a sauce for pasta by wrapping the crabs in cheesecloth and crushing them through a sieve. The juices as well as the crushed shell, which remains in the cheesecloth, are used for the broth. This bag is called a* "pupatella."

Soak the mussels for 30 minutes in a bowl of cold water containing the squeezed lemon halves and a large pinch of coarse salt.

Drain the mussels and rinse them under cold running water. Pour 2 tablespoons of the oil and the water into a skillet and set the skillet over low heat. Add the mussels, raise the heat to high, cover the skillet, and cook for 2 minutes. By this time, the mussels should be open (discard any that are still closed). Use a slotted spoon or a skimmer to transfer the mussels to a serving platter. Save the juices from the skillet for later use.

Finely chop the garlic and parsley together on a cutting board. Transfer the mixture to a crockery or glass bowl and add the bread crumbs, 2 tablespoons of the oil, and pepper to taste. Mix very well.

Preheat the oven to 400°F.

Remove the mussels from their shells. Detach the two halves of the shells, saving the larger ones and discarding the smaller ones. Place the mussels themselves in a small bowl. Lightly oil a round baking dish that is large enough to hold all the saved mussel shells in one layer.

Take 3 to 4 tablespoons of the juices from the skillet, add them to the bread crumb mixture, and mix well. On each half-shell, place one or two mussels and cover them with the bread crumb mixture. Drizzle some of the remaining oil over each stuffed shell. Bake for 10 minutes.

Remove from the oven, drizzle the lemon juice over the baked mussels, and serve hot.

impepata di cozze

PEPPERY MUSSELS I

SERVES 4

2 pounds mussels in the shell, scrubbed very well

Coarse-grained salt

1 large lemon, cut in half

3/4 cup extra-virgin olive oil

2 tablespoons cold water

1 large clove garlic, peeled

Juice of 1 large lemon

Abundant freshly ground black pepper

15 large sprigs Italian parsley, leaves only, coarsely chopped

TO SERVE

1 lemon, cut into wedges

Sprigs of Italian parsley

Soak the mussels for 30 minutes in a bowl of cold water containing a large pinch of coarse salt and the squeezed lemon halves. Rinse the mussels many times under cold running water to be sure there is no more sand in them.

Drain the mussels and rinse them under cold running water. Place a casserole containing the oil and the 2 tablespoons cold water over very low heat for 1 minute, then add the mussels and the garlic. Raise the heat to medium-high, cover the casserole, and cook for about 4 minutes.

By this time, the mussels should all be open and almost ready (discard any mussels that are still closed). Add the lemon juice, pepper, and chopped parsley. Mix very well for a few seconds, then transfer the mussels and sauce to a serving platter. Serve with the lemon wedges and parsley sprigs.

VARIATIONS

1. Omit the garlic.

2. Another method for cooking even more peppery mussels: Place the drained, soaked mussels in a large skillet with no oil or water, sprinkle them with a lot of freshly ground black pepper, and let rest for at least 30 minutes. Then set the skillet over high heat and cook, covered, for about 4 minutes. At the very last moment before removing the skillet from the heat, add the parsley. Serve hot, with a generous squeeze of lemon juice.

impepatella di cozze

PEPPERY MUSSELS II

SERVES 4

2 pounds mussels in the shell, scrubbed very well

Coarse-grained salt

1 large lemon, cut in half

2 tablespoons extra-virgin olive oil

Freshly ground black pepper

20 large sprigs Italian parsley, leaves only, finely chopped

Juice of 1 large lemon

OPPOSITE: Impepata di Cozze *(Peppery Mussels I) is shown here.*

Soak the mussels for 30 minutes in a large bowl of cold water containing a large pinch of coarse salt and the squeezed lemon halves. Rinse the mussels many times under cold running water to be sure there is no more sand in them.

Drain the mussels and rinse them under cold running water. Place a casserole containing 1/4 cup cold water over medium heat, add the mussels, cover, and cook until they are all open, about 4 minutes. Discard any that are still closed. Add the oil, abundant pepper, and the parsley and mix very well.

Transfer the mussels with their juices to a serving platter, pour the lemon juice over them, and serve hot.

alici o sarde "arraganate"

SARDINES WITH OREGANO

SERVES 4

- 1/4 cup extra-virgin olive oil
- 8 fresh sardines, about 1 pound total, cleaned, boned, heads and tails removed
- Coarse-grained salt
- I large lemon, cut in half
- 10 sprigs Italian parsley, leaves only
- 2 large cloves garlic, peeled
- 10 leaves fresh oregano, or a large pinch of dried oregano
- Salt and freshly ground black pepper

Preheat the oven to 400°F and use a little of the oil to lightly coat a round glass baking dish. Soak the sardines for 5 minutes in a bowl of cold water containing a little coarse salt and the squeezed lemon halves.

Drain and rinse the sardines and pat them dry with paper towels. Arrange the sardines like the spokes of a wheel in the baking dish. Finely chop the parsley and garlic together on a cutting board, sprinkle the mixture over the sardines, and season with the oregano, salt, and pepper. Pour the remaining oil over the top and bake for 15 minutes.

Serve the sardines hot, directly from the baking dish.

VARIATION

Before baking, sprinkle 2 tablespoons bread crumbs over the sardines.

bucatini basilico, aglio, e acciughe

PASTA WITH BASIL, GARLIC, AND ANCHOVIES

SERVES 4 TO 6

- 20 large fresh basil leaves
- 10 sprigs Italian parsley, leaves only
- 1 large clove garlic, peeled
- 1/2 cup extra-virgin olive oil
- 2 whole anchovies preserved in salt, boned and rinsed under cold running water; or 4 anchovy fillets packed in oil, drained
- Coarse-grained salt
- 1 pound dried *bucatini* or *perciatelli*, preferably imported Italian
- 2 tablespoons capers preserved in wine vinegar, drained
- Salt and freshly ground black pepper

This simple pasta dish is from Salerno.

Finely chop the basil, parsley, and garlic all together on a cutting board. Place a large skillet containing the oil over low heat and a large pot of cold water for the pasta over medium heat.

When the oil in the skillet is warm, remove the skillet from the heat, add the anchovies, and mash them with a fork.

When the water for the pasta reaches a boil, add coarse salt to taste, then the pasta, and cook for 8 to 11 minutes, depending on the brand (1 minute less than for normal al dente).

Meanwhile, place the skillet with the anchovies back on low heat, add the chopped herbs, and lightly sauté for 1 minute. Add the capers and season with salt and pepper.

2 heaping tablespoons very fine unseasoned bread crumbs, preferably homemade, lightly toasted

TO SERVE

Sprigs of fresh basil

When the pasta is ready, drain it and transfer it to the skillet containing the sauce, adding 1/2 cup of the pasta water. Mix very well and let the water be absorbed by the pasta. Taste for salt and pepper. Sprinkle the bread crumbs over the pasta, mix again, and transfer to a warm serving platter.

Serve hot, with sprigs of basil.

zuppa di vongole

ZUPPA OF CLAMS

SERVES 4 TO 6

- 2 pounds small clams, such as Manila clams, cockles, or littlenecks, in the shell
- Coarse-grained salt
- 1 large lemon, cut in half
- 6 tablespoons extra-virgin olive oil
- 2 tablespoons cold water
- Salt and freshly ground black pepper
- 1 cup dry white wine
- 1 1/2 pounds ripe tomatoes; or 1 1/2 pounds drained canned tomatoes, preferably imported Italian
- 3 cloves garlic, peeled and finely chopped
- 15 sprigs Italian parsley, leaves only
- Large pinch of hot red pepper flakes (optional)

TO SERVE

- Several *crostini*, lightly fried in olive oil
- Several fresh basil leaves

Soak the clams for 30 minutes in a bowl of cold water containing a little coarse salt and the squeezed lemon halves. Rinse the clams several times under cold running water.

Drain the clams and rinse them again under cold running water. Heat the oil in a nonreactive casserole over medium heat, and when the oil is warm, raise the heat and add the clams and the water. Season them with salt and pepper, cover the casserole for 2 minutes, then add the wine and let it evaporate for 1 minute.

By this time, the clams should be open (discard any that are still closed). Using a slotted spoon, transfer the clams to a serving platter and cover the platter to keep them warm.

Lower the heat to medium. Add the tomatoes to the juices left in the casserole and cook for a few minutes, then add the garlic and parsley and simmer for 15 minutes, stirring several times with a wooden spoon. Season again with salt and pepper and add the red pepper flakes if using. Return the clams to the pot, mix very well, and cook for 2 minutes more.

Serve hot, with the fried *crostini* and basil leaves.

zuppa di arselle alla napoletana

CLAM SOUP, NEAPOLITAN STYLE

SERVES 4

- 2 pounds very small clams, such as Manila clams or cockles, in the shell
- Coarse-grained salt
- 3/4 cup extra-virgin olive oil
- 4 large cloves garlic, peeled and finely chopped
- 15 large sprigs Italian parsley, leaves only, finely chopped
- Salt and freshly ground black pepper
- 4 slices country-style bread, lightly toasted and rubbed with a clove of garlic
- 1/2 cup heated vegetable broth or completely defatted chicken broth, preferably homemade, if needed

TO SERVE

Italian parsley sprigs

ABOVE: *Select very small clams.*

Soak the clams for 30 minutes in a bowl of cold water containing a little coarse salt. Rinse the clams several times under cold running water.

Drain the clams, rinse them again under cold running water, and place them in a skillet over medium heat. Cover the skillet and cook for 4 minutes. By this time, all the clams should be open (discard any that are still closed).

Using a slotted spoon, transfer the clams to a crockery or glass bowl and cover the bowl with aluminum foil so they do not dry out. Pour all the juices from cooking the clams into a small bowl and reserve.

Add the oil to the skillet, leaving it over medium heat. When the oil is warm, add the garlic and parsley. Sauté for a few minutes; the garlic should be still light in color.

Return the clams to the skillet, lightly season with salt and pepper, and cook, stirring every so often with a wooden spoon, for about 5 minutes. Add the reserved juices from the clams and cook for 5 minutes more.

If you do not have a lot of juice, spoon some of the broth over the bread placed in individual soup bowls. Ladle the clams and all the liquids from the skillet over the slices of bread, and serve hot with parsley sprigs.

spaghetti o vermicelli con le vongole al sugo

SPAGHETTI OR VERMICELLI AND CLAMS IN TOMATO SAUCE

SERVES 4 TO 6

1 1/2 pounds small clams, such as Manila clams, cockles, or littlenecks, in the shell

Coarse-grained salt

1 lemon, cut in half

1/2 cup extra-virgin olive oil

3 large cloves garlic, peeled and finely chopped

Salt and freshly ground black pepper

Very large pinch of hot red pepper flakes (up to 1/2 teaspoon)

1 1/2 pounds ripe tomatoes, blanched (see page 263), skin and seeds removed, cut into large pieces; or 1 1/2 pounds drained canned tomatoes, preferably imported Italian, seeded

1 pound dried spaghetti, preferably imported Italian

15 sprigs Italian parsley, leaves only, coarsely chopped

TO SERVE

10 sprigs Italian parsley, leaves only, or several fresh basil leaves

Soak the clams for 30 minutes in a bowl of cold water containing 1 tablespoon coarse salt and the squeezed lemon halves. Rinse the clams several times under cold running water.

Drain the clams and rinse them again under cold running water. Heat the oil in a nonreactive casserole over medium heat, and when the oil is warm, add the garlic and clams. Raise the heat, season with salt, pepper, and the red pepper flakes to taste, and cover the casserole. Cook for 5 minutes, or until all the clams are open (discard any that are still closed). Transfer the clams, using a slotted spoon, to a serving platter.

Immediately add the tomatoes to the casserole, lower the heat, and cook for about 15 minutes, stirring every so often with a wooden spoon. Remove the clams from their shells and discard the shells.

Bring a large pot of cold water to a boil over medium heat, add coarse salt to taste, then add the pasta and cook it until al dente, 9 to 12 minutes depending on the brand.

Meanwhile, add the parsley to the casserole, mix very well, and let simmer for about 5 minutes more. Add the shelled clams and simmer the sauce for 2 more minutes.

Drain the pasta into a large bowl, add all the clam sauce, mix very well, then transfer everything to a large warmed serving platter. Sprinkle with the parsley or basil, and serve hot.

VARIATION

This dish is often served with the clams left in their shells.

spaghetti o vermicelli con le vongole in bianco

SPAGHETTI OR VERMICELLI IN CLAM SAUCE

SERVES 4 TO 6

1 1/2 pounds small clams, such as Manila clams, cockles, or littlenecks, in the shell

Coarse-grained salt

1 lemon, cut in half

3/4 cup extra-virgin olive oil

3 large cloves garlic, peeled and finely chopped

1 pound dried vermicelli or spaghetti, preferably imported Italian

Salt and abundant freshly ground black pepper

20 large sprigs Italian parsley, leaves only, coarsely chopped

TO SERVE

10 sprigs Italian parsley, leaves only

I know it is very difficult to convince restaurateurs, but adding even a drop of heavy cream completely destroys this dish. The combination of the oil and the juices coming out from the clams as they open and cook forms a wonderful emulsion that is the only sauce you need to toss with the pasta.

Soak the clams for 30 minutes in a bowl of cold water containing 1 tablespoon coarse salt and the squeezed lemon halves. Rinse the clams several times under cold running water.

Drain and rinse the clams again under cold running water. Place a stockpot of cold water over medium heat to cook the pasta, and place a large skillet containing the oil and garlic over medium heat.

When the oil is warm and barely starts sautéing the garlic, raise the heat to high, add the clams, and cover. Cook for 2 minutes, shaking the skillet several times.

By this time, the water for the pasta should be boiling. Add coarse salt to taste, then add the pasta and cook for 8 to 11 minutes, depending on the brand (1 minute less than for normal al dente).

Season the clams well with salt and pepper and add the parsley. By this time, all the clams should be open (discard any that are still closed). Cover the skillet and cook for 4 minutes more, mixing frequently.

Drain the pasta, add it to the skillet, and mix very well to coat the pasta with the juices.

Transfer the contents of the skillet to a large serving platter, sprinkle with the parsley, and serve hot, with the clams still in their shells.

VARIATION

Even though this is a "white" sauce, some people add three or four whole cherry tomatoes.

OPPOSITE: *Spaghetti in Clam Sauce.*

This is the traditional version of *Acqua Pazza* or "crazy water," which is made from *mazzamma*, a mixture of cheap, tiny fish. Cooking the fish from the beginning in the oil and water emulsion forms a sauce that is used as a topping for bread. Nowadays, this technique is also used with larger fish served whole, with the emulsion as a sauce. However, the original recipe remains dear to old Neapolitans.

acqua pazza

"CRAZY WATER"

SERVES 4 TO 6

1 pound *mazzamma* (tiny fish or whitebait)

Coarse-grained salt

1 lemon, cut in half

4 cherry tomatoes

1 cup cold water

1/2 cup extra-virgin olive oil

2 large cloves garlic, peeled and finely chopped

Salt and freshly ground black pepper

15 sprigs Italian parsley, leaves only, coarsely chopped

Hot red pepper flakes to taste

TO SERVE

4 to 6 slices country-style bread, about 3/4 inch thick

Preheat the oven to 375°F. Meanwhile, soak the tiny fish for 30 minutes in a bowl of cold water containing a little coarse salt and the squeezed lemon halves.

Place the cherry tomatoes on a cookie sheet and bake for 15 minutes. Remove the tomatoes from the oven, let them cool for 10 minutes, then cut them in half.

Drain the fish and rinse them under cold running water. Place a casserole containing the water and oil over medium heat, and when the liquid starts simmering, add the garlic, tomatoes, and fish. Season with salt and pepper, and cook for about 5 minutes. By this time, the fish will have almost dissolved, and a beautiful emulsion from the combination of water and oil will have formed.

Add the parsley and season with red pepper flakes, mix well, and ladle the soup over the slices of bread placed in individual soup bowls.

zuppa di pesce alla napoletana

FISH SOUP, NEAPOLITAN STYLE

SERVES 6

- $1^{1}/_{2}$ pounds clams in the shell, preferably Manila clams or cockles
- $1^{1}/_{2}$ pounds mussels in the shell, scrubbed very well
- 3 pounds assorted fish, such as grouper, porgy, or sea bass, with heads on, cut into large pieces
- 2 tablespoons coarse-grained salt
- 2 lemons, cut in half
- $^{3}/_{4}$ cup extra-virgin olive oil
- 1 tablespoon cold water
- 6 large cloves garlic, peeled and finely chopped
- 3 pounds ripe tomatoes, cut into large pieces; or 3 pounds undrained canned tomatoes, preferably imported Italian
- Salt and freshly ground black pepper

TO SERVE

- 20 large sprigs Italian parsley, leaves only, coarsely chopped
- 6 *friselle* (Neapolitan toasted half rolls) or *crostini* (small squares of country-style bread toasted or lightly fried in olive oil)

Place the clams and mussels in a bowl of cold water; place all the other fish in a separate bowl of cold water. To each bowl add 1 tablespoon coarse salt and two squeezed lemon halves. Let rest for 30 minutes.

Drain the clams and mussels, rinse them under cold running water, and place them in a skillet with 2 tablespoons of the oil and the tablespoon of cold water. Cover the skillet and set it over medium heat. After 4 to 5 minutes, the clams and mussels will be open (discard any that are still closed). Drain the shellfish, saving all the juices, and place them on a serving platter, covering the platter so they do not dry out.

Pour the remaining 10 tablespoons oil into a large nonreactive casserole and place it over medium heat. When the oil is warm, add the garlic and sauté for 1 minute. Strain the reserved shellfish juices and add them to the casserole, along with the fish heads. Cook for 3 to 5 minutes, then add the tomatoes, season with salt and pepper, and simmer for at least 1 hour, stirring every so often with a wooden spoon.

Pass the contents of the casserole through a food mill into a second casserole, using the disk with the smallest holes. Set this casserole over medium heat, taste for salt and pepper, then drain and rinse the fish and add them according to their cooking times.

When all the fish are in the soup and are almost cooked, put in the reserved shellfish and cook for 1 minute longer.

Serve hot with abundant chopped parsley, ladling fish and broth into individual soup bowls over the *friselle* or *crostini*.

VARIATION

In other parts of Campania, some *calamari* (squid) and *seppie* (cuttlefish), cut into rings, are added to the casserole.

In Naples, a very strong distinction is made between *baccalà* and *stoccofisso* (stockfish). Both are big cod that has been salted and dried, but with the *baccalà,* the pieces of cod are preserved in salt and compressed in wooden barrels, while the *stoccofisso* is salted and air-dried. The latter acquired the name "stockfish" because the air-drying makes it as hard as a stick. The preferred part of any cod is the so-called *mussilo,* which refers to the thick back part of the fish.

zuppa di code di stocco

BACCALÀ SOUP

SERVES 4

- 4 ounces soaked *stocco* or *baccalà*
- 1 all-purpose potato, about 4 ounces, peeled and cut into 1/2-inch cubes, left soaking in a bowl of cold water
- 6 cups cold water
- 1 large clove garlic, peeled and cut into quarters
- 4 cherry tomatoes
- 2 tablespoons extra-virgin olive oil
- Freshly ground black pepper
- 10 sprigs Italian parsley, leaves only, coarsely chopped
- Salt

TO SERVE

- 4 slices country-style bread, toasted on both sides
- Freshly ground black pepper (optional)
- Hot red pepper flakes (optional)

Be sure there are no bones left in the *stocco*, then cut it into 1-inch pieces and place them in a medium-sized casserole. Drain the potato cubes and add them to the casserole. Pour in the cold water and add the garlic and the tomatoes. Place the casserole over medium heat and simmer for 15 minutes. Add the oil, pepper to taste, and parsley. Simmer for 30 minutes more. By this time, the stocco should be rather soft, the potatoes should be almost dissolved, and the water reduced by one third.

Taste for salt. Remove from the heat and let the broth rest a few minutes before ladling it over the toasted bread placed in individual soup bowls. Sprinkle with more freshly ground black pepper and/or red pepper flakes if using, and serve.

RIGHT: Baccalá *for sale, filleted or chopped in small pieces.*

baccalà alla napoletana

BACCALÀ, NEAPOLITAN STYLE

SERVES 4 TO 6

1 1/2 pounds soaked *baccalà*, cut into pieces about 3 inches square

1 cup unbleached all-purpose flour

2 cups vegetable oil (preferably a mixture of half sunflower oil, half corn oil)

1/2 cup extra-virgin olive oil

Fine salt

FOR THE TOMATO SAUCE

3 large cloves garlic, peeled and left whole

5 tablespoons extra-virgin olive oil

1 1/2 pounds ripe tomatoes, blanched (see page 263), skin and seeds removed, cut into large pieces; or 1 1/2 pounds drained canned tomatoes, preferably imported Italian, seeded

Salt and freshly ground black pepper

Hot red pepper flakes to taste

1/4 cup capers preserved in wine vinegar, drained

3 ounces Gaeta olives, pitted

TO SERVE

15 sprigs Italian parsley, leaves only

Be sure there are no bones left in the *baccalà*, then flour all the pieces. Heat the vegetable oil and the olive oil in a skillet over medium heat until the oil mixture is hot, about 375°F. (If the oil is much hotter, the coating of the fish will become golden too quickly while the inside remains uncooked.) Fry the fish until golden all over, about 2 minutes on each side, sprinkle with fine salt to taste, then transfer the fish to a serving platter lined with paper towels and let rest until needed.

PREPARE THE TOMATO SAUCE: Place a nonreactive casserole containing the garlic and the oil over medium heat; the casserole should be large enough to hold all the fish in one layer. When the garlic is golden all over, add the tomatoes and cook for 10 minutes, stirring every so often with a wooden spoon. Season with salt, pepper, and red pepper flakes to taste. Cook for 5 minutes more, then add the capers and olives and the fried fish. Simmer for 15 minutes, turning the fish three or four times.

Transfer the sauce and fish to a warmed serving platter, sprinkle the parsley all over, and serve hot.

NOTE: If you have a lot of the tomato sauce left over, you can use it as a sauce for pasta.

RIGHT: *Like* baccalá, stoccofisso *is pieces of salt-dried cod; however, stocco is air-dried while baccalá is dried in a barrel.*

pomodorini e coda di rospo

MONKFISH AND CHERRY TOMATOES

SERVES 4 TO 6

1 pound cherry tomatoes, preferably the so-called grape cherry tomatoes, very well washed and left whole, stems removed

1 1/2 pounds boned monkfish, cut crosswise into 1-inch slices

Coarse-grained salt

1 lemon, cut in half

20 sprigs Italian parsley, leaves only

4 large cloves garlic, peeled

1/4 cup extra-virgin olive oil

1 teaspoon fine salt

1/2 teaspoon freshly ground black pepper

Hot red pepper flakes to taste

TO SERVE

4 to 6 slices country-style bread, lightly toasted

10 sprigs Italian parsley, leaves only

12 large fresh basil leaves

Preheat the oven to 375°F. Carefully rinse the tomatoes and arrange them in one layer in a jelly-roll pan. Place the pan in the oven for 10 minutes. Then remove the tomatoes and let them cool for 30 minutes.

Meanwhile, cut each slice of fish in half. Soak the fish pieces for 30 minutes in a bowl of cold water with a little coarse salt and the squeezed lemon halves. Rinse the fish pieces under cold running water, pat them dry with paper towels, and place them in a crockery or glass bowl. Cut the cooled tomatoes in half and add them to the fish.

Finely chop the parsley and garlic together on a cutting board, and sprinkle the mixture over the tomatoes. Season with the oil, salt, pepper, and red pepper flakes to taste. Gently mix all the ingredients together, cover the bowl with plastic wrap, and refrigerate for at least 1 hour, mixing the ingredients once or twice.

Place a large skillet that has a lid over medium heat, and when the pan is very hot, add the fish mixture. Cover the skillet and cook for 5 minutes, shaking the pan several times to be sure nothing sticks to the bottom. By this time, the fish should be cooked and the tomatoes will have fallen apart to form a rather rich sauce.

Taste for salt and pepper, mix very well, and spoon the hot mixture over the bread slices placed on individual serving plates. Sprinkle with the parsley and basil leaves, and serve.

RIGHT: *Fresh "grape" tomatoes, still on the vine, are your best choice for this dish.*

pesce al forno alla napoletana

BAKED WHOLE FISH, NEAPOLITAN STYLE

SERVES 4 TO 6

1 whole fish such as grouper, red snapper, sea bass, or striped bass, about 3 pounds, cleaned, with head and tail on

Coarse-grained salt

1 large lemon, cut in half

1 small stalk celery

1 small carrot, scraped

1 bay leaf

20 sprigs Italian parsley, leaves only

1 quart cold water

1 1/2 pounds all-purpose potatoes

10 tablespoons extra-virgin olive oil

1 1/2 pounds cherry tomatoes, cut in half

Salt and freshly ground black pepper

4 large garlic cloves, peeled

TO SERVE

Italian parsley, leaves only

Fresh basil leaves

Soak the fish for 30 minutes in a bowl of cold water containing a little coarse salt and the squeezed lemon halves.

Drain the fish, rinse it under cold running water, then cut it crosswise into 2-inch strips. Save the head and the tail.

Place the celery, carrot, bay leaf, and a few of the parsley leaves in a pot with the cold water. Place the pot over medium heat, and when the water reaches a boil, add coarse salt to taste, then the reserved head and tail of the fish. Let boil for 10 minutes; strain the water and discard the fish pieces and all the vegetables. Return the water to the pot and bring it to a boil again.

Meanwhile, peel the potatoes and cut them into 1/2-inch-thick slices. Parboil the potatoes in the broth for 4 minutes, then drain them and place them on paper towels to absorb excess liquid.

Place a skillet containing 4 tablespoons of the oil over medium heat, and when the oil is warm, add the cut-up tomatoes and sauté for 5 minutes, stirring with a wooden spoon; season with salt and pepper. Transfer the tomatoes and all their juices to a crockery or glass bowl and let rest until cool, about 30 minutes.

Use 1 tablespoon of the oil to heavily coat a glass baking dish. Preheat the oven to 400°F.

Arrange the potatoes in the baking dish. Season with a little salt and pepper. Finely chop the remaining parsley and the garlic together on a cutting board, and transfer the mixture to a small crockery or glass bowl. Add the remaining 5 tablespoons oil, and season with salt and pepper to taste. Mix very well. Arrange the fish pieces over the potatoes, sprinkle half of the parsley mixture over them, and season again with salt and pepper. Place the tomatoes over everything, sprinkle the remaining parsely mixture on top, and bake for 30 minutes.

Serve with the parsley and basil leaves.

triglie stufate

STEWED RED MULLET

SERVES 4

4 red mullets, about 6 ounces each, cleaned, heads and tails left on

Large pinch of coarse-grained salt

1 lemon, cut in half

1/4 cup extra-virgin olive oil

1 very large clove garlic, peeled and finely chopped

1 pound ripe tomatoes, blanched (see page 263), skin and seeds removed; or 1 pound drained canned tomatoes, preferably imported Italian, seeded

Salt and freshly ground black pepper

Large pinch of hot red pepper flakes

1 cup vegetable oil (preferably a mixture of half sunflower oil, half corn oil)

About 1 cup unbleached all-purpose flour

TO SERVE

10 sprigs Italian parsley, leaves only, coarsely chopped

1 lemon, cut into wedges

Soak the fish for 30 minutes in a bowl of cold water containing the coarse salt and the squeezed lemon halves.

Meanwhile, to prepare the sauce, heat the olive oil in a skillet over medium heat. When the oil is warm, add the garlic and sauté for 10 seconds, then add the tomatoes, season with salt, pepper, and red pepper flakes, and simmer for 15 minutes, stirring every so often with a wooden spoon.

Drain the fish, rinse them under cold running water, and pat them dry with paper towels.

Heat the vegetable oil in a second skillet over medium heat, and when the oil is hot, about 370°F, lightly coat the fish with the flour and cook them, two at a time, for 30 seconds on each side, or until light in color. Transfer them to a serving platter lined with paper towels to absorb excess oil, then fry the remaining fish.

Arrange the fish in the skillet containing the tomato sauce, and simmer for 1 minute on each side.

Serve the fish hot with some of the sauce, the parsley sprinkled all over, and the lemon wedges.

orata al forno

BAKED *DORADE*

SERVES 4

2 *dorades* (also called sea bream), about 1 pound each, cleaned, with head and tail on

Coarse-grained salt

1 lemon, cut in half

1/4 cup extra-virgin olive oil

4 large cloves garlic, peeled and left whole

15 sprigs Italian parsley, leaves only, coarsely chopped

Salt and freshly ground black pepper

1/2 cup red wine vinegar, or the juice of 2 lemons

TO SERVE

Italian parsley, leaves only

Soak the dorades for 30 minutes in a bowl of cold water containing a large pinch of coarse salt and the squeezed lemon halves.

Preheat the oven to 400°F.

Heavily oil a baking dish made of glass, china, or terra-cotta, but not metal. Drain the fish, rinse them under cold running water, and pat dry with paper towels. Using the garlic, half of the parsley, and salt and pepper to taste, season the insides of each fish and arrange them both in the prepared baking dish. Pour the remaining oil and the vinegar or lemon juice over the fish, and season again with salt and pepper.

Bake for 25 minutes, or longer if each fish is bigger than 1 pound, basting them every so often with the juices in the dish. The fish should be thoroughly cooked but not overcooked.

Transfer the fish and all their juices to a serving platter, sprinkle with the parsley leaves, and serve.

RIGHT: *A customer being served at the fish market.*
OPPOSITE: *Whole red mullet for sale.*

MOTORICAMBI
AUTORICAMBI
STUDIO

pesce al cartoccio alla napoletana

FISH BAKED IN A PAPER BAG, NEAPOLITAN STYLE

SERVES 4

1 whole fish such as grouper or red snapper, about 2 pounds, cleaned, with head and tail on

Coarse-grained salt

1 large lemon, cut in half

4 large cloves garlic, peeled

15 sprigs Italian parsley, leaves only

2 teaspoons fresh rosemary leaves

Large pinch of dried oregano

Pinch of dried thyme

Salt and freshly ground black pepper

1/4 cup extra-virgin olive oil, plus extra for the parchment

TO SERVE

2 tablespoons freshly squeezed lemon juice

1 lemon, cut into wedges

Soak the fish for 30 minutes in a bowl of cold water containing coarse salt to taste and the squeezed lemon halves.

Preheat the oven to 400°F.

Finely chop the garlic, parsley, and rosemary together on a board, and transfer the mixture to a small bowl. Add the oregano and thyme, season with salt and pepper, pour in the 1/4 cup oil, and mix very well.

Drain the fish, rinse it under cold running water, and pat it dry with paper towels. Lightly oil a piece of parchment paper or aluminum foil. Drizzle 1 tablespoon of the parsley mixture over the center of the parchment and place the fish on top. Pour half of the remaining mixture into the cavity of the fish and the other half over the fish. Wrap the fish and place it on a jelly-roll pan. Bake for 15 minutes on each side, or longer if the fish is bigger than 2 pounds.

When the fish is ready, transfer it to a serving platter, pour the lemon juice over it, and serve, boned, with the lemon wedges.

OPPOSITE: *The harbor of Procida. This quiet, beautiful, and very picturesque isle supports an unusually reserved life, including a colony of serious artists and not many tourists. Its volcanic soil is used to grow orange orchards and vineyards.*

vermicelli al sugo di pesce alla marinara

PASTA WITH FISH SAUCE, SAILOR'S STYLE

SERVES 4

1 recipe *Pesce alla Marinara* (opposite)

Coarse-grained salt

3/4 pound dried long pasta, such as vermicelli, preferably imported Italian

1/4 cup extra-virgin olive oil

ABOVE: Vermicelli al Sugo di Pesce alla Marinara.

Prepare the *pesce alla marinara* up to the point when the fish and tomatoes are removed from the oven. Do not yet sprinkle the dish with the chopped parsley.

While the fish is baking, bring a pot of cold water to a boil over medium heat, add coarse salt to taste, then the pasta, and cook it for 8 to 11 minutes, depending on the brand (1 minute less than for normal al dente).

When the fish is ready, transfer it to a serving platter, leaving the tomatoes and juices in the baking dish, and cover the platter with aluminum foil to keep the fish warm.

Transfer the cherry tomatoes and all the juices from the fish to a skillet, add the oil, and set the skillet over low heat. Drain the pasta, add it to the skillet, mix very well, and lightly sauté for less than a minute.

Sprinkle the parsley over the vermicelli, mix very well, and transfer everything to a serving platter. Serve the pasta immediately, followed by the fish (not at the same time).

pesce alla marinara

BAKED FISH, SAILOR'S STYLE

SERVES 4

- 3/4 pound cherry tomatoes
- 1 whole sea bass (*dorade* or *branzino*, also called *spigola*), about 1 1/2 pounds, cleaned, with tail and head on
- Large pinch of coarse-grained salt
- 1 large lemon, cut in half
- 1/4 cup extra-virgin olive oil
- Salt and freshly ground black pepper
- Very large pinch of dried oregano leaves
- 2 very large cloves garlic, peeled, left whole or coarsely chopped

TO SERVE

- 20 sprigs Italian parsley, leaves only, coarsely chopped

Quite frequently, the juices from the baked fish and the cherry tomatoes are used to dress some vermicelli (see Vermicelli al Sugo di Pesce, *opposite).*

Wash the cherry tomatoes well and pat them dry with paper towels. Soak the fish for 30 minutes in a bowl of cold water containing the coarse salt and the squeezed lemon halves.

Preheat the oven to 400°F. Meanwhile, drain the fish, rinse it under cold running water, and pat it dry with paper towels. Pour 2 tablespoons of the oil into a glass baking dish and place the fish in it. Arrange the tomatoes around it, then season with salt, pepper, and oregano, and add the garlic. Drizzle the remaining 2 tablespoons oil over the fish. Bake for about 15 minutes, or more if the fish is larger. The fish should be completely cooked and soft to the touch.

Remove the baking dish from the oven, sprinkle the parsley over the fish, and serve hot.

RIGHT: *Use a whole sea bass for this dish,* Pesce alla Marinara.

calamari al limone

SQUID WITH LEMON JUICE

SERVES 4 TO 6

- 1 1/2 pounds of the smallest squid (stomachs and tentacles intact) you can find, already cleaned
- 1 heaping teaspoon coarse-grained salt
- 1 large lemon, cut in half
- 2 medium-sized carrots, scraped
- 2 large stalks celery
- 1/4 cup extra-virgin olive oil
- 2 large cloves garlic, peeled and left whole
- Fine salt and freshly ground black pepper
- Large pinch of hot red pepper flakes
- About 1/4 cup completely defatted chicken broth, preferably homemade
- Juice of 1 large lemon
- 15 sprigs Italian parsley, leaves only, coarsely chopped

Soak the squid for 30 minutes in a bowl of cold water containing the coarse salt and the squeezed lemon halves.

While the squid is soaking, finely chop the carrots and celery together on a cutting board. Heat the oil in a heavy casserole, preferably flameproof terra-cotta or enamel, over medium heat. When the oil is lukewarm, add the garlic and sauté for 1 minute, or until lightly golden. Add the chopped vegetables and season with fine salt, pepper, and the red pepper flakes.

Drain the squid and rinse it under cold running water. Arrange the squid over the vegetables, cover the casserole, and cook for at least 45 minutes without stirring. By this time, the squid should be very tender and still juicy. Mix very well and cook for 2 to 3 minutes more, uncovered if there is too much liquid. Add the lemon juice, mix very well, and remove the casserole from the heat.

Sprinkle the parsley all over, mix again, and transfer everything to a serving platter. Serve hot.

RIGHT: *Lemons still attached to the tree branch.*

minestra di "polpetielli e fagioli"

OCTOPUS AND BEAN SOUP

SERVES 6 TO 8

1 cup dried *cannellini* (white kidney beans), picked over

5 tablespoons extra-virgin olive oil

Coarse-grained salt

1 pound whole octopuses, as small as possible, cleaned, with skin on

1 large lemon, cut in half

1 whole anchovy preserved in salt, boned, rinsed under cold running water, and cut into small pieces; or 2 anchovy fillets packed in oil, drained and cut into small pieces

1 pound fresh tomatoes, blanched (see page 263), skin and seeds removed, cut into small pieces; or 1 pound drained canned tomatoes, preferably imported Italian, cut into small pieces

2 large cloves garlic, peeled and finely chopped

Salt and freshly ground black pepper

10 large sprigs Italian parsley, leaves only, coarsely chopped

Soak the beans in a bowl of cold water overnight. The next morning, drain the beans, rinse them under cold running water, then place them in a casserole along with 2 quarts cold water. Add 1 tablespoon of the oil and set the casserole over medium heat. Simmer until the beans are cooked and soft, about 45 minutes. Add coarse salt to taste, mix very well, and simmer for 5 minutes more.

Drain the beans, saving the water. Put the beans in a crockery or glass bowl, and place wet paper towels over them to prevent them from becoming too dry.

Meanwhile, soak the octopuses. If they are small, leave them whole. If they are larger than 2 inches, cut them into 2-inch pieces and place them in a bowl of cold water containing coarse salt to taste and the squeezed lemon halves for 30 minutes.

Drain the octopuses and rinse them well under cold running water. Heat the remaining 4 tablespoons oil in a nonreactive casserole, preferably flameproof terra-cotta or enamel, over medium heat. When the oil is just lukewarm, add the anchovies, remove the casserole from the heat, and mash the anchovies with a fork.

Place the octopuses, tomatoes, and garlic in the casserole containing the anchovy mixture. Tightly cover the casserole, first with a piece of parchment paper, then with its lid so that no steam escapes. Set the casserole over medium heat and cook, without removing the lid, from 1 to 2 hours depending on the size of the octopuses. The octopuses should be very soft and juicy.

Taste for salt and pepper, then add the beans and enough cooking water from the beans to cover everything by 1/4 inch. Simmer for 2 minutes, add the parsley, mix very well, and serve hot, directly from the casserole.

This recipe is described as *"alla Luciana"* because it was traditionally made in the quarter of Santa Lucia, which was one of the main fishing areas in Naples and is now becoming one of the most desirable places to live. In the old days, the octopus would have been soaked and then cooked in seawater.

polpi "alla luciana"

OCTOPUS IN THE STYLE OF SANTA LUCIA

SERVES 6 TO 8 AS AN APPETIZER

1 whole octopus, about 1 1/2 pounds, cleaned, with the skin on

Coarse-grained salt

1 large lemon, cut in half

1/2 cup extra-virgin olive oil

Juice of 1 large lemon

Salt and freshly ground black pepper

2 medium-sized cloves garlic, peeled and finely chopped

15 sprigs Italian parsley, leaves only, coarsely chopped

Soak the octopus for 30 minutes in a bowl of cold water containing coarse salt to taste and the squeezed lemon halves.

Drain the octopus, rinse it well under cold running water, and place it in a heavy casserole, preferably flameproof terra-cotta. Add enough cold water to cover the octopus by about 2 inches and season with coarse salt. Cover the casserole with a piece of wax paper or parchment paper, then place the lid on top. Be sure the pot is completely sealed. (You can even prepare a "rope" of dough—just flour mixed with water—and press it around the edges of the lid to seal it.)

Set the casserole over medium heat and simmer for about 1 1/2 hours.

Once the octopus is cooked and very soft, let it rest in its own liquid until cool, about 1 hour. If you want to remove the skin, transfer the octopus to a cutting board and lift off the skin with your fingers; return the octopus to the poaching liquid and rub to remove any remaining pieces of skin. (In Italy, most of the time we eat the octopus with the skin left on.)

Cut the octopus into pieces and arrange it on a serving platter. Season with the oil, lemon juice, salt, abundant pepper, and the garlic. Mix very well, then sprinkle the parsley over all.

You may serve it immediately or cover the platter until you are ready to serve.

polpo al sugo

STEWED OCTOPUS

SERVES 4

2 medium-sized whole octopuses *veraci* (see photo, far right), about 1 pound each, cleaned, with the skin on

Large pinch of coarse-grained salt

1 lemon, cut in half

2 pounds ripe but not overripe tomatoes, cut into large pieces; or 2 pounds cherry tomatoes, cut in half; or 2 pounds drained canned tomatoes, preferably imported Italian

3 ounces Gaeta olives, pitted

3 large cloves garlic, peeled and left whole

5 heaping tablespoons capers preserved in wine vinegar, drained

15 sprigs Italian parsley, leaves only, coarsely chopped

5 large fresh basil leaves, left whole

1/2 cup extra-virgin olive oil

3/4 tablespoon salt

1/2 teaspoon freshly ground black pepper

Large pinch of hot red pepper flakes

TO SERVE

Fresh basil leaves, torn into thirds

Fresh Italian parsley leaves

Soak the octopuses for 30 minutes in a bowl of cold water containing the coarse salt and squeezed lemon halves.

Place the tomatoes, olives, garlic, capers, parsley, and basil in a crockery or glass bowl. Add the oil, salt and pepper, and red pepper flakes. Mix very well and let marinate, covered, in the refrigerator until needed.

Drain and rinse the octopuses very well under cold running water, and pat them dry with paper towels.

Place the octopuses in a heavy nonreactive casserole, preferably flameproof terra-cotta, then add the tomato mixture. Cover the casserole: It should be so tightly covered that no steam can escape. This can be accomplished by laying a piece of parchment paper over the casserole and then placing the lid on top. (Alternatively, you can prepare a rather stiff dough, mixing unbleached flour and water, shape it into a long rope, and seal the casserole by pinching this dough around the edges of the lid.)

Set the casserole over medium heat and simmer for 1 1/2 hours. By this time, the octopuses should be very soft and juicy, and a full-bodied tomato sauce will have formed. Cut the octopuses into pieces and serve with the sauce, with the basil and parsley sprinkled on top.

VARIATION

This dish may be used to dress pasta, such as *perciatelli*, spaghetti, or vermicelli to make *perciatelli al sugo di polpo*.

ABOVE: Polpi veraci *or "real octopus" (right) have two rows of suckers on their tentacles, while the* polpi sinischi *(left) have only one, which makes them much less desirable.*

CHAPTER SIX

il gran fritto alla napoletana

Il Gran Fritto alla Napoletana (the Grand Neapolitan Fried Course) and Bologna's *Gran Bollito Misto* (the Grand Boiled Course) are two old and important traditions in Italian cooking. *Il Gran Fritto*, of which a wide array of dishes can be considered a part, is not an antipasto, although it is eaten before the meal, often as something to snack on while the rest of the meal is being prepared.

I know many sophisticated diners who dismiss these courses as anything but grand, declaring *Il Gran Fritto* nothing more than a bunch of simple, uninspired fried dishes and *Il Gran Bollito Misto* just a collection of bland boiled meats. However, to understand why Italians consider these courses so important is to gain a privileged insight into Italian *cucina*.

Both the boiled and fried courses call for their own special battery of techniques. These traditional procedures must be followed strictly to ensure the correct results. Perfect boiling is not as straightforward as it might seem: Mastering the subtle techniques and flavor combinations used in *Il Gran Bollito Misto* is actually a grand endeavor.

The fact that successful frying also demands knowledge and skill was demonstrated by Caterina de' Medici, who introduced this Italian art to French courtiers in the mid-sixteenth century. The Neapolitan expression *frijenno magnanno*—or "fry and eat"—aptly describes the best way to prepare and serve fried foods. This method requires continuous frying so that each dish may be brought to the table in its proper order, still hot, light, and crisp—never greasy.

In the old days, Italian towns were full of little fry stands or shops known as *friggitorie*, where food was fried on demand and sold hot. In most towns, the fry shops served mainly fried fruits and other desserts, but in Naples they offered a great variety of fried dishes, including fried vegetables, fish, and savory pastries. Today Neapolitans continue to consume the same wide range of fried dishes, which they make at home or buy from the remaining *friggitorie*. Following are some popular examples:

- Anchovies or sardines lightly coated in flour then fried.
- *Frittelle di Alghe*, seaweed fritters.
- Zucchini sticks or slices of eggplant, fried in batter when prepared at home or in flour when store-bought.
- *"Scurilli"* (zucchini blossoms, page 179), dipped in batter and fried, or coated with flour and egg, then fried.
- *Sedano Fritto* (fried celery, page 186).
- *Carciofi Fritti o Dorati* (golden-fried artichokes, page 187).
- Hard-boiled egg yolks dipped in *balsamella* (béchamel sauce) before frying.
- Small pieces of cheese, especially buffalo-milk mozzarella (page 194), coated with bread crumbs and fried.
- *"Crocché" di Patate* (potato croquettes, page 184), stuffed or unstuffed, and coated with bread crumbs before frying.
- *Palle di Riso* (rice balls, page 181), fried.
- *Tittoli*, small thick triangles of polenta, coated with cornmeal before frying (the name refers to roof tiles, which share the reddish color of this dish).
- *Mannelle*, small pieces of fried dough that are shaped like hands.
- *Panzarotti*, boiled rice and potatoes mixed with chopped parsley and coated with bread crumbs before frying.
- *Zitoni Ripieni*, or stuffed and fried *zitoni*. (For recipe, see *Bugialli on Pasta*, pages 338–339.)

PRECEDING PAGES: *A selection of small fried dishes make up* Il Gran Fritto alla Napoletana, *or the Grand Fried Course.*

pasta cresciuta con gli "scurilli" *or* zeppole con fiori di zucca

ZUCCHINI BLOSSOM *ZEPPOLE*

MAKES 24

1 recipe *Pasta Cresciuta* batter (page 210)

24 large zucchini blossoms

TO FRY THE *ZEPPOLE*

1/4 cup extra-virgin olive oil

3 cups vegetable oil (preferably a mixture of half sunflower oil, half corn oil)

TO SERVE

Fine salt

1 large lemon, cut into wedges

ABOVE: *The author at a vegetable stand.* Il Gran Fritto *often includes a wide range of fried vegetables.*

Prepare the batter and let it rest until ready. Meanwhile, clean the zucchini blossoms by removing and discarding the pistils; do not cut off the stems. Lightly rinse the blossoms in cold running water and immediately dry them with paper towels. Let the zucchini blossoms rest wrapped in paper towels slightly dampened with cold water.

FRY THE *ZEPPOLE*: Heat the olive oil and vegetable oil in a large skillet over medium heat, and when the oil mixture is hot, about 400°F, dip each blossom in the batter and fry it until golden all over, about 30 seconds.

Transfer the blossoms to a serving platter lined with paper towels to absorb excess oil. When all the blossoms are on the platter, remove the paper towels, sprinkle some fine salt over the blossoms, and serve hot with the lemon wedges.

VARIATIONS

1. Insert 1 teaspoon of ricotta, seasoned with a little salt and pepper, into each blossom before dipping it into the batter.
2. Insert a very small piece of mozzarella and, if desired, a quarter of an anchovy fillet into each blossom before dipping it into the batter.

zeppole all'acciuga
or pasta cresciuta con acciughe

ANCHOVY *ZEPPOLE*

MAKES ABOUT 20

Coarse-grained salt

1 medium all-purpose potato

2 cups unbleached all-purpose flour, plus 1/2 cup for kneading

1 ounce fresh compressed yeast, or 2 envelopes active dry yeast

1 cup lukewarm milk for fresh yeast, or warm milk for dry

2 tablespoons extra-virgin olive oil, or 2 tablespoons (1 ounce) unsalted butter or lard, at room temperature

Fine salt

6 whole anchovies preserved in salt, boned, rinsed under cold running water, and cut into fourths; or 12 anchovy fillets packed in oil, drained, and cut into fourths

1 tablespoon extra-virgin olive oil

TO FRY THE *ZEPPOLE*

1/2 cup extra-virgin olive oil

1 1/2 cups vegetable oil (preferably a mixture of half sunflower oil, half corn oil)

TO SERVE

Fine salt

1 lemon, cut in half

Bring a small pot of cold water to a boil over medium heat. Add coarse salt to taste, then the potato, and cook until very soft, about 40 minutes. Drain the potato, peel it, and pass it through a potato ricer into a small crockery or glass bowl, using the disk with the smallest holes.

Place the flour in a bowl and make a well in the flour. Dissolve the yeast in the milk and pour it into the well. Measure out 2 tablespoons of the riced potato and add it to the well, along with the olive oil or the butter or lard and fine salt to taste (keep in mind that the anchovies will be salty).

Use a wooden spoon to thoroughly mix together all the ingredients in the well. Start adding the flour from the edges of the well, a little at a time, until all the flour is incorporated and a rather thick dough forms. Cover the bowl with a cotton dish towel and let it rest in a warm place away from drafts until the dough doubles in size, about 45 minutes.

Pour the 1/2 cup of flour out onto a pastry board, place the dough on top, and lightly knead it, incorporating more flour. Keep kneading until the dough is smooth but still very light to the touch. Sprinkle the anchovies over the dough and gently knead to distribute the anchovy pieces throughout. Heavily oil a crockery or glass bowl, place the dough in it, and oil the top of the dough as well. Cover the bowl with a cotton dish towel and let it rest in a warm place until doubled in size, about 1 hour.

RIGHT: *Anchovies, cut into fourths, have been sprinkled on top of the risen* pasta cresciuta *dough.*

FRY THE *ZEPPOLE*: Heat the olive oil and the vegetable oil together in a deep fryer over medium heat. When the oil mixture is hot, about 375°F, lightly oil a measuring tablespoon so the dough does not stick and use it to gently drop the dough into the hot oil by heaping tablespoons.

Do not fry more than five or six spoonfuls of dough at a time because the *zeppole* will puff up a lot. Fry the *zeppole* for 1 minute, or until lightly golden all over, moving them around with a strainer-skimmer and turning them several times.

Use the skimmer to transfer the *zeppole* to a serving platter lined with paper towels to absorb excess oil. When all the *zeppole* are on the platter, remove the paper towels and sprinkle the *zeppole* with fine salt and a few drops of lemon juice and serve hot.

palle di riso *or* crocchette di riso

RICE BALLS

MAKES ABOUT 15

Coarse-grained salt

1 cup rice, preferably Italian Arborio

6 tablespoons freshly grated aged local pecorino or Pecorino Romano cheese

1 extra-large egg

Salt and freshly ground black pepper

About 1 cup very fine unseasoned bread crumbs, preferably homemade, lightly toasted

1/4 cup extra-virgin olive oil

2 cups vegetable oil (preferably a mixture of half sunflower oil, half corn oil)

TO SERVE

Fine salt

Bring a pot of cold water to a boil over medium heat, add coarse-grained salt to taste, then add the rice and simmer for 16 minutes. Drain the rice and let it rest in the colander to cool for at least 1 hour.

Transfer the rice to a crockery or glass bowl, and add the cheese, egg, and salt and pepper to taste. Mix very well. Shape heaping tablespoons of the rice mixture into balls, then coat them with the bread crumbs.

Heat the olive oil and the vegetable oil in a skillet over medium heat. When the oil mixture is hot, about 375°F, fry the rice balls in batches until very light in color all over.

Transfer the cooked *palle* to a serving platter lined with paper towels to absorb excess oil. Repeat until all the rice balls are shaped and cooked, then remove the paper towels.

Serve the rice balls hot, with a little fine salt sprinkled over them.

"crocché" di patate

POTATO CROQUETTES

MAKES ABOUT 20

Coarse-grained salt

1 pound all-purpose potatoes

2 tablespoons (1 ounce) unsalted butter

2 heaping tablespoons freshly grated Parmigiano

Grated peel of half a lemon

2 extra-large eggs, lightly beaten

5 large sprigs Italian parsley, leaves only, finely chopped

Salt and freshly ground black pepper

TO FRY THE CROQUETTES

3 extra-large eggs

Fine salt

1/4 cup extra-virgin olive oil

2 cups vegetable oil (preferably a mixture of half sunflower oil, half corn oil)

About 1 cup unbleached all-purpose flour

About 1 cup very fine unseasoned bread crumbs, preferably homemade, lightly toasted

TO SERVE

Fine salt

1 lemon, cut into thin slices

Bring a pot of cold water to a boil over medium heat. Add coarse salt to taste, then add the potatoes and cook until they are soft, about 35 minutes depending on their size.

Immediately peel the potatoes and pass them through a potato ricer, using the disk with the smallest holes, into a crockery or glass bowl. Add the butter and mix with a wooden spoon until well combined. Add the Parmigiano, lemon peel, eggs, and parsley and mix again. Season with salt and pepper and mix again.

Very lightly beat the three eggs with a fork and add a pinch of fine salt. Shape the "*crocché*" by rolling heaping tablespoons of the potato mixture between the palms of your hands to make small balls.

FRY THE CROQUETTES: Heat the olive oil and vegetable oil in a deep fryer or heavy casserole. When the oil mixture is hot, about 400°F, quickly dip the "*crocché*" first in the eggs, then in the flour, again in the eggs, and finally in the bread crumbs. Fry in batches until very light golden all over. Transfer the cooked "*crocché*" to a serving platter lined with paper towels to absorb excess oil.

When all the "*crocché*" are on the platter, remove the paper towels, sprinkle a little fine salt over them, and serve hot with the lemon slices.

PRECEDING PAGES: *On the road from Naples to Paestum, at the beginning of the Amalfi coast, sits Vietri, where the famous ceramics are produced. Most of the dishes used in this book are authentic pieces from Vietri. Notice that the dome and the bell tower of San Giovanni Battista are almost completely covered with decorated Majolica tiles.*

frittelle di cicenielli

CICENIELLI FRITTERS

MAKES ABOUT 20

3/4 pound *cicenielli* or *bianchetti*

1 lemon, cut in half

Coarse-grained salt

10 sprigs Italian parsley, leaves only

2 medium-sized cloves garlic, peeled

2 cups unbleached all-purpose flour

1/2 ounce fresh compressed yeast, or 1 envelope active dry yeast

1 1/2 cups lukewarm water for fresh yeast or warm water for dry

Fine salt

TO FRY THE FRITTERS

1/4 cup extra-virgin olive oil

2 cups vegetable oil (preferably a mixture of half sunflower oil, half corn oil)

TO SERVE

Fine salt

1 lemon, cut into wedges

Cicenielli *means "small as chickpeas," an apt description for these tiny fish. They are deep-fried in batter in this recipe, but they may also be used as a pizza topping. The extremely white* cicenielli *are baby* alici, *or anchovies.*

Wash the *cicenielli* very well under cold running water, then soak them for 10 minutes in a bowl of cold water with the squeezed lemon halves and a little coarse salt. Drain and rinse the fish under cold running water, then pat them dry with paper towels. Let them rest, wrapped in paper towels in the refrigerator, until you need them.

Finely chop the parsley and garlic together on a cutting board, transfer to a bowl, and set aside until needed.

Place the flour in a medium-sized bowl and make a well in the flour. Dissolve the yeast in the water and pour it into the well. Add a pinch of fine salt, then start incorporating the flour a little at time, mixing with a wooden spoon. When all the flour is incorporated, let the batter rest, covered, for 10 minutes.

Combine the parsley mixture with the *cicenielli*, season with fine salt, and add the mixture to the batter. Mix very well and let the batter rest for at least 30 minutes. By this time, it will have become very spongy.

FRY THE FRITTERS: Heat the olive oil and the vegetable oil in a large skillet over medium heat. When the oil mixture is hot, about 375°F, spoon out heaping tablespoons of the batter and fish into the oil and fry until lightly golden all over. Transfer the fritters to a serving platter lined with paper towels to absorb excess oil.

When all the fritters are on the platter, remove the paper, sprinkle fine salt over them, and serve hot with the lemon wedges.

sedano fritto

FRIED CELERY

SERVES 4 TO 6
AS AN APPETIZER

1 large bunch celery

Coarse-grained salt

3 extra-large eggs

2 tablespoons freshly grated aged local pecorino or Pecorino Romano cheese

Very large pinch of hot red pepper flakes

Salt

1/4 cup extra-virgin olive oil

2 cups vegetable oil (preferably a mixture of half sunflower oil, half corn oil)

1 1/2 cups unbleached all-purpose flour

TO SERVE

Fine salt

1 lemon, cut into wedges

Clean the celery, discarding the outer dark green stalks and the leaves. Cut the celery stalks into 3-inch pieces and soak them for 30 minutes in a bowl of cold water containing a pinch of coarse salt.

Use a fork to lightly beat the eggs with the cheese, red pepper flakes, and salt to taste in a crockery or glass bowl.

Heat the olive oil and vegetable oil in a skillet over medium heat. Drain the celery, pat it dry with paper towels, and place it in a colander. Sprinkle the flour over the celery, and shake the colander several times until the excess flour falls out and the celery is evenly coated with flour.

When the oil mixture is hot, about 375°F, dip each piece of celery in the egg mixture and fry it until it is golden all over. Do not fry more than six or seven pieces at a time.

Transfer the fried celery to a serving platter lined with paper towels to absorb excess oil. When all the celery is on the platter, remove the paper towels.

Serve the fried celery hot, with a little fine salt sprinkled all over and the lemon wedges.

carciofi fritti o dorati

GOLDEN-FRIED ARTICHOKES

SERVES 4 TO 6
AS A VEGETABLE

3 large artichokes

2 lemons, cut in half

About 3/4 cup unbleached all-purpose flour

2 extra-large eggs

Pinch of fine salt

1/4 cup extra-virgin olive oil

1 1/2 cups vegetable oil (preferably a mixture of half sunflower oil, half corn oil)

TO SERVE

Fine salt

1 lemon, cut into wedges

Soak the artichokes for 30 minutes in a large bowl of cold water containing the squeezed lemon halves. Clean the artichokes, removing the tough outer leaves, chokes, and hair (see page 263). Cut them into eighths and put them back in the acidulated water until needed.

Drain the artichokes, put them in a large colander, and sprinkle the flour over them. Vigorously shake the colander so all the excess flour falls through the holes and the artichokes are perfectly coated. Lightly beat the eggs with the fine salt in a small bowl.

Heat the olive oil and vegetable oil in a skillet over medium heat. When the oil mixture is hot, about 375°F, dip each piece of artichoke in the beaten egg and fry it for about 1 minute, or until golden (*dorati*) all over. Transfer the artichoke pieces to a serving platter lined with paper towels to absorb excess oil.

When all the artichokes are on the platter, remove the paper towels and serve the artichokes immediately, with a little salt sprinkled over them and the lemon wedges.

RIGHT: *The famous* carciofi di Paestum, *a round artichoke that is one of the best tasting in all of Italy.*

CHAPTER SEVEN

buffalo-milk mozzarella

In the gastronomy of Campania, the main roles are played by vegetables and cheese. There is not a specific cheese course in the Neapolitan diet, because cheese is eaten—in different ways—at almost every meal. And the cheese that Neapolitans prefer is mozzarella.

Mozzarella di bufala (made from the milk of water buffaloes) is a D.O.C. product (*Denominazione di Origine Controllata*, or government-controlled area of origin) only when it is produced in the Campania region. If it is produced elsewhere, the cheese is no longer a D.O.C. product. Of course, like balsamic vinegar, which is produced in regions other than Emilia-Romagna and, although not D.O.C., can still be sold as real balsamic vinegar, other regions in Italy produce good buffalo-milk mozzarella. Still the most wonderful *mozzarella di bufala* comes from Campania, especially the area surrounding the town of Caserta and the lands around Paestum. It is said that the latter cheese is, as the Italians say, a little bit "*sciapa*," meaning less salty. No matter where it is from, this mozzarella obviously must be made from 100-percent buffalo milk from animals that are allowed to wander freely across the land, rest next to ponds, and eat mainly fresh grass.

The preferred shape for *mozzarella di bufala* is the classic roundish ball. The tiny, roundish "*ovuli*," or "*ovule*" (as they are called in Neapolitan dialect), are known as *bocconcini* in northern Italy. Mozzarella also appears in very large round or oval shapes or in a braided form called *treccia*. The round form in the classic size is preferred because it remains just juicy enough—not too dry, not too wet. The size maintains the "onion" texture perfectly, with many well-separated layers. It is *mozzata*, the rope of the curd torn by hand, that gives the name *mozzarella* to the cheese.

Buffalo-milk mozzarella is not to be confused with *fiordilatte*, a mozzarella cheese produced with cow's milk, or only a very low percentage of buffalo milk. It is used most often for cooking because it does not shed a lot of liquid while cooking.

Most everyone agrees that you can best taste the full flavor of mozzarella the day after it is made. But when there is talk about the temperature at which mozzarella must be served, I have heard many different opinions, but most would say that it should not be eaten straight from the refrigerator, but rather at room temperature, sitting until the very last moment in its *acquetta* or brine, not milk. And then: Should it be slightly lukewarm, kept for a few seconds next to a pot of lukewarm water once it is removed from its brine? I could go on and on.

When seated in a restaurant in Naples, the waiter asks you if you want "something" while waiting for the first course. An immensity of mixed appetizers arrives, mostly deep-fried vegetables along with a whole mozzarella, even if you are by yourself. The cheese is completely "naked," with at the most two basil leaves not very close to it. Not even a little oil dripped over it? Not even a tiny tomato? "Taste it as it is," was the answer I received, "then you can tell me if you need to add something." I deserved such an answer. The taste was absolutely superb.

In addition to eating mozzarella as an appetizer or a dessert cheese, it also is used in many wonderful dishes, combined primarily with vegetables. I think everyone knows the celebrated *Insalata Caprese*, in which slices of mozzarella alternate with slices of tomatoes and basil leaves, with just a few drops of extra-virgin olive oil drizzled all over. But the cooked dishes with vegetables will be less familiar.

What is considered the best preparation of mozzarella is the "*buriello*." In the old days, there were two different methods, one "*in lancella*," in which a *lancella*, small terra-cotta amphora mainly used for water, was filled with cream with some small balls of mozzarella, or "*in pane*" (in a loaf), in which the cream and the small balls of mozzarella were wrapped in a layer of more mozzarella. Today the outer layer is made of *scamorza*, a mild, mozzarella-like cheese.

Even as we honor the buffalo-milk mozzarella, we cannot forget the other cheeses from Naples and the Campania region. There is *provola affumicata* (smoked provola), a cheese made from whole cow's milk; and the so-called *burrino incamiciato*, similar to the burrata from the Apulia region. This is formed by mixing butter with coarsely chopped cheese, and then wrapping the mixture—like a bag—in a casing of *scamorza*.

Provolone also is a frequent ingredient, cooked in many Neapolitan dishes. It may be prepared with buffalo milk as well as the usual cow's milk and may be used fresh or aged. When it is fresh, its aroma and taste is very "personal," smooth, and quite rich. Aged provolone is mainly used as a seasoning.

Finally we have the "*caciocavallo,*" which is a semi-hard aged cheese made with whole cow's milk, similar to provolone, but with a very different shape. There are different theories about the origin of its name. I think the old and very exotic idea that the milk used came from mares must be discarded. (*Giumenta* is the feminine of *horse*, *cavallo* in Italian.) A second idea is that the cheese is arranged as a pair, one on each end of a stick, making it *a cavallo* ("on horseback"), similar to the pommel horse used in gymnastics. A third theory is that, mainly in the Calabria region, the cheese-makers used to mold small horse-shaped figures with the just-prepared cheese. And the last theory goes back to the time when the shepherds would come down from the mountains where they had produced the cheese and place the cheese *a cavallo*—still tied two by two—over the back of the horse.

PRECEDING PAGES: *The grounds of the Royal Palace of the Old Kingdom of Naples in Caserta, not far from Naples itself.*

the making of mozzarella

When you watch mozzarella cheese being made, you clearly understand and appreciate the combination of love, pride, and technical mastery that goes into the process. The people involved do not work; they follow a ritual, going from one step to the next, until finally the ball of mozzarella emerges, coming out of their hands almost as if it were rising from the blue sea alongside the Amalfi Drive.

Mozzarella, when cut open, resembles a thick strip wrapped into a ball. Italians refer to this type of curd as *pasta filata*, or "layered curd." In mozzarella production, the curds that are formed after the milk has been cooked with rennet are crumbled and placed on a slanted table to allow the whey to run off. The crumbled curds begin to dry and ferment naturally. But after about three hours, the solidified curd is cut into long strips, returned to the kettle, and covered with boiling water. As the strips float to the top of the kettle, bunches of them are seized, quickly torn to pieces, and formed into balls of one-half pound to one pound in weight.

(Smaller balls of about one-quarter pound are called *bocconcini* or "little mouthfuls.") It is the tearing action, *mozzare* in Italian, that gives the cheese its name. The balls of torn curd are placed in cold water for several minutes and then transferred to a light brine for ten to twelve hours. Once removed, they are kept in their own whey and may be eaten immediately or up to two weeks later.

Other cheeses of southern Italy share the fascinating technique of layering, in which the curd is cut into strips before being pressed together. This group of cheeses includes *treccia*, *scamorze*, *caciocavallo*, *provola*, and *provolone*, among others.

Variations in the same basic technique distinguish provolone and mozzarella. After the milk has been cooked for provolone, the curds are not crumbled, but rather placed directly on a slanted table to drain. They are left to dry and ferment for a longer period than the mozzarella curds—one to three days, depending on the weather. (The *casaro*, or cheese-maker, knows by touch when the curd is ready.) As with mozzarella, the provolone curd is cut into long strips, placed in a kettle, and covered with boiling water. But the bunches of strips, once seized from the water, are cut with a knife rather than torn. Then they are formed into a huge sausage shape that is quickly bathed in cold water. They are immediately placed in a strong brine for six to twelve hours, depending on the local custom. At this point, the provolone is either smoked or tied up like a sausage and left to age.

Buffalo milk is heated and pasteurized, then the rennet is added, mixed very well, and left to rest in a huge vat for about 5 hours to create perfect *cagliata* (curd).

All the curds are transferred to a perforated stainless-steel table so the excess water can run off. Here, the *cagliata* is cut into large pieces.

The large pieces of curd are ground and transferred to a large cherry wood container called a *comuencina*. Next hot water will be added, then drained, changing the very grainy texture to a smooth one.

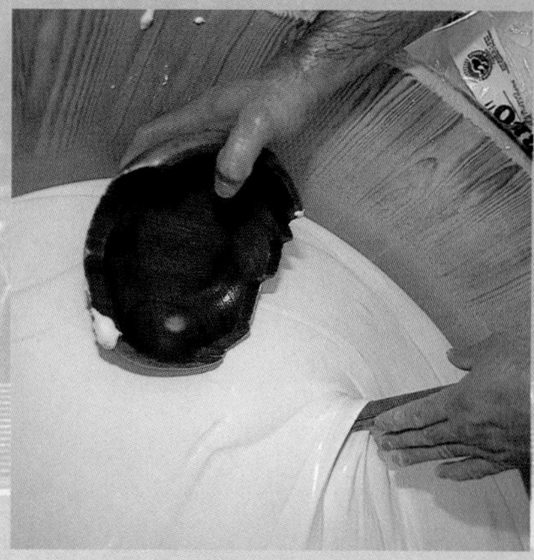

A small cherry wood bowl is used to remove excess water as it rises to the top. Then the *cagliata* is mixed and pieces are removed for molding using the same cherry wood bowl.

Molding the mozzarella by hand takes two people: The one on the left holds the piece of *cagliata*, while the one on the right tears and shapes it.

Before being wrapped in plastic bags for sale, the mozzarelle are placed in a container with cold water for 10 minutes, then transferred to another large container filled with brine for a 3-hour rest.

mozzarella impanata

BREADED MOZZARELLA

SERVES 4 TO 6 AS AN APPETIZER, 2 TO 4 AS A MAIN COURSE

12 *bocconcini* (1-inch balls of cow's milk mozzarella); or 12 slices buffalo-milk mozzarella, preferably imported Italian, about 1 inch thick

4 extra-large eggs

Salt and freshly ground black pepper

1/4 cup extra-virgin olive oil

2 cups vegetable oil (preferably a mixture of half sunflower oil, half corn oil)

About 2 cups very fine unseasoned bread crumbs, preferably homemade, lightly toasted

TO SERVE

Fine salt

1 large lemon, cut into wedges

When preparing this recipe, you must be sure the bread crumbs, if they are not homemade, are still very dry and crisp so they do not absorb a lot of oil.

Let the *bocconcini* or the mozzarella slices rest on paper towels for at least 1 hour to dry completely.

Using a fork, lightly beat the eggs in a small bowl with a pinch of salt and a twist of black pepper.

Heat the olive oil and the vegetable oil in a skillet over medium heat. When the mixture is hot, about 375°F, dip each piece of mozzarella in the eggs and immediately coat it with the bread crumbs. Fry until very light in color all over, about 1 minute.

Remove from the skillet and transfer to a serving patter lined with paper towels to absorb excess oil. When all the mozzarella pieces are fried and on the platter, remove the paper towels, sprinkle some fine salt over the mozzarella, and serve hot, with lemon wedges.

mozzarella ai ferri

GRILLED MOZZARELLA

SERVES 4 TO 6

- 12 *bocconcini* (1-inch balls of cow's milk mozzarella), left whole; or 12 slices buffalo-milk mozzarella, preferably imported Italian, about 1 inch thick
- Branches of rosemary, sage, bay leaves, and oregano, for the coals
- 1/4 cup extra-virgin olive oil
- Salt and freshly ground black pepper

When using very fresh mozzarella, you must be sure to let the slices rest on paper towels until all the juices from the cheese are completely absorbed. That way, you should have no problems during grilling.

Let the *bocconcini* or mozzarella slices rest on paper towels in the refrigerator for at least 2 hours before using them so they are completely drained.

On an outdoor grill, prepare the hot ashes, placing all the branches of aromatic herbs on them. Lightly oil the grill and place the mozzarella on it. Grill for about 4 minutes. The mozzarella should be barely cooked and not browned at all.

Transfer to a serving platter, drizzle a little of the oil over it, and season with a pinch of salt and freshly ground black pepper. Serve hot.

VARIATION

You can cook the mozzarella in the oven instead of on the grill. Wrap the *bocconcini* or mozzarella slices and the branches of aromatic herbs together in cheesecloth, then place the bundle on paper towels in the refrigerator to drain.

Preheat the oven to 400°F and discard the herbs and cheesecloth before baking the mozzarella for about 20 minutes.

OPPOSITE: *Smoked* scamorza *is another Neapolitan favorite. It's a cow's milk cheese that uses the same preparation techniques as mozzarella.*

Though Neapolitan in origin, this dish has become very popular in Rome, and almost all the restaurants there have it on the menu. But the Neapolitans complain that the Romans do not follow the proper step-by-step preparation when making this dish. "Too fast, too easy," they say. "They do not have the patience and a humble enough attitude!" After eating this dish prepared with Neapolitan love, I can say it's a superior experience.

mozzarella in carrozza

MOZZARELLA "IN A CARRIAGE," NEAPOLITAN STYLE

SERVES 4 TO 6

- 2 mozzarelle (1/2 pound each), preferably buffalo-milk mozzarella imported from Italy
- 12 slices white bread, crusts removed
- About 1/2 cup milk
- 3 extra-large eggs
- Fine salt
- 1/4 cup extra-virgin olive oil
- 2 cups vegetable oil (preferably a mixture of half sunflower oil, half corn oil)
- About 2 cups very fine unseasoned bread crumbs, preferably homemade, lightly toasted

TO SERVE

- Salt

THE CLASSIC NEAPOLITAN WAY: Cut the mozzarella into six 1/2-inch-thick slices and let them rest on paper towels for at least 30 minutes so they dry out.

Cut the slices of bread the same size as the mozzarella and lay them out on paper towels or wax paper. Drizzle 3/4 tablespoon of the milk over each slice of bread, then the same amount of milk over each mozzarella slice. Make six sandwiches, placing a slice of mozzarella between two slices of bread. Gently press the sandwiches so the cheese is completely attached to the bread.

Using a fork, lightly beat the eggs in a small bowl with a little salt. Heat the olive oil and the vegetable oil in a small skillet over medium heat. When the oil mixture is hot, about 375°F, dip each sandwich into the eggs, then coat it with the bread crumbs. Lightly fry until golden all over.

Use a slotted spatula to transfer the fried *mozzarella in carrozza* to a serving dish lined with paper towels to absorb excess oil.

When all the sandwiches are ready, remove the paper towels and serve hot, with a little salt sprinkled on top.

THE SHORTCUT: After putting the sandwich together, soak the *mozzarella in carrozza* in the milk, then dip it in the eggs, coat it with the bread crumbs, and fry it.

involtini di verza

MOZZARELLA BUNDLES

SERVES 4 OR 8

- 1 small savoy cabbage, just large enough to provide 8 large white leaves
- Coarse-grained salt
- 1 mozzarella (1/2 pound), preferably buffalo-milk mozzarella imported from Italy
- 1 very small clove garlic, peeled and finely chopped
- 5 sprigs Italian parsley, leaves only, coarsely chopped
- Salt and freshly ground black pepper
- 1/4 cup extra-virgin olive oil
- 2 cups tomato sauce without hot pepper, such as "*Pommarola*" *alla Napoletana* (page 96)

TO SERVE

- Fresh basil sprigs

Bring a pot of cold water to a boil over medium heat, add coarse salt to taste and then the eight cabbage leaves. Cook the leaves for 2 to 3 minutes, or until quite soft. Transfer them to a bowl of cold water, then place them on a layer of paper towels.

Coarsely chop the mozzarella, add the garlic and parsley, season with salt and pepper, and mix very well.

Remove the large vein from each cabbage leaf, then lightly overlap the two halves to make a full leaf. Place an eighth of the mozzarella stuffing on top of each leaf, fold it like a package, and tie with white string.

Heat the oil in a nonreactive medium-sized casserole, preferably flameproof terra-cotta or enamel, over medium heat, and when the oil is warm, add the bundles and sauté for 20 seconds, turning them once. Pour in the tomato sauce, taste for salt and pepper, and simmer, covered, for 5 minutes, turning the bundles twice.

Remove the strings and serve the mozzarella bundles hot, with the basil sprigs.

ABOVE: *Mozzerelle resting in the brine.*

carciofi ripieni di mozzarella

ARTICHOKES STUFFED WITH MOZZARELLA

SERVES 4

4 large artichokes

1 lemon, cut in half

10 sprigs Italian parsley, leaves only

2 large cloves garlic, peeled

1 mozzarella (1/2 pound), preferably buffalo-milk mozzarella imported from Italy, cut into pieces

2 tablespoons freshly grated Parmigiano

1 extra-large egg

Salt and freshly ground black pepper

4 heaping teaspoons very fine unseasoned bread crumbs, preferably homemade, lightly toasted

TO BAKE THE ARTICHOKES

About 3/4 cup completely defatted chicken or vegetable broth, preferably homemade

1/4 cup extra-virgin olive oil

The sweetness of the cheese stuffing blends very well with the slightly sour aftertaste of the artichokes.

Soak the artichokes for 30 minutes in a bowl of cold water containing the squeezed lemon halves. Clean the artichokes (see page 264), saving the stems and discarding the tough outer leaves, the chokes, and the hair. Use your fingers to enlarge the cavity of each artichoke.

Preheat the oven to 375°F.

Trim the saved artichoke stems, removing and discarding the darker outer parts, and cut the trimmed stems into pieces. Use a meat grinder (or knife) to very finely chop the parsley, garlic, mozzarella, and artichoke stems all together into a crockery or glass bowl. Add the grated Parmigiano and the egg, and season with salt and pepper. Mix very well with a wooden spoon.

Fill the prepared artichokes with the stuffing and sprinkle a heaping teaspoon of bread crumbs over each.

BAKE THE ARTICHOKES: Arrange the artichokes in a casserole, pour in the broth, then drizzle the oil all over. Cover the casserole and bake for 45 minutes. By this time, the artichokes should be completely cooked and almost all the liquid will have evaporated.

Transfer the artichokes with their juices to a serving platter and serve warm.

mozzarella e melanzane

MOZZARELLA AND EGGPLANT CASSEROLE

SERVES 6 TO 8

4 eggplants, not more than 10 ounces each

Coarse-grained salt

1/4 cup extra-virgin olive oil

2 cups vegetable oil (preferably a mixture of half sunflower oil, half corn oil)

Unbleached all-purpose flour

1 mozzarella (1/2 pound), preferably buffalo-milk mozzarella imported from Italy, cut into slices

FOR THE TOMATO SAUCE

2 1/2 pounds cherry tomatoes

6 tablespoons extra-virgin olive oil

3 cloves garlic, peeled and finely chopped

Salt and freshly ground black pepper

4 extra-large eggs

Several fresh marjoram leaves

TO SERVE

Several fresh basil leaves

Peel the eggplants, then cut them into 3/4-inch-thick slices. Place the slices on a serving platter, sprinkle some coarse salt over them, then place a second platter as a weight on top. Let rest for 1 hour.

Rinse the eggplants very well under cold running water and pat them dry with paper towels.

Heat the olive oil and the vegetable oil in a large skillet over medium heat. When the oil mixture is hot, about 375°F, lightly flour the eggplant slices and fry them until golden all over, about 2 minutes.

Transfer the fried eggplant to a serving platter lined with paper towels to absorb excess oil. When all the eggplant is on the platter, lightly oil a large glass baking dish. Arrange a layer of eggplant slices in the dish and place a slice of mozzarella on top of each eggplant slice. Cover each slice of mozzarella with one more slice of eggplant.

PREPARE THE TOMATO SAUCE: Place the cherry tomatoes on a cookie sheet and bake for 15 minutes. Set a nonreactive medium-sized casserole, preferably flameproof terra-cotta or enamel, containing the oil over medium heat, and when the oil is warm, add the garlic and lightly sauté it for 1 to 2 minutes; the garlic should still be very light in color. Add the tomatoes, raise the heat, and sauté for 10 minutes, seasoning with salt and pepper.

Transfer the sauce to a crockery or glass bowl and let it rest until cool, about 30 minutes.

Preheat the oven to 375°F.

Use a fork to lightly beat the eggs with a pinch of salt. Pour the egg mixture into the cooled tomato sauce, add the marjoram, mix very well, and carefully pour everything over the eggplant in the baking dish. Bake for 20 minutes.

Remove from the oven and serve hot, with the fresh basil leaves.

mozzarella e uova

MOZZARELLA AND EGGS

SERVES 4 TO 6

1 mozzarella (1/2 pound), preferably buffalo-milk mozzarella imported from Italy

4 extra-large eggs

Pinch of fine salt

1 tablespoon extra-virgin olive oil

Cut the mozzarella into 1/2-inch-thick slices and let them rest on paper towels for at least 30 minutes to dry out.

Use a fork to lightly beat the eggs in a small bowl with the fine salt. Heat an 8-inch omelet pan containing the oil over medium heat. Be sure the pan is very well seasoned because mozzarella sticks easily. Remove the extra oil, and when the pan is heated evenly, add the eggs and let them cook over low heat for 1 minute.

Arrange all the mozzarella slices over the eggs and start shaking the pan to be sure nothing sticks. Use a fork to prick the eggs to help the still very loose eggs run under the mozzarella. Cook until the eggs are completely set, about 4 minutes. By this time, the mozzarella will be melting a little.

Slide the "frittata" onto a round serving platter and serve hot.

ABOVE: *A* cagliata *(curd) of mozzarelle is lifted to make a perfect filo (string).*

pennette e pomodorini alla sorrentina

PASTA AND CHERRY TOMATOES WITH MOZZARELLA

SERVES 6

1 1/2 pounds cherry tomatoes, preferably the so-called grape cherry tomatoes, very well washed and left whole

1/2 cup extra-virgin olive oil

1/4 cup cold water

6 large cloves garlic, peeled and coarsely chopped

Salt and freshly ground black pepper

Large pinch of dried oregano

Coarse-grained salt

1 pound dried short tubular pasta, such as *pennette*, preferably imported Italian

TO SERVE

2 mozzarelle (1/2 pound each), preferably buffalo-milk mozzarella imported from Italy, drained and cut into small cubes

Abundant fresh basil leaves

Preheat the oven to 375°F.

Place the cherry tomatoes in a large glass baking dish, preferably made of flameproof terra-cotta. Add the oil, water, and garlic. Season with salt, pepper, and oregano and bake for 45 minutes, or until the tomatoes are very soft and a lot of juice emerges.

Bring a large pot of cold water to a boil over medium heat, add coarse salt to taste, then the pasta, and cook until al dente, 9 to 12 minutes depending on the brand.

Drain the pasta and add it to the baking dish containing the tomatoes. Mix very well and serve hot, topped with the mozzarella cubes and basil leaves.

VARIATIONS

1. Finely chop fifteen sprigs Italian parsley, leaves only, then mix them with two cloves garlic, peeled and finely chopped. Sprinkle over the pasta before serving.

2. Cut the cherry tomatoes in half, add the olive oil plus fifteen sprigs Italian parsley, leaves only, finely chopped, mixed with two cloves garlic, peeled and finely chopped. Refrigerate for 1 hour before sautéing the mixture on the burner.

CHAPTER EIGHT

neapolitan pizza and the savory pastries

DI SEM
RASOLE
IRA

Without a doubt, preparing a perfect pizza is an art. It is not easy to successfully produce a dish so balanced and self-sufficient using only a few common ingredients. Today the *pizzaiolo*, or pizza-maker, is a member of a specialized profession, and he really dedicates his life to producing what has become the most famous dish in Italian cuisine. Always smiling, almost dancing while he works, it is the amazing ability of the *pizzaiolo* to "understand" a piece of dough and know how to turn it into a wonderful pizza.

Yes, you have to "understand" that a common piece of pizza dough changes completely as it is worked by different people. And in the old days, the *pizzaiolo*'s shop—which could have been large or small, with nice tables or just benches—was more than a place to eat. It was a meeting place where you could see people from all levels of society brought together by this magic piece of dough.

Much has been written about the origin of the pizza, but I believe the identifying characteristic of the Neapolitan pizza is that it represents the first time a piece of dough or a thick batter was given a topping—be it simple or complex—rather than being stuffed. There are many different types of flatbreads eaten in different countries that possibly predate the pizza. These represent varied approaches to a stretched dough or thick batter that would be baked, grilled, or fried. Most were either plain or lightly stuffed, primarily with aromatic herbs and then later with vegetables or meat, but they never had a topping.

In Italy, these flatbreads were called *schiacciate*, and like pizza, they were baked directly on stones or terra-cotta and flavored with herbs, the most common being rosemary. These breads are documented in early Renaissance cookbooks, but if we look to archeological sources, we might suspect that this method was already used by the Etruscans and the ancient Romans. A fresco

IL PIZZAIUOLO.

in an Etruscan tomb shows a person kneading and stretching a piece of dough, ready to place it in a wood-burning oven. (Since the real *focacce* are baked in a greased pan, they are not considered ancestors of pizza.)

In his late-eighteenth-century cookbook, *Il Cuoco Galante (The Gallant Cook),* Vincenzo Corrado, who, with Cavalcanti, is the other great gastronome of the Kingdom of Naples, includes only one mention of pizza. That is a recipe for *Pizzette alla Fiorentina*, which are small pizzas with rosemary, but no tomatoes. Ripe red tomatoes were still quite a new ingredient Corrado's time, but in the early nineteenth century, they found their "habitat"—not only in the fields all around Naples, but on top of a piece of dough as well. When baked together in a wood-burning brick oven, the Neapolitan pizza was born.

Still, as we study old manuscripts, we must realize that this "invention" was most likely an accident, as most inventions and discoveries are. Pizza probably came into being while someone was searching for a new food for the poor and working classes of Naples. Tomatoes were by now abundant in the region, so it makes sense that they would be used to complete a filling dish for the common man.

Today pizza is stretched, first with a very short and thin rolling pin, then by "playing" with the disk of dough in the air on top of the fingers, just as a skilled *giocoliere* (juggler) would. This stretches the dough more in the center, leaving it thicker all around the edges and forming what is called the *cornicione*. Because of this rim, when the topping is placed on the dough, it naturally spreads all over, but remains inside the crust while baking. Traditionally the dough was stretched only on a flat surface, first by rolling it out with a roundish piece of wood, and then using the palm of the hand and the fingers to form a center that was quite thin, leaving it much thicker around the edges. The real Neapolitan pizza has a dough that is neither extremely thin and uniformly crusty nor uniformly thick, gummy, and gluey.

From the beginning, you could order a whole pizza or one slice of a larger one. The first toppings used were abundant chopped garlic and olive oil, the so-called *coll'aglio e l'oglio*. Another favorite topping in the early days was lard and fresh anchovies or the tiny fresh fish called *cecenielli* (see page 185); sometimes a few small clams (*vongole veraci*) were added. The fish fully cooked as the pizza was baking. This topping fell out of favor as tomatoes and mozzarella became the principal ingredients, but preserved anchovies held on.

Today the classic toppings are:

ALLA MARINARA: Garlic, tomatoes, oregano, and oil.

MARGHERITA (named, as everyone knows, for the wife of Umberto I, King of Italy): Olive oil, mozzarella, basil, and tomatoes.

ROMANA: Olive oil, oregano or basil, tomatoes, mozzarella, and some anchovies.

IN BIANCO: Not as popular as those listed above, this pizza is topped with sheep's milk cheese (pecorino), lard or olive oil, and a lot of black pepper. *Scamorza* or mozzarella may be substituted for the pecorino. The crucial omission is tomatoes—hence the name *bianco*.

All the extravagant toppings consisting of many ingredients are more recent innovations. The first ones were called *quattro stagioni* (four seasons), with each quarter having a different topping, and *capricciosa*, which allowed any mixture of ingredients. By now there are no limits to what may be used as a topping, but the classic toppings remain the most popular, and for good reason.

OPPOSITE: *A historical illustration of a pizza-maker.*
PRECEDING PAGES: *One of the cities many pizzerie.*

Neapolitan pizza is completely different from all the other pizza found on the market these days. The very thin, crusty and flaky pizzas are not the Neapolitan style, nor are the uniformly thick and gummy ones. The traditional way of eating pizza was to fold it into quarters. A current stylish trend in Naples is to eat it with a fork and knife, discarding the *cornicione*, or edge of the rim around the pizza. Perhaps this method will pass as quickly as other fads.

pizza alla napoletana

NEAPOLITAN PIZZA

MAKES 8 PIZZAS ABOUT 8 INCHES IN DIAMETER

- 5 cups unbleached all-purpose flour
- 1 ounce fresh compressed yeast, or 2 envelopes active dry yeast
- 2 cups lukewarm water for fresh yeast or warm water for dry
- Large pinch of fine salt

To prepare a real Neapolitan pizza, a wood-burning brick oven is essential, but lining the middle shelf of your oven with unglazed terra-cotta tiles (the kind used for flooring) is a very good substitution; just be aware that you have to preheat the oven for at least double the usual time because the tiles must be very hot. Do not flour or oil the tiles, or wet them with cold water. This terra-cotta lining not only bakes the pizza perfectly; it gives off the particular, intense smell of pizza baked in a professional wood-burning brick oven.

Place the flour in a mound and make a well in it. Dissolve the yeast in the water, pour it into the well, and add the salt. Using a wooden spoon, first stir the salt into the yeast mixture, then start adding flour from the rim of the well. When a thick batter is formed, start working with your hands, incorporating more flour, until a rather uniform dough forms. At this point, not all the flour is incorporated. Transfer the dough to a very well floured bowl, cover it with a dish towel, and let rest in a warm place away from drafts until doubled in size, about 1 hour.

When the dough is ready, divide it into eight pieces and knead each piece for 1 minute.

Line the oven with unglazed terra-cotta tiles as described above, and preheat it, taking at least twice the usual time, to 450°F.

To stretch the dough into a disk that is very thin in the center and thicker all around the rim, or *cornicione*, is an art. The very good *pizzaioli* (pizza-makers) in Naples stretch the dough over one of their fingers and rotate it in the air to achieve the perfect shape. But this technique is not for everybody: Using a thin, very short rolling pin in the beginning, then stretching the dough with your fingers produces very good results. This method, though less artful and dramatic, is perfectly authentic and was for a long time the way pizza dough was stretched.

Once the dough is stretched to the desired thickness, transfer it to a paddle and arrange the topping that you have chosen over the dough, remembering to keep the topping inside the *cornicione*. In the oven the *cornicione* will puff up and all the topping will remain in the center. Be sure the bottom of the pizza dough is completely dry. With a brusque movement, slide the pizza off the paddle and onto the hot tile. Bake for 4 to 5 minutes. Serve hot with any of the classic toppings described on page 205.

ABOVE: *A proud pizza-maker displays his art.* **OPPOSITE:** *The real Neapolitans eat pizza folded into fourths* a libretto *(like a small book). If a pizza is folded over before baking, it becomes a calzone. Eating the inside portion of the pizza and discarding the high outer ring of dough is a recent affectation; it is not traditional.*

le pizzette fritte ripiene alla napoletana

FRIED PIZZAS WITH STUFFING, NEAPOLITAN STYLE

MAKES 6 STUFFED PIZZAS

FOR THE DOUGH

3 cups unbleached all-purpose flour

1 ounce fresh compressed yeast, or 2 envelopes active dry yeast

1 cup lukewarm water or milk for fresh yeast or warm water or milk for dry

1 potato, about 4 ounces, boiled in salted water, peeled, and finely riced

2 tablespoons extra-virgin olive oil or melted lard

Fine salt

FOR THE STUFFING

6 ounces provolone or unsmoked *scamorza*, cut into small pieces

1 cup whole-milk ricotta

1/4 pound pancetta or Neapolitan salami, coarsely ground or cut into very small pieces

Salt and freshly ground black pepper

TO FRY THE *PIZZETTE*

1 cup vegetable oil (preferably a mixture of half sunflower oil, half corn oil)

1/2 cup extra-virgin olive oil

TO SERVE

Fine salt

PREPARE THE DOUGH: Arrange 2 cups of the flour in a mound on a board and make a well in it. Dissolve the yeast in the water or milk and pour it into the well. Add the riced potato, along with the oil and fine salt to taste, and mix the ingredients in the well together. Use a wooden spoon to incorporate flour from the edges of the well, a little at a time.

When a rather thick batter has formed, use your hands to incorporate more flour. Knead the dough in a folding motion until it is smooth and elastic, about 5 minutes. Place the dough in a well-floured bowl, cover it with a cotton dish towel, and let it rest in a warm place away from drafts for about 45 minutes, or until doubled in size.

PREPARE THE STUFFING: In a crockery or glass bowl, combine the provolone, ricotta, and ground pancetta, and season with salt and pepper. Let the stuffing rest, covered, in the refrigerator until needed.

When the dough has risen, return it to the board and start kneading in a folding motion, incorporating the remaining cup of flour, until the dough is very smooth and the texture of the riced potatoes has completely disappeared, about 2 minutes.

Divide the dough into twelve equal pieces. Roll each piece out into a disk about 1/8 inch thick, then let the disks rest, covered with a cotton dish towel, for 5 minutes.

FRY THE *PIZZETTE*: Heat the vegetable oil and olive oil in a skillet over medium heat. Spread one-sixth of the stuffing in the center of six of the disks, leaving a 1-inch border. Place the remaining disks on top of the stuffing and seal the edges, using the tines of a fork.

When the oil mixture is hot, about 375°F, use a fork to prick each *pizzetta* twice on top, and fry one or two at a time until lightly golden on both sides, about 1 minute.

Transfer the fried *pizzette* to a platter lined with paper towels to absorb excess oil. When all the *pizzette* are ready, remove the paper towels, sprinkle with a little fine salt, and serve hot.

le pizzette fritte aperte alla napoletana

FRIED PIZZAS WITH TOPPING, NEAPOLITAN STYLE

MAKES 12 PIZZAS

FOR THE DOUGH

1 recipe Fried Pizza dough (page 208)

TO FRY THE *PIZZETTE*

1 cup vegetable oil (preferably a mixture of half sunflower oil, half corn oil)

1/2 cup extra-virgin olive oil

FOR THE TOPPING

1 large mozzarella, about 1 pound, preferably buffalo-milk mozzarella, sliced very thin

About 1 1/2 cups *"Pommarola" alla Napoletana* (page 96)

About 6 tablespoons extra-virgin olive oil

Salt and freshly ground black pepper

Abundant fresh basil leaves

Prepare the pizza dough according to the directions on page 208; when you are finished, you should have twelve disks, 1/8 inch thick, resting under a cotton dish towel for 5 minutes.

FRY THE *PIZZETTE*: Heat the vegetable oil and olive oil in a skillet over medium heat. When the oil mixture is hot, about 375°F, use a fork to prick each *pizzetta* twice on top, and fry one or two at a time until lightly golden on both sides, about 1 minute. Transfer the fried *pizzette* to a platter lined with paper towels to absorb the excess oil.

TOP THE *PIZZETTE*: When all the *pizzette* are fried and on the platter, top each one with a slice of mozzarella, about 3 tablespoons of the tomato sauce, a few drops of olive oil, a little salt and pepper, and the basil. Serve immediately.

NOTE: If you prefer a melted cheese topping, place all the toppings but the basil leaves on the *pizzette* and bake them in an oven preheated to 375°F for 10 minutes. Remove the *pizzette* from the oven, add the basil leaves, and serve hot.

VARIATIONS ON THE TOPPING

1. Sprinkle fresh or dried oregano over the mozzarella.

2. Add anchovy fillets, cut into small pieces, and fresh tomato slices to the topping.

pizza finta

MOCK PIZZA

SERVES 4

6 tablespoons extra-virgin olive oil

Enough 1/2-inch-thick slices country-style bread, crusts removed, to line the bottom of a 10-inch pie plate

6 ounces mozzarella, preferably buffalo-milk mozzarella imported from Italy, cut into 1/2-inch-thick slices

Salt and freshly ground black pepper

2 large pinches of dried oregano leaves

2 whole anchovies preserved in salt, boned, rinsed under cold running water, and cut into fourths; or 4 anchovy fillets packed in oil, drained and cut into fourths

2 large fresh basil leaves

3/4 pound ripe tomatoes, cut into 1/2-inch-thick slices

A focaccia is related to a pizza, but it is stretched with a rolling pin and baked in a greased pan. Like a focaccia, Pizza Finta *is baked in a pan.*

Preheat the oven to 400°F. Use some of the oil to lightly grease a 10-inch pie plate.

Arrange the bread slices on the bottom of the pie plate, then cover them with the mozzarella slices and season with salt, pepper, and some of the oregano. Distribute the anchovies over the mozzarella, and the basil leaves over the anchovies. Top everything with the tomato slices. Season again with salt, pepper, and oregano. Drizzle the remaining oil over all.

Bake for 20 minutes, until the tomatoes are cooked and rather soft and the bread is lightly golden. Serve hot.

pasta cresciuta

RISEN BATTER

MAKES ABOUT 2 1/2 CUPS BATTER

2 1/3 cups unbleached all-purpose flour

Large pinch of fine salt

1/2 ounce fresh compressed yeast, or 1 envelope active dry yeast

2 cups lukewarm water for fresh yeast or warm water for dry

This is the most common thick batter used for frying or as a binder for fritters (see page 179). Yeast, rather than large amounts of egg white, is the leavening agent.

Sift the flour into a bowl, add the salt, and mix very well. Make a well in the flour. Dissolve the yeast in 1 cup of the water. Pour the dissolved yeast into the well and use a wooden spoon to incorporate some of the flour from all sides. Keep working until almost all the flour is used. At that point, add the remaining 1 cup water and keep mixing until a very smooth, almost translucent batter forms.

Let the batter rest, covered, in a warm place away from drafts until doubled in size, about 1 hour. The *pasta cresciuta* is now ready to be used for different dishes, such as *pasta cresciuta con gli "scurilli"* (zucchini blossom zeppole).

OPPOSITE: Focaccia al Formaggio.

focaccia al formaggio

CHEESE FOCACCIA

SERVES 8 TO 10

FOR THE SPONGE

1 cup plus 1 tablespoon unbleached all-purpose flour

1 ounce fresh compressed yeast, or 2 envelopes active dry yeast

2/3 cup lukewarm water for fresh yeast, or warm water for dry

1 tablespoon unsalted butter, very soft

Fine salt

FOR THE DOUGH

2 cups unbleached all-purpose flour

1/2 cup lukewarm water

Fine salt to taste

6 tablespoons (3 ounces) unsalted butter, very soft

6 heaping tablespoons freshly grated Parmigiano

TO BAKE THE FOCACCIA

Enough unsalted butter to heavily butter the pan

1 1/2 tablespoons extra-virgin olive oil

TO SERVE

Extra-virgin olive oil

Fine salt

This dough resembles the starting point of a very rustic puff pastry: The technique of turning is used, but there is no resting in between. In the old days, pure and usually homemade lard flavored with bay leaves was the fat used instead of butter. Careful attention must be paid to the cheese; it absolutely must be very finely grated or it will not completely amalgamate with the dough and will have a tendency to burn while baking.

PREPARE THE SPONGE: Place 1 cup of the flour in a medium-sized bowl and make a well in it. Dissolve the yeast in the water and pour it into the well. Add the butter, and start mixing the ingredients in the well, using a wooden spoon. Add fine salt to taste. Gradually mix in the flour from the edges of the well until it is all incorporated. Sprinkle the remaining tablespoon of flour over the sponge.

Cover the bowl with a cotton dish towel and let it rest in a warm place away from drafts until doubled in size, about 1 hour.

PREPARE THE DOUGH: Arrange the 2 cups flour in a mound on a board and make a well in the flour. Transfer the sponge to the well, add the water, and start mixing, using a wooden spoon. When the sponge is combined with the water, start incorporating the flour from the edges of the well. Use your hands to knead the dough in a folding motion, absorbing more flour. Keep kneading for 3 to 4 minutes more, until the dough is elastic and smooth. Use a rolling pin to stretch the dough into a rectangle about 15 by 10 1/2 inches.

Heavily butter a jelly-roll pan. Use a brush to grease the top of the dough with 2 tablespoon of the soft butter. Sprinkle 2 heaping tablespoons of the grated cheese over the dough. Fold the dough in half and gently roll it back out to the original rectangular shape. Butter the top for the second time and sprinkle with 2 more heaping tablespoons of the cheese. Fold and roll the dough out again, brushing it with the remaining butter and sprinkling it with the remaining cheese. Then stretch it out for the fourth time.

Carefully transfer the focaccia to the prepared jelly-roll pan. Cover it with parchment paper, then place a cotton dish towel over it. Let the focaccia rest until doubled in size, about 2 hours.

BAKE THE FOCACCIA: Preheat the oven to 400°F. When it is ready, lightly brush the top of the focaccia with the 1 1/2 tablespoons oil and bake it for 30 minutes, or until it is puffed up, very golden on top, and rather crisp. Drizzle some oil over it and serve sprinkled with fine salt.

ciro
RISTORANTE ciro PIZZERI

focaccia alle cipolle

ONION FOCACCIA

SERVES 12 AS AN APPETIZER

FOR THE TOPPING

2 pounds yellow onions, cleaned and cut into thin slices

1/4 cup extra-virgin olive oil

2 tablespoons (1 ounce) unsalted butter

2 cups dry white wine

Salt and freshly ground black pepper

Large pinch of dried oregano

FOR THE SPONGE

1 1/2 cups plus 1 tablespoon unbleached all-purpose flour

1 1/2 ounces fresh compressed yeast, or 3 envelopes active dry yeast

1 cup lukewarm water for fresh yeast, or warm water for dry

Pinch of fine salt

FOR THE DOUGH

3 1/2 cups unbleached all-purpose flour

1 tablespoon extra-virgin olive oil

1 cup lukewarm water

1 teaspoon salt

TO BAKE THE FOCACCIA

7 tablespoons extra-virgin olive oil

TO SERVE

3 tablespoons extra-virgin olive oil

Freshly ground black pepper

Soak the onions in a bowl of cold water for 30 minutes.

MAKE THE TOPPING: Place the oil and butter in a large skillet. Drain the onions, add them to the skillet, and place over medium heat. Sauté for 10 minutes, stirring every so often with a wooden spoon. Add 1 cup of the wine, season with salt, pepper, and oregano, and cook for 40 minutes, adding the remaining 1 cup wine as needed. The onions should be very soft and almost all the liquid will be incorporated. Transfer the onions to a crockery or glass bowl to cool for about 30 minutes.

PREPARE THE SPONGE: Place 1 1/2 cups of the flour in a medium-sized bowl and make a well in the flour. Dissolve the yeast in the water and pour it into the well. Add the fine salt and stir with a wooden spoon until all the flour is incorporated. Sprinkle the remaining 1 tablespoon flour over the sponge, then cover the bowl with a cotton dish towel and put it in a warm place away from drafts. Let the sponge stand until it has doubled in size, about 1 hour.

PREPARE THE DOUGH: When the sponge is ready, arrange the 3 1/2 cups of flour on a board, make a well in the flour, and add the oil, water, salt, and the sponge in the well. Start mixing with your hands, incorporating all the flour and kneading the dough in a folding motion until it is elastic, about 5 minutes.

Use 4 tablespoons of the oil to heavily coat a jelly-roll pan. With a rolling pin, stretch the dough to fit the prepared pan, and place it in the pan. Drizzle the remaining 3 tablespoons oil over the top, prick the dough all over with a fork, cover it with plastic wrap, and let it rest in a warm place until doubled in size, about 1 hour.

BAKE THE FOCACCIA: Preheat the oven to 375°F. When the dough is ready, remove the plastic wrap and bake for 20 minutes. Drain the onions, discarding the liquid, and spread them on top of the half-baked focaccia. Bake for another 20 minutes. Remove the pan from the oven, transfer the focaccia to a board, and slice.

Drizzle the oil over the slices and season with pepper. Serve hot.

OPPOSITE: *The Borgo Marinari features restaurants and cafés that were once fashionable meeting places for Neapolitans and foreign tourists.*

This dish can be traced directly back almost to the Renaissance, when a slice of bread or a savory flat bread was used as a plate to hold meat, fish, fowl, or vegetables, and then discarded. Now, the *brioscia* is eaten together with the selected vegetable, which can vary according to your taste and seasonal availability. The center hole is filled with the vegetable (in the photograph opposite, it is a pepper casserole, *Peperoni in Casseruola*, page 54), and most of the time, the filled *ciambella* is served as a main course. The *ciambella* may be prepared in advance and eaten at room temperature; the vegetable filling should be just cooked and still hot.

la ciambella di brioscia

BRIOCHE RING

SERVES 6 TO 8

FOR THE SPONGE

1 cup plus 1 tablespoon unbleached all-purpose flour

1 ounce fresh compressed yeast, or 2 envelopes active dry yeast

3/4 cup lukewarm water for fresh yeast or warm water for dry

Pinch of fine salt

FOR THE DOUGH

4 tablespoons (2 ounces) unsalted butter, melted

3 extra-large eggs

2 cups unbleached all-purpose flour

1/2 cup lukewarm milk

Salt and freshly ground black pepper

3 ounces freshly grated Parmigiano

2 ounces coarsely grated provolone cheese

3 ounces boiled ham, cut into slices less than 1/2 inch thick, then cut into thin strips

TO BAKE THE *CIAMBELLA*

2 tablespoons (1 ounce) unsalted butter, at room temperature, for the pan

OPPOSITE: La Ciambella di Briosca *filled with a pepper mixture.*

PREPARE THE SPONGE: Place 1 cup of the flour in a medium-sized bowl and make a well in it. Dissolve the yeast in the water and pour it into the well. Add the fine salt and start mixing the ingredients in the well, using a wooden spoon. Gradually mix in the flour from the edges of the well until it is all incorporated. Sprinkle the remaining 1 tablespoon flour over the sponge. Cover the bowl with a cotton dish towel and let rest in a warm place away from drafts until doubled in size, about 1 hour.

PREPARE THE DOUGH: When the sponge is ready, pour the melted butter into the bowl of an electric mixer fitted with a paddle attachment. Start mixing the butter on medium speed and incorporate the eggs one at a time; then add the sponge. When the sponge is completely amalgamated, add the flour, a little at a time, alternating with the milk. When all the flour and milk is added, mix for 2 minutes more or until the dough is smooth and very shiny. Lift the paddle, cover the bowl with a cotton dish towel, and let it rest until doubled in size, about 1 hour.

Uncover the bowl, return the paddle, and season the dough with salt and pepper. Add the Parmigiano, provolone, and ham. Mix again for 2 minutes.

Heavily butter a 4-quart ring mold and pour the batter into the mold. Cover the ring mold with a cotton dish towel and leave until the batter has doubled in size, about 1 hour.

BAKE THE *CIAMBELLA*: Preheat the oven to 375°F. When the oven is ready, bake the *ciambella* for 25 minutes or more; it should be golden and very spongy to the touch. Remove the mold from the oven and let it rest on a wire rack for about 15 minutes before unmolding the *ciambella* onto a round serving platter.

Serve hot or at room temperature, with the vegetable you prefer.

tortano con i cicoli

SAVORY PASTRY WITH *CICOLI*

SERVES 8 TO 10

FOR THE SPONGE

1 cup plus 1 tablespoon unbleached all-purpose flour

1/4 cup semolina flour

1 ounce fresh compressed yeast, or 2 envelopes active dry yeast

1 cup lukewarm water for fresh yeast or warm water for dry

Large pinch of fine salt

FOR THE DOUGH

3 1/2 cups unbleached all-purpose flour, plus extra for the mold

1/4 cup semolina flour

1 cup lukewarm water

Salt

1 heaping tablespoon plus 2 tablespoons butter or lard, at room temperature

FOR THE STUFFING

8 tablespoons (4 ounces) lard or unsalted butter, at room temperature

Abundant freshly ground black pepper

1/2 pound *cicoli* (small pieces of pork rind, cooked until crisp)

PLUS

2 tablespoons extra-virgin olive oil

PREPARE THE SPONGE: Combine 1 cup of the all-purpose flour with the semolina flour in a medium-sized bowl and make a well in the center. Dissolve the yeast in the water, then pour the mixture into the well along with the salt. Use a wooden spoon to gradually incorporate all the flour. Sprinkle the remaining 1 tablespoon flour over the top, cover the bowl with a cotton dish towel, and let it rest in a warm place away from drafts until doubled in size, about 1 hour.

PREPARE THE DOUGH: When the sponge is ready, combine 3 1/2 cups of the all-purpose flour with the semolina flour and arrange the mixture in a mound on a board. Make a well in the center and add the sponge, as well as the water, salt, and butter.

Mix all the ingredients in the well together with a wooden spoon, then start mixing with your hands, incorporating the flour from the rim of the well. When almost all the flour is incorporated, start kneading in a folding motion, until the dough becomes quite elastic and smooth. Use 2 tablespoons of the butter and some all-purpose flour to coat a 4-quart ring mold.

STUFF THE *TORTANO*: Using a rolling pin, stretch the dough into a rectangle about 24 by 12 inches. Use a brush to coat the dough rectangle with the heaping tablespoon of butter, sprinkle with abundant pepper, and arrange the *cicoli* over all.

Starting from the long side, roll the dough into a rather thick rope. Carefully transfer the dough rope to the prepared ring mold and seal the ends together. Brush the dough with the oil, cover the mold with parchment paper, and let rest in a warm place away from drafts until doubled in size, about 1 hour.

Preheat the oven to 375°F. When the dough is ready, remove the parchment paper and bake for 45 minutes. The top should be golden, but soft to the touch. Serve the *tortano* warm or let it rest for a few hours until it reaches room temperature.

VARIATION

Instead of using the lard, pepper, and *cicoli* stuffing, fill the dough with provola, provolone, eggs, and salami. (This is the most common filling for a *tortano ripieno*, or stuffed *tortano*.)

gattò di santa chiara

SANTA CHIARA SAVORY BREAD

SERVES 8

FOR THE SPONGE

1 1/2 cups plus 1 tablespoon unbleached all-purpose flour

1 1/2 ounce fresh compressed yeast, or 1 envelope active dry yeast

1 cup lukewarm water for fresh yeast or warm water for dry

Pinch of fine salt

FOR THE DOUGH

1/2 pound all-purpose potatoes

Coarse-grained salt

4 1/2 tablespoons lard or unsalted butter

2 3/4 cups unbleached all-purpose flour, plus extra for the pan

2 extra-large eggs, lightly beaten

1/4 pound ham, sliced very thin, then cut into thin strips

6 ounces mozzarella, preferably buffalo-milk mozzarella imported from Italy, drained very well, patted dry with paper towels, and cut into thin slices

PREPARE THE SPONGE: Place the flour in a small bowl, and make a well in the center. Dissolve the yeast in the water and pour it into the well. Add the fine salt, then use a wooden spoon to incorporate all the flour. Sprinkle the remaining 1 tablespoon flour over the sponge. Cover the bowl and let the sponge rest in a warm place away from drafts until doubled in size, about 1 hour.

PREPARE THE DOUGH: Boil the potatoes in water containing a pinch of coarse salt until very soft, about 25 minutes. Immediately peel and pass them through a potato ricer into a small bowl, using the disk with the smallest holes. Use 1/2 tablespoon of the lard or butter to grease the bottom and sides of a 10-inch springform pan; then dust it with flour.

When the sponge is ready, arrange the 2 3/4 cups flour in a mound on a pastry board and make a large well in the center. Place the eggs and the remaining 4 tablespoons lard or butter in the well. Start mixing with a wooden spoon, incorporating some of the flour from the edges of the well. Add the sponge and use your hands to incorporate the sponge into the flour. Add the riced potatoes, mix very well, and start kneading the dough in a folding motion, incorporating all but 1/2 cup of the flour. Keep kneading until the dough is elastic and very smooth, about 5 minutes, incorporating the remaining 1/2 cup flour. Distribute the strips of ham over the dough and knead again for 2 minutes, incorporating all the ham into the dough.

Divide the dough into two pieces and use your hands to shape both pieces into disks the size of the springform pan. Place one of the disks on the bottom of the pan. Arrange the mozzarella slices over the dough, but do not allow the cheese to reach the sides of the pan. Fit the second disk of dough over the mozzarella, and press very well with your fingers all around the edges so the two layers of dough are well sealed. Cover the mold and let it rest in a warm place away from drafts until the dough has doubled in size, about 1 1/2 hours.

Preheat the oven to 375°F. When the oven is ready, bake the *gattò* for 40 minutes, or until the top is golden and the sides are completely detached from the springform; it should be very spongy to the touch. Open the springform and let the *gattò* rest for at least 15 minutes before unmolding it onto a serving platter. To serve the *gattò*, slice it like a cake.

gattò di patate

SAVORY POTATO CAKE

SERVES 8 TO 10

- $2^{1}/_{2}$ pounds all-purpose potatoes
- Coarse-grained salt
- Enough extra-virgin olive oil to heavily oil the mold
- About $^{1}/_{4}$ cup very fine unseasoned bread crumbs, preferably homemade, lightly toasted
- 3 ounces freshly grated local pecorino or Pecorino Romano cheese
- 3 ounces prosciutto, coarsely ground or cut into very small pieces
- 10 sprigs Italian parsley, leaves only, coarsely chopped
- 4 extra-large eggs
- Salt and freshly ground black pepper
- $^{1}/_{2}$ pound buffalo-milk mozzarella, preferably imported Italian, drained very well, patted dry with paper towels, and cut into thin slices
- 3 ounces provolone cheese, shredded with a hand cheese grater
- About 6 pats unsalted butter

The dough for this savory pastry is made completely with potato rather than yeast. However, even some yeast doughs in Campania and Calabria have a little potato added.

Boil the potatoes in salted boiling water until very soft, about 45 minutes. Skin the potatoes while they are still very hot, then pass them through a potato ricer into a crockery or glass bowl, using the disk with the smallest holes.

Preheat the oven to 375°F. Heavily oil the bottom and sides of a 10-inch springform pan and coat it with some of the bread crumbs.

Add the pecorino to the potatoes and mix very well using a wooden spoon. Then add the prosciutto, parsley, and the eggs, one at a time, mixing very well. Season with salt and pepper, keeping in mind that the provolone cheese to be added is quite salty.

Arrange half of the potato mixture in the springform pan to make an even layer. On top of this layer arrange all the slices of mozzarella, but do not let the cheese reach the sides of the pan—keep it 1 inch away. Sprinkle the provolone over the mozzarella. Make one more layer of potato, using the rest of the mixture, and be sure that the two layers of potatoes are sealed all around the pan by pressing the edges of the top layer down.

Level the top of the potatoes and sprinkle the remaining bread crumbs over all. Arrange the pats of butter on top, wrap the sides and bottom of the pan in aluminum foil so it does not leak, and bake for 40 minutes. When it is done, the *gattò* should be golden on top, completely detached from the sides of the pan, and rather soft to the touch.

Transfer the *gattò*, still in the pan, to a rack and let it rest for at least 15 minutes. Then transfer the pan to a round serving platter, open the mold, and lift it off, leaving the *gattò* on the platter.

The *gattò* may be served immediately or allowed to rest until completely cool. Slice it like a cake to serve.

OPPOSITE: *Vesuvius is shown behind this* Gattò di Patate.

taralli col pepe

PEPPERY *TARALLI*

MAKES 16

FOR THE SPONGE

3/4 cup plus 1 tablespoon unbleached all-purpose flour

1/2 ounce fresh compressed yeast, or 1 envelope active dry yeast

1/2 cup lukewarm water for fresh yeast or warm water for dry

Pinch of fine salt

FOR THE DOUGH

2 cups unbleached all-purpose flour

1/2 cup lukewarm water

Fine salt

2 teaspoons coarsely ground black pepper

4 tablespoons (2 ounces) unsalted butter or lard, at room temperature

PREPARE THE SPONGE: Place the 3/4 cup flour in a medium-sized bowl and make a well in the center. Dissolve the yeast in the water and pour it into the well. Use a wooden spoon to mix the flour with the dissolved yeast. Add the fine salt and mix again. Sprinkle the remaining 1 tablespoon of flour over the mixture. Cover the bowl with a cotton dish towel and let it rest in a warm place away from drafts until doubled in size, about 1 hour.

PREPARE THE DOUGH: When the sponge is ready, arrange the 2 cups flour in a mound on a board and make a well in the center. Place the sponge in the well and add the water, fine salt to taste, the pepper, and the butter. Using a wooden spoon, mix together all the ingredients in the well, then start incorporating the flour from the edges of the well. Use your hands to knead the dough in a folding motion, absorbing more flour. Keep kneading for 2 to 3 minutes more, or until the dough is quite elastic and smooth. Divide the dough into four pieces. Use the palms of your hands and your fingers to stretch each piece of the dough into a rope about 3/4 inch thick.

To shape the *taralli*, twist two ropes of dough together, then cut the twisted ropes into 8-inch pieces and bend each piece to form a ring. Seal by pressing the two ends together. Each 8-inch piece becomes an individual *tarallo*, roughly resembling a pretzel. Repeat the same procedure with all the other ropes of dough.

Transfer the *taralli* to a baking dish lined with parchment paper and cover them with another piece of parchment. Let rest for 1 hour in a warm place away from drafts.

When they are ready, remove the top layer of parchment paper, place the baking dish in the oven, and heat the oven to 325°F (do not preheat the oven). Bake for 70 minutes.

Remove the baking dish from the oven, transfer all the *taralli* to a wire rack, and let them rest until cool, about 1 hour. *Taralli* may be prepared several days in advance.

VARIATION

Sprinkle some almonds, blanched and cut into slivers, over the *taralli* before baking them.

OPPOSITE: Taralli *are small rings of dough baked until they are very crisp; sometimes they are parboiled first. They are found in all the regions that belonged to the Kingdom of Naples. There are different types of* taralli*: savory ones with a lot of ground black pepper or anise or fennel seeds;* taralli con la sugna, *with a lot of lard; and* taralli nasprati, *dipped in sugar icing. The name* taralli *comes from the word taralla, meaning "ring."*

taralli con i finocchietti

TARALLI WITH FENNEL SEEDS

MAKES 24

FOR THE SPONGE

3/4 cup plus 1 tablespoon unbleached all-purpose flour

1/2 ounce fresh compressed yeast, or 1 envelope active dry yeast

1/2 cup lukewarm water for fresh yeast or warm water for dry

Pinch of fine salt

FOR THE DOUGH

2 1/2 cups unbleached all-purpose flour

1/2 cup lukewarm water

4 teaspoons fennel seeds

1 tablespoon unsalted butter or lard, at room temperature

Fine salt

PREPARE THE SPONGE: Place 3/4 cup of the flour in a medium-sized bowl and make a well in the center. Dissolve the yeast in the water and pour it into the well. Use a wooden spoon to mix the flour with the dissolved yeast. Add the salt and mix again. Sprinkle the remaining tablespoon of flour over the mixture. Cover the bowl with a cotton dish towel and let it rest in a warm place away from drafts until doubled in size, about 1 hour.

PREPARE THE DOUGH: When the sponge is ready, arrange the 2 1/2 cups flour in a mound on a board and make a well in the center. Place the sponge in the well and add the lukewarm water, the fennel seeds, and the butter; season with fine salt to taste. Using a wooden spoon, mix together all the ingredients in the well; then start incorporating the flour from the edges of the well. Use your hands to knead the dough in a folding motion, absorbing more flour. Keep kneading for 2 to 3 minutes more or until the dough is quite elastic and smooth. Divide the dough into six pieces. Use the palms of your hands and your fingers to stretch each piece of dough into a thin rope, about 3/4 inch thick. Cut the ropes into 5-inch-long pieces, and then bend each piece to form a ring, pinching the ends together to seal them.

Transfer the *taralli* to a baking dish lined with parchment paper and let rest, uncovered, for 1 hour or more, until doubled in size.

When they are ready, bring a large pot of cold water to a boil over medium heat. Remove it from the heat and use a skimmer to gently transfer the *taralli*, a few at a time, from the baking dish to the almost boiling water. Let the *taralli* rest in the water for a few seconds, then transfer them to a new baking dish lined with parchment paper.

When all the *taralli* are parboiled and in the baking dish, place the dish in the oven; then heat the oven to 325°F (do not preheat the oven). Bake for 70 minutes.

Remove the dish from the oven, transfer the *taralli* to a wire rack, and let them rest until cool, about 30 minutes, before serving. *Taralli* may be prepared several days in advance.

CHAPTER NINE

the myth and fantasy of *sfogliatelle* and other classic desserts

CROSTATA
DI
MELE
£5000 B.

There are hundreds of bakeries and coffee shops spread all over Naples, serving the pastries for which the city is famous, along with wonderful coffee made in big espresso machines. Besides the renowned *sfogliatelle*, *cannoli*, and other treats that are eaten all year round, there are many desserts traditionally tied to specific holidays. So at Easter the shops will feature *pastiera* (page 248), and at Christmas mounds of *struffoli*, small balls of honey-dipped fried dough, will fill the bakery windows.

Via Toledo is the longest street in Naples, connecting Piazza Trieste e Trento to Piazza Dante, by way of the Quartieri Spagnoli, the Spanish Quarters. A walk through this, the heart of the city, along streets lined with *bassi* (apartments that are entered directly from street level), hung with laundry, and crowded with *scugnizzi*, the young boys who spend most of their time playing and eating in the streets, offers a glimpse into the day-to-day life of the famously superstitious Neapolitans. Hanging outside the door of the *bassi* you'll often see a bird cage; if death should pass through the streets it would take the birds before the humans. Bingo, or *lotto* in Italian, represents a significant part of the family budget. And for good luck (presumably at *lotto* and in general), shop owners and restaurateurs keep a bit of salt in all the corners of the main room, or place a large bowl of salt at the entrance—it is said that there are three kinds of salt in Naples: fine salt, coarse salt, and salt to be used *contro il malocchio*, against the evil eye.

Continuing through the center of the city, you'll pass the Caffe Gambrinus and come to the Galleria Umberto, built in 1887, with its iron and glass dome and its spectacular marble floor; during the heyday of vaudeville and even today it is one of the most popular meeting places in the city. And in the old days, from the galleria artists could enter the Salone Margherita, the most famous *café chantant* in Naples.

This part of the city is dotted with piazzas. Piazza del Plebiscito, opposite the Palazzo Reale and once used as a fairgrounds, was in large part built by the Frenchman Gioacchino Murat, who in 1808 was sent by Napoleon to rule Naples. The reign of Murat, who was known in France and abroad as a true bon vivant, led to a sudden infusion of French chefs, who adapted traditional French techniques to please their new clientele and to exploit Neapolitan ingredients. Off Piazza Trieste e Trento, on Via Toledo, is the San Carlo opera house, which was commissioned by Carlo III, the first Bourbon king of Naples, in 1737, when Naples was the center of musical culture in Europe. Some of the most important operas by Pergolesi, Rossini, and Donizetti premiered at the San Carlo theater.

Via Toledo was the center of a "war" among famous Neapolitan pastry shops at the end of the 1800s that also included Pintauro, with his *sfogliatelle* and *zeppoli*; Caflish, a Swiss who moved to Naples via Livorno and Rome; Scaturchio, who came from the nearby region of Calabria with a repertoire that included some of his native pastries; and finally Attanasio.

Pintauro's shop is still in operation, as is Scaturchio's, which is famous not only for its *sfogliatelle*, but also for its *cioccolatini* (little chocolates). Known as *ministeriali*, these are prepared with chocolate, cream of ricotta, rum, and some other ingredients that have never been revealed. Caflish has only recently closed, but Gay Odin, another Swiss chocolatier, remains from the old days.

And always with the pastry, there is coffee. I don't know why, but coffee in Naples tastes completely different than anywhere else. This is possibly because of the water, or perhaps—as it is often said—because of the love and devotion that goes into its preparation. Coffee of the highest quality is found all over Naples. Made with modern espresso machines, its taste is rich, full-bodied, and complex. Most of the coffee bars have their own secret mixture of beans.

The ritual for service starts with the cups that rest in boiling water before they are placed under the spout of the espresso machine—Neapolitans will never accept an espresso if the cup has not been very well heated in advance. A glass of water always accompanies a cup of espresso; you drink it before the coffee so that the palate is cleansed to appreciate the full flavor of the coffee. By tradition, a tip is left to pay for the water, even though it is free.

The famous but humble coffee maker known as *la Napoletana* consists of two small cylinder-shaped pots, one with a spout and a handle, the other with only a handle. The coffee, ground extremely fine, is placed in a perforated, basketlike container that fits inside the spouted half. As you prepare the coffee, the container without the spout is filled with water and sits on the bottom. Then the spouted container holding the coffee is placed on top and screwed to the bottom. The pot is set over the heat, and when the water reaches a boil, it is removed from the flame and immediately turned over so the spouted half is now on the bottom. As the water starts to drip through the ground coffee, a small brown-paper cone called a *cupariello* or *coppetiello* is placed over the spout so the aroma of the coffee remains inside. Once all the water has passed through, the coffee is ready to pour.

This method of coffee making is so characteristic of Naples that Eduardo de Filippo, the most famous of the city's actors and playwrights, wrote a play that carefully describes the art of the *Napoletana* and the importance of the *cupariello*.

ABOVE: *An espresso at Caffe Rosati is an experience. Most Neapolitans love sugar in their espresso (as do most Italians). Here, the sugar comes in the form of "cream," a mixture of sugar and coffee that is whipped together and poured on top of the espresso.*
OPPOSITE: *The famous humble coffee maker known as* la Napoletana.
PRECEDING PAGES: *A glass case in a* pasticceria *displays a staggering assortment of Neapolitan pastries and cookies.*

At 5 AM, even during the winter, in all twelve quartieri of Naples, *il caffettiere ambulante* (the coffee vendor) starts working. In his baskets, he brings what he needs to keep the coffee, as well as the cups and glasses, warm. Sometimes he added *Rosolio liqueur* to the coffee.

Even if the coffee sold by these vendors is not the top quality that you can get from the shops (and may have extra water added), you can be sure it is real coffee, not a concoction made from barley or dried fava beans or from *liquorizia*.

IL CAFFETTIERE AMBULANTE

cannoli alla napoletana

CANNOLI, NEAPOLITAN STYLE

MAKES ABOUT 18

FOR THE FILLING

- 1 cup cold water
- 1 cup granulated sugar
- 1 pound whole-milk ricotta, drained very well
- 1 tablespoon confectioners' sugar
- Pinch of ground cinnamon
- 3 ounces glacéed citron, cut into small pieces
- 3 ounces glacéed orange peel, cut into small pieces
- 1 tablespoon rose water

FOR THE PASTRY SHELLS

Cannoli *are perhaps the best-known southern Italian pastries; unfortunately, they are too often encountered in commercial versions that don't do them justice. To experience this pastry at its best, use crisp, freshly made pastry shells and this authentic Neapolitan filling—enriched ricotta flavored with cinnamon, rose water, and glacéed fruit. There are many different sizes of* cannoli *molds; try your local kitchen supply store or Italian market.*

PREPARE THE FILLING: Put the water and granulated sugar into a heavy saucepan and simmer until a heavy, but still colorless, syrup is formed, about 45 minutes. Transfer the syrup to a crockery or glass bowl and let it rest until cool but still fluid, about 1 hour.

Put the ricotta in a crockery or glass bowl. When the syrup has cooled, add it to the bowl and mix together very well with a wooden spoon. Add the confectioners' sugar and cinnamon, and mix well. Cover the bowl and refrigerate it for about 2 hours.

12 ounces (about 2 1/2 cups) unbleached all-purpose flour

3 extra-large eggs

4 tablespoons (2 ounces) unsalted butter, at room temperature

About 1/2 cup dry Marsala

TO FRY THE *CANNOLI*

1 quart vegetable oil (preferably a mixture of half sunflower oil, half corn oil)

4 tablespoons (2 ounces) unsalted butter

TO SERVE

About 1/3 cup confectioners' sugar

Remove the ricotta mixture from the refrigerator and pass it through a strainer into a bowl. Add the glacéed fruits and rose water, and mix very well. Cover again and refrigerate until needed.

PREPARE THE SHELLS: Arrange the flour in a mound on a board and make a well in the center. Separate two of the eggs. Place the two egg yolks, one whole egg, and the butter in the well and add the Marsala. (Save the egg whites for later use.) Mix all the ingredients in the well with a fork until they are combined. Incorporate almost all the flour little by little. Then start kneading the dough, continuing until it is elastic and smooth, about 10 minutes.

Let the dough rest, wrapped in a cotton dish towel, for about 30 minutes in a cool place or on the bottom shelf of the refrigerator.

Use a rolling pin or a hand-cranked pasta machine to roll the dough into a square or rectangle not more than 1/8 inch thick. Place the dough on a floured board. Using a jagged pastry cutter, cut the pastry into squares. The sides of the squares should be a little shorter than the length of your cannoli molds. Lightly beat the reserved egg whites with a fork for 1 minute.

Turn a pastry square diagonally to resemble a diamond. Place the *cannoli* mold at one point of the diamond and roll the pastry onto the mold to form a tube, being careful not to press the pastry with your fingers. Brush the opposite end of the diamond with the beaten egg whites to seal the pastry together. Leave the mold inside the pastry. Repeat with all the other cannoli molds.

FRY THE *CANNOLI*: Heat the vegetable oil and butter in a skillet over medium heat. When the butter is melted and the oil is heated to about 375°F, put in three or four *cannoli*. Let the *cannoli* fry slowly until very light golden all over, about 1 minute.

Use a large strainer-skimmer to transfer the *cannoli* from the fryer to a serving platter lined with paper towels to absorb excess oil. Let rest until completely cool, about 20 minutes.

To remove the *cannoli* from the molds, contract each mold by gently pinching it at one end, where the metal is not covered with pastry. The contracted mold will detach from the pastry and can be eased out. Let the shells sit on paper towels to be sure all the oil is drained off.

Using a pastry bag without a tip, fill each *cannolo* by piping the filling into both open ends. Transfer the *cannoli* to a serving dish, sprinkle the confectioners' sugar over them using a fine-mesh sieve, and serve.

frittelle di agrumi

ORANGE AND LEMON FRITTERS

MAKES ABOUT 12

FOR THE BATTER

1 cup unbleached all-purpose flour

Pinch of salt

1 teaspoon orange extract, or 1 drop if imported Italian extract

3/4 cup whole milk

3 extra-large eggs

FOR THE FRUIT

1 large, thin-skinned lemon, washed very well, ends removed and the rest cut into 6 slices

1 large, thin-skinned orange, washed very well, ends removed and the rest cut into 6 slices

1/2 cup granulated sugar

1/4 cup cold water

1 teaspoon orange extract, or 1 drop if imported Italian extract

TO FRY THE *FRITTELLE*

1 cup vegetable oil (preferably a mixture of half sunflower oil, half corn oil)

1/4 cup extra-virgin olive oil

TO SERVE

1/2 cup granulated sugar

Grated peel of 1 large orange

PREPARE THE BATTER: Sift the flour into a crockery or glass bowl and make a well in the center, adding the salt. Pour the orange extract and the milk into the well and add one of the eggs. Separate the two remaining eggs and set the whites aside for later use. Add the egg yolks to the well in the flour.

Use a wooden spoon first to mix all the ingredients in the well together, then to incorporate the flour from the edges, a little at a time. When all the flour has been incorporated, keep mixing until a very smooth batter forms, about 2 minutes. Let the batter rest, covered, for at least 1 hour.

PREPARE THE FRUIT: Place the lemon and orange slices on a platter and sprinkle 1/4 cup of the sugar over them. Cover the platter and refrigerate it for 30 minutes.

When the fruit slices are ready, place a skillet containing the water, the remaining 1/4 cup sugar, and the orange extract over medium heat. As soon as the liquid starts bubbling, add the orange and lemon slices with all their juices. Simmer for about 10 minutes or until a rather thick but still absolutely colorless syrup has formed.

Transfer the syrup-coated lemon and orange slices, one by one, to a serving platter lined with parchment paper and let them rest until cool, about 30 minutes.

FRY THE *FRITTELLE*: When ready to fry the fritters, heat the vegetable oil and the olive oil in a skillet over medium heat until rather hot, about 365°F. While the oil heats, beat the reserved egg whites until soft peaks form and fold them into the batter. Combine the 1/2 cup sugar and the grated orange peel in a small bowl.

Dip the slices of fruit in the batter and fry them, a few at a time, until golden all over, about 30 seconds. Transfer the cooked fritters to a serving platter lined with paper towels to absorb excess oil.

When all the fruit is on the platter, remove the paper towels and serve hot, sprinkled with the orange-flavored sugar.

zeppole semplici

SIMPLE *ZEPPOLE*

MAKES ABOUT 16

FOR THE DOUGH

1 cup cold water

2 tablespoons (1 ounce) unsalted butter

1/2 cup plus 1 tablespoon dry white wine or dry Marsala

Pinch of salt

12 ounces (about 2 1/2 cups) unbleached all-purpose flour

3 extra-large eggs

4 extra-large egg yolks

1/2 tablespoon olive oil

TO FRY THE *ZEPPOLE*

2 cups vegetable oil (preferably a mixture of half sunflower oil, half corn oil), or 4 cups vegetable oil if frying the *zeppole* in 2 skillets

TO SERVE

1 cup lukewarm honey

1/2 cup *diavolilli* (colored candy sprinkles)

Follow the procedure for preparing the dough for *zeppole di San Giuseppe* (page 263), using the ingredients listed here, up to the step where the dough is left to rest for 1 hour.

When the dough is ready, take 2 heaping tablespoons of it and use your fingers to roll out a short rope about 3/4 inch in diameter. Seal the two ends to make a small ring. Repeat with the remaining dough.

To fry the *zeppole*, follow the same technique as for *zeppole di San Giuseppe* (page 263).

When all the *zeppole* are cooked and on the serving platter, dip each one in the lukewarm honey and place it on a clean serving platter.

Drizzle the remaining honey over all and sprinkle with the *diavolilli*. Serve warm.

RIGHT: *This small stand prepares a refreshing lemon drink.*

In the early afternoon when the heat was at its peak, the *sorbettari* (sorbet man) wandered through the busy downtown where his customers gathered. He was always dressed in very colorful, bright, and extravagant costumes to match the colors of his merchandise.

It seems that these *sorbettari* became very popular outside Naples, and many of them migrated not only to other parts of Italy, but even spread throughout Europe, where they taught the art of making *sorbetti*. "Ice cold like a rock in the containers, but immediately melting in your mouth," was the golden standard, according to Mastiani. Other *ambulanti* who sold refreshments included the *acquaioli*, who sold ice cold water, sometimes flavored with orange or lemon juice, and maybe a Calabrian punch flavored with lemon or the flowers of the sambuca plant.

sorbetto di fragole

STRAWBERRY SORBET

SERVES 8 TO 10

- 1 pint ripe strawberries, washed and stems removed
- 1/2 cup superfine sugar
- 1/4 cup confectioners' sugar
- 1 1/4 cups heavy cream

Cut the strawberries into quarters and put them in a crockery or glass bowl. Sprinkle the superfine sugar and confectioners' sugar over them and refrigerate, covered, for at least 1 hour. When ready, mix the strawberries with a wooden spoon, breaking up most of them. Depending upon your preference, leave the strawberries as they are or pass them through a food mill into a small bowl, using the disk with the smallest holes.

Using a cold wire whisk and an ice-cold metal bowl, lightly whip the cream. Add the strawberry mixture and continue whipping the cream until it is quite firm. Ladle the *sorbetto* into individual freezer-safe glasses and place them in the freezer for at least 2 hours before serving.

VARIATION

An alternative way of making *sorbetto* is to pass the strawberries through a food mill, using the disk with the smallest holes, then prepare a rather thick syrup by bringing both sugars and 1 cup cold water to a simmer over medium heat. Chill the syrup, and when it is cold, whip the cream. Incorporate the pureed strawberries into the syrup, then the whipped cream. Spoon the *sorbetto* into individual freezer-safe glasses and freeze.

la torta di mandorle di capri *or* la caprese

ALMOND-CHOCOLATE TORTE

SERVES 8 TO 10

6 ounces (about 1 1/4 cups) whole unblanched almonds

2 ounces (about 1/2 cup) whole shelled walnuts

1 cup plus 1 heaping tablespoon granulated sugar

Unsalted butter and unbleached flour, for the cake pan

1/2 pound bittersweet chocolate

2 sticks (8 ounces total) unsalted butter, at room temperature

8 extra-large eggs

1 teaspoon sweet orange extract, or 2 drops if imported Italian extract

TO SERVE

1/2 cup plus 1 tablespoon granulated sugar

Grated peel of a large, thick-skinned orange

2 cups heavy cream

1 teaspoon confectioners' sugar

This is the torte that is eaten in the coffee shops and bars all along the famous Piazzetta *in Capri, the perfect place to sit sipping a cappuccino or an aperitif, but more important, a place to see who is in the city, and to be seen by them. This pastime is almost a passport to becoming a true resident of the isle.*

Preheat the oven to 375°F. Blanch the almonds for a few seconds in boiling water, remove the skins, and dry them in the oven for 10 minutes. Finely grind the almonds and walnuts together with the 1 cup granulated sugar in a blender or food processor until the mixture has the texture of a very fine flour.

Butter and lightly flour the bottom and sides of a round cake pan that is 10 inches in diameter and 3 inches high. Place a piece of parchment paper on the bottom of the pan. Melt the chocolate by placing it in a metal bowl and setting it over a pot of boiling water. Remove the melted chocolate from the heat and allow it to cool for about 30 minutes.

Place the soft butter in the bowl of an electric mixer fitted with the paddle attachment. Separate six of the eggs and set the egg whites aside for later use. Start mixing, adding the egg yolks one at a time. When all the yolks are incorporated, start adding the nut flour, a heaping tablespoon at a time. Then add the orange extract and the cooled melted chocolate. Add the remaining two whole eggs and keep mixing for 1 minute more. Transfer the thick batter to a large bowl.

Using a copper or metal bowl and a wire whisk, beat the reserved egg whites together with the remaining 1 tablespoon sugar until stiff. Gently fold the egg whites into the batter, using a rubber spatula in a folding motion. Pour the contents of the bowl into the prepared pan and bake for 45 minutes. The top of the torte should be lightly crusty, and the sides should be completely detached and rather soft and moist to the touch. Remove the torte from the oven and let it rest in the pan on a rack for 15 minutes before unmolding it onto a serving platter. Cover the platter with a metal bowl and let stand until completely cool before serving.

When ready to serve, mix the 1/2 cup granulated sugar with the orange peel. Whip the cream together with the remaining 1 tablespoon granulated sugar and the confectioners' sugar, using a chilled metal bowl and a wire whisk. Slice the torte into wedges and serve it with the whipped cream. Using a fine sieve,top the cream with the orange-flavored sugar.

crostata alla napoletana

CHOCOLATE-APRICOT TORTE, NEAPOLITAN STYLE

SERVES 8

FOR THE APRICOTS

1 pound dried apricots, preferably Turkish, left whole

2 cups dry white wine

2 cups cold water

FOR THE CRUST

10 tablespoons (5 ounces) unsalted butter, at room temperature

3 ounces (about 3/4 cup) sugar

2 extra-large egg yolks

Grated peel of 1 small lemon

8 ounces (about 1 3/4 cups) unbleached all-purpose flour

FOR THE CUSTARD CREAM

3 extra-large egg yolks

5 tablespoons granulated sugar

1 tablespoon potato starch

1 cup lukewarm milk

1 cup heavy cream

1/4 cup unsweetened cocoa powder

2 extra-large eggs

PLUS

3 tablespoons granulated sugar

PREPARE THE APRICOTS: Place the whole apricots in a casserole containing the wine and water, and simmer over medium heat for 30 minutes. By this time, the apricots should be soft but still whole, and the liquid will be completely incorporated. Let rest until cool, about 30 minutes.

MAKE THE CRUST: Place the butter with the sugar in a crockery or glass bowl and use a wooden spoon to incorporate them; mix in a rotating motion until the butter is almost whipped. Add the egg yolks and lemon peel and mix well again.

Place the flour in a mound on a board, make a well in the center, and put the butter and sugar mixture in the well. Use a wooden spoon to incorporate some of the flour from the edges of the well, then use your hands to work in the remaining flour, trying to avoid a kneading motion. When all the flour is incorporated, wrap the dough in a cotton dish towel and let it rest in a cool place or on the bottom shelf of the refrigerator for 30 minutes.

PREPARE THE CUSTARD CREAM: Place the egg yolks in a crockery or glass bowl, then add the sugar and potato starch. Mix well with a wooden spoon until the yolks turn a lighter color. Add the milk, mix well, then add the heavy cream and mix again.

Transfer the mixture to a saucepan and place it over medium heat. Stir constantly with a wooden spoon until the custard completely coats the spoon and is very close to boiling. Absolutely do not allow it to boil. Remove the pan from the heat, sprinkle the cocoa powder over the custard, and incorporate it very well. Transfer the chocolate custard to a crockery or glass bowl and let it rest until cool, about 30 minutes.

Preheat the oven to 375°F. Lightly butter a tart pan with a removable bottom that is 11 inches in diameter and 1 1/2 inches high.

Take two large pieces of parchment paper. Lay one out on a board, place the dough in the center, then cover it with the second piece of parchment. Use a rolling pin to stretch the dough into a round about 16 inches in diameter. Gently flip the dough round into the buttered pan and press down the bottom. Remove the custard cream from the refrigerator, add the two whole eggs, and mix well with a wooden spoon. Pour the mixture

There are three different types of chestnut vendors: *che ha bottega*, who has a small shop; *a posta fisso* (shown in this illustration), who has a permanent stand, always in the same place; and finally *il castagnaro ambulante*, who travels all around the city to sell chestnuts. The first type sells shelled or unshelled raw chestnuts; the second one sells the so-called *bruciate*, or chestnuts roasted over hot ash; and the third one sells baked chestnuts.

The small chestnut shops and stands are located next to *taverne* (wine bars), perfectly situated to serve all the wine-saturated but famished people as they exit. The traveling chestnut vendor had two roles: first to sell the baked chestnuts and second to serve as a sort of traveling clock. Because *il castagnaro* walked from one street to the next at exactly the same time every day, people could watch his movements to figure out what time it was.

into the pan, level it with a spatula, then arrange half of the cooked apricots in a layer on top, reserving the remaining apricots for later use. Sprinkle the 3 tablespoons sugar over the apricot layer. Using a scalloped pastry wheel, cut off the extra pastry hanging over the edge of the pan. Bake the *crostata* for 40 minutes.

Remove the *crostata* from the oven, let it cool for 30 minutes, then remove it from the pan. Transfer the *crostata* to a serving dish and let it rest until completely cool, about 40 minutes. Coarsely chop the remaining apricots, spread them over the *crostata*, and serve.

The celebrated Neapolitan version of *Zuppa Inglese*, with its classic oval shape, is very different from the northern version, in which the dessert is tinted red by the addition of the Florentine liqueur *Alkermes*.

I was very lucky to have met a very old pastry-maker, not a famous pastry chef, but rather someone who had spent most of his life preparing this classic dessert. He told me all about the special shape, and the love and care that should be taken in the creation of this cake. As he described how to soak the layers of sponge cake in rum, I asked him, "What about the *Alkermes*?" He looked at me and with a half-smile on his face and replied, "Too Florentine!"

Once the layering was completed, he told me to wrap the cake very tightly in a very fine linen (today we would use cheesecloth) and keep it wrapped overnight. But, he warned, that does not mean you forget the layers of the cake until the next morning: You must always check them carefully to be sure the wrapping is neither too tight nor too loose, so the layers of the sponge cake, cream, and syrup end up very well integrated, with just enough rum to give the cake a wonderful aroma all the way through. The next morning, he would finish the cake with a covering of meringue, another classic Neapolitan touch.

zuppa inglese alla napoletana

NEAPOLITAN RUM CAKE

SERVES 8 TO 10

FOR THE SPONGE CAKE

6 extra-large eggs, separated

8 ounces (about 1 1/4 cups) granulated sugar

Grated peel of 1 lemon

Pinch of fine salt

2 ounces potato starch

2 ounces (about 1/3 cup) unbleached all-purpose flour

About 1 tablespoon unsalted butter, to coat the cake pan

FOR THE PASTRY CREAM

6 extra-large egg yolks

1/2 cup granulated sugar

1 1/2 tablespoons potato starch

1 1/2 cups lukewarm whole milk

PREPARE THE SPONGE CAKE: At least 2 days before assembling the dessert, make the cake. Use a wooden spoon to mix the egg yolks and the sugar in a crockery or glass bowl until the sugar is completely incorporated and the egg yolks turn a lighter color. Add the lemon peel and salt and mix again. In a separate bowl, combine the potato starch with the flour and start adding this mixture, a little at a time, to the bowl containing the egg mixture. Stir continuously with a wooden spoon.

Butter a double cake pan that is 10 inches in diameter, with sides higher than 2 inches, and preheat the oven to 375°F.

Use a wire whisk and a copper or metal bowl to beat the egg whites until soft peaks form, and fold the egg whites gently into the batter. Pour the batter into the prepared pan and bake for about 40 minutes. The cake should be golden on top but very spongy to the touch. Let the cake rest on a rack until cool before unmolding it onto a serving platter.

PREPARE THE PASTRY CREAM: Using the ingredients and quantities listed here, make the pastry cream according to the directions on page 265. Transfer the cooked pastry cream to a crockery or glass bowl, let rest until cool, then refrigerate, covered, until needed.

FOR THE SYRUP

1 cup cold water

3/4 cup granulated sugar

2 drops freshly squeezed lemon juice

1/2 cup maraschino liqueur

PLUS

About 1 tablespoon unsalted butter, to coat the serving platter

About 1/2 cup *amarena* jam (made with sour Italian cherries, available at Italian markets or specialty food stores)

6 extra-large egg whites

2 heaping tablespoons confectioners' sugar

ABOVE: Zuppa Inglese, *Neapolitan style.*

MAKE THE SYRUP: Place the water, sugar, and lemon juice in a small saucepan over low heat and simmer for about 35 minutes, or until a rather thick syrup forms. Let the syrup cool, then add the maraschino liqueur.

Lightly butter an oval ovenproof serving platter. Cut the sponge cake into 1/2-inch-thick slices, place them in a jelly-roll pan, and pour the aromatic syrup over the slices.

To assemble the cake, carefully transfer a third of the slices to the buttered serving platter. Spread a third of the pastry cream over the cake slices, and then spread a very thin layer of the jam over the cream, using about a third of it. Repeat this procedure twice.

Preheat the oven to 150°F, then beat the egg whites with the confectioners' sugar until stiff. Spread the egg whites over the cake on the serving platter and bake for a few minutes, until a golden meringue forms. Remove the *zuppa Inglese* from the oven and let it cool completely before serving it.

VARIATION

Instead of using pastry cream and *amarena* jam, cover the maraschino-soaked sponge cake with alternating layers of ricotta, chocolate sauce, and sliced fresh strawberries.

The term *babà* is believed to be of Polish origin, but the origin of the cake itself is uncertain, although it has long been a part of the Italian repertoire. A homemade *babà* is quite a different experience from the commercial product: Deliciously light and yeasty cake with raisins is cut in half and filled with pastry cream. Traditionally rum-flavored syrup is poured on top to create an extremely moist and flavorful cake.

babà alla crema

BABÀ LAYER CAKE

SERVES 8 TO 10

1/2 pound raisins

2 cups lukewarm milk

1 1/4 pounds (4 cups) unbleached all-purpose flour, sifted

2 ounces fresh compressed yeast, or 4 envelopes active dry yeast

2/3 cup lukewarm water for fresh yeast or warm water for dry

2 sticks (8 ounces total) unsalted butter

2 tablespoons granulated sugar

6 extra-large eggs

FOR THE PASTRY CREAM

4 extra-large egg yolks

6 tablespoons granulated sugar

3 teaspoons potato starch

1 cup cold milk

Small piece of orange peel

FOR THE SYRUP

1 cup water

1/2 cup granulated sugar

1 cup light rum

PLUS

About 2 tablespoons orange or lemon syrup (available at Italian markets or specialty food stores)

Soak the raisins in a small bowl with the lukewarm milk for 30 minutes.

Place 1 1/2 cups of the sifted flour in a crockery or glass bowl, and make a well in the center. Dissolve the yeast in the water and pour the mixture into the well. Mix with a wooden spoon until all the flour is incorporated. Sprinkle 1 tablespoon of the remaining flour over the sponge. Cover the bowl with a cotton dish towel and let it stand in a warm place away from drafts until the sponge has doubled in size, about 1 hour.

Meanwhile, melt the butter in the top of a double boiler, remove it from the heat, and let it cool. Drain the raisins, discarding the milk, and dry them on paper towels.

When the sponge has doubled in size, add the sugar, stirring constantly with a wooden spoon always in the same direction. Add the eggs, one by one, and then the cooled melted butter. Add the remaining flour, a little at a time, until it is all incorporated and a very smooth, thick batter has formed. Add the raisins and mix carefully.

Butter a 3-quart ring mold or a tube pan that is 10 inches in diameter. Pour the batter into the mold. Cover the mold with a cotton dish towel and let it rest in a warm place away from drafts until doubled in size, about 1 hour.

PREPARE THE PASTRY CREAM: With the ingredients listed here, make the pastry cream following the directions on page 265. Transfer the pastry cream to a crockery or glass bowl, let it cool for about 30 minutes, then cover the bowl with buttered parchment paper and refrigerate the custard to cool it completely.

Preheat the oven to 400°F.

OPPOSITE: *A mouthwatering display of cakes.*

PREPARE THE SYRUP: Put the water and sugar in a heavy saucepan over low heat. Simmer for about 35 minutes, or until a light syrup has formed. (If the syrup is not to be used immediately, it may be stored in the refrigerator until needed.) Add the rum just before using and mix thoroughly.

When the dough is ready, remove the towel and place the mold in the oven for about 40 minutes. Do not open the oven door until at least 25 minutes have passed. If the crust becomes too brown, put a piece of aluminum foil over the mold. Remove the *babà* from the oven and let it cool for about 20 minutes.

Unmold the *babà* and transfer it to a rack to cool completely. With a slicing knife, cut the cake in half horizontally. Moisten the mold with the orange syrup. Fit the top half of the cake back into the mold and spread pastry cream over it. Then fit the other half of the *babà* over the filling. If the cake will not be served immediately, place aluminum foil over the ring mold and let it stand until needed (it can be stored this way for several hours).

When ready to serve the *babà*, carefully unmold the cake onto a serving platter. Spoon the syrup over the cake and cut it into slices.

pizza di amarene

SOUR CHERRY "PIZZA"

SERVES 8

FOR THE PASTRY (*PASTA FROLLA*)

8 ounces (about 1 1/2 cups) unbleached all-purpose flour

8 tablespoons (4 ounces) unsalted butter, at room temperature, cut into pats

3 ounces (about 1/2 cup) sugar

2 extra-large eggs

1 extra-large egg white

FOR THE PASTRY CREAM

4 extra-large egg yolks

1/2 cup granulated sugar

1 tablespoon potato starch

1 1/2 cups heavy cream

PLUS

Unsalted butter, for the tart pan

2 ounces drained *amarene* (sour Italian cherries in syrup, available at Italian markets or specialty food stores)

PREPARE THE *PASTA FROLLA*: Place the flour in a mound on a board and make a well in the center. Add the butter, sugar, whole eggs, and egg white. Rapidly combine all these ingredients, using a metal dough scraper so the dough is not affected by the heat of your hands (see Note). Wrap the dough in plastic wrap and refrigerate for 1 hour.

PREPARE THE PASTRY CREAM: Using the ingredients and quantities listed, make the pastry cream according to the directions on page 265. Transfer the cooked pastry cream to a crockery or glass bowl and let rest until cool, about 30 minutes.

Preheat the oven to 375°F and very lightly butter a 9-inch tart pan with a removable bottom. Place the dough between two pieces of parchment paper and use a rolling pin to stretch it into a disk about 12 inches in diameter. Remove the top piece of parchment paper from the dough and flip the pastry over the tart pan. Carefully remove the other piece of parchment paper, then pass a rolling pin over the tart pan to cut off the excess pastry.

Using a fork, make several punctures in the bottom of the pastry, then place a piece of parchment paper on top and fill it with pastry weights or dried beans to keep the crust from puffing up while baking. Refrigerate the tart pan for 30 minutes, then bake it for 15 minutes.

Remove the parchment paper and the beans from the tart pan and let the pastry rest in the tart pan until cool, about 30 minutes.

Fill the crust with the pastry cream and arrange the cherries on top. Bake the tart for 15 minutes, or until the pastry cream sets. Let the "pizza" rest in the tart pan for about 15 minutes before serving.

NOTE: The pastry—*pasta frolla*, or short pastry—is very delicate. The heat either from your hands or from overworking the dough when you try to stretch it can make it fall apart. If this happens, you can save the dough by adding one egg white and restretching it.

the making of *sfogliatelle*

As is the case with most of the desserts of southern Italy, the incredible pastry known as the sfogliatelle *was born in monasteries and convents. Nuns, young girls of the nobility whose destiny was separated from the everyday life of Naples, played the greatest role in developing the* sfogliatelle *and then spreading its secret. The convent of Croce di Lucca was not only considered a desirable placement for high-born girls, it also produced a celebrated pastry while keeping the girls safely hidden from public view.*

From the monasteries and convents, the "secret" of making these pastries spread to the city, to one of the most famous pastry shops to open in the late nineteenth century: Pintauro, run by the man who invented the *sfogliatelle frolle*, the variety made of short pastry.

Pintauro's *sfogliatelle* became one of the classic forms (page 243); the other was *sfogliatelle ricce* (page 242), with a shell made of a dough similar to puff pastry. Other versions have also become popular. The convent of Santa Rose "refined" the *ricce*; they use the same stuffing, but add some pastry cream on top as well as a glazed amarena cherry. Another type of *sfogliatelle*, the very small one, is called *monachina*—tiny nun—in tribute to its convent origins. But the innovations do not stop here. Today a large cake in the shape of a huge *sfogliatella* is served in some restaurants, and the absolute latest fashion is a *sfogliatella* with a savory stuffing.

To best appreciate any kind of *sfogliatella*, but especially the *sfogliatelle ricce*, it must be eaten when it is just baked, warm and fresh out of the oven. Only then will you completely experience the *sfogliatella*'s intense and voluptuous taste. In the old days, once the pastries became cold, the *sfogliatella* makers would remove the stuffing, discard the shell, and save the stuffing for the following day. Unfortunately, such care is not taken these days, and there are large factories that provide bakeries with the shell already prepared and partially baked. If the extremely thin layer of pastry wrapped around the stuffing does not break or crumble when you bite into it, but remains almost intact like a strip of rubber, you will know that your *sfogliatella* is factory-made.

After you have made a thick "rope" by rolling up all the pastry layers and allowing them to rest overnight, continue with the following steps:

SFOGLIATELLE RICCI

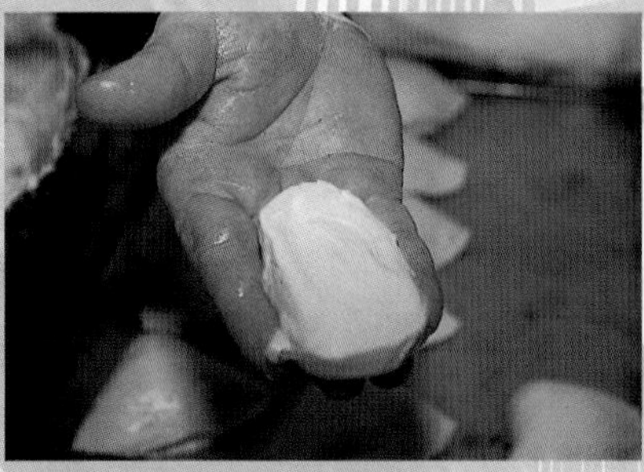

1. Cut a slice of the long rope of layered pastry.

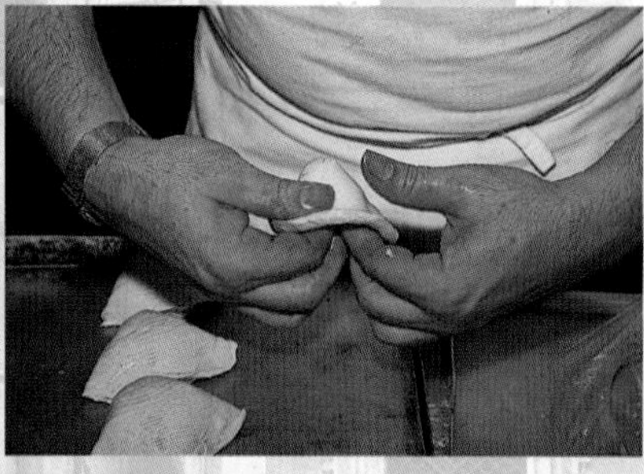

2. Shape the slice into a cone by carefully sliding out the layers of pastry.

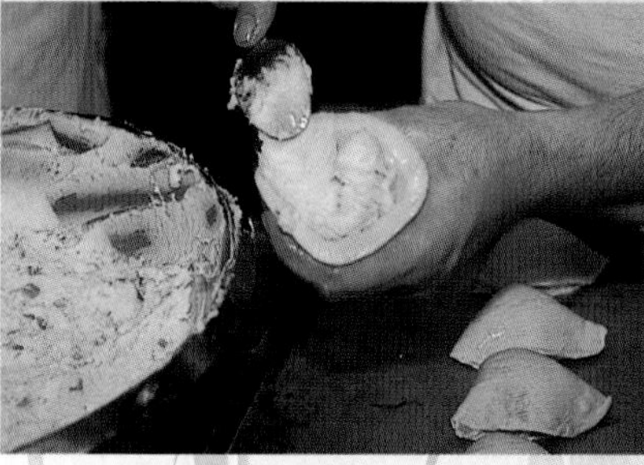

3. Stuff each *sfogliatella*.

4. Place the stuffed *sfogliatelle* in a jelly roll pan.

5. Brush the *sfogliatelle* with a little melted lard or butter (see recipe, page 242) and bake them for about 15 minutes or more until crisp and golden.

6. The baked *Sfogliatelle Ricci*—golden and incredibly crisp.

SFOGLIATELLE FROLLE

1. Detach a piece (about 3 ounces) of the *pasta frolla*—the pastry that gives this type of *sfogliatella* its name.

2. Roll out each piece of *pasta frolla* (called "*pettola*" in Neapolitan dialect).

3. Place the stuffing on the circle of dough, then stretch half the pastry over the stuffing. Finish the edges with a pastry cutter and bake the *sfogliatelle* for about 15 minutes or more until crisp and golden.

4. The baked *Sfogliatelle Frolle*.

OPPOSITE: *This is an unusual type of* sfogliatelle, *called* aragostina *(little lobster) or* coda d'aragosta *(lobster tail) because of its shape. It is shown in the garden opposite the* passeggiata, *which is along the coast.*

The shell of this type of sfogliatelle *is made from the same dough as* sfogliatelle ricce, *but before baking, a piece of brioche pastry* (pasta bomboloni) *is inserted inside. While baking, the inner pastry expands quite a bit, giving the outside pastry the typical shape of a lobster tail. These* sfogliatelle *are usually stuffed with whipped cream.*

sfogliatelle ricce

LAYERED *SFOGLIATELLE*

FOR THE FILLING

1 recipe of the filling from *Sfogliatelle Frolle* (page 243)

FOR THE PASTRY

2 cups unbleached all-purpose flour

2 cups hard-wheat flour (such as Manitoba from Canada)

1 teaspoon honey

Pinch of salt

1 1/2 cups cold water

PLUS

1 cup (8 ounces) lard or butter, melted and at room temperature

TO SERVE

Confectioners' sugar

Prepare the filling with the ingredients and quantities listed on page 243 and let it rest, covered, in the refrigerator, until needed.

PREPARE THE PASTRY: Combine the all-purpose flour and the hard-wheat flour and arrange the mixture in a mound on a cutting board. Make a well in the flour and add the honey, salt, and water. Use a fork to mix together the ingredients in the well, then gradually add flour from the edges of the well until all but about 1/2 cup of flour is incorporated. Knead the dough with your hands, using a folding motion, until all the flour is absorbed and the dough is smooth and elastic but firm, about 4 minutes. Wrap the dough in plastic wrap and refrigerate for about 2 hours.

When the dough is ready, divide it into 4 pieces and use a hand-cranked pasta machine to stretch each piece into a very thin, long layer about 6 inches wide, reaching the last notch on the pasta machine.

Cut each layer of pastry into pieces about 18 inches long. Place 1 piece of pastry on a sheet of parchment paper. Use a brush to completely coat the top of the pastry with melted lard. Place another piece of pastry over the first and again brush it with lard. Continue this procedure, adding a layer of pastry and brushing with lard until all the pieces of pastry are used.

Starting from one of the 6-inch-wide ends, tightly roll the pile of pastry into a single roll. Wrap the roll in a cotton dish towel and refrigerate it for at least 4 hours, or even overnight.

Preheat the oven to 375°F.

At this point continue by following the steps in the photos on page 240.

As the *sfogliatelle* come out of the oven, sprinkle them with confectioners' sugar. Serve warm.

sfogliatelle frolle

SFOGLIATELLE OF SHORT PASTRY

FOR THE PASTRY (*PASTA FROLLA*)

3 1/2 cups unbleached all-purpose flour

3/4 cup granulated sugar

12 tablespoons (6 ounces) lard or unsalted butter, at room temperature

Scant 1/2 cup cold water

Pinch of fine salt

Grated peel of 1 lemon

1 extra-large egg yolk

FOR THE FILLING

3 cups cold whole milk or water

Pinch of coarse-grained salt

6 ounces (about 3/4 cup) semolina flour

6 ounces whole-milk ricotta, drained very well

12 ounces (about 1 1/2 cups) superfine sugar

Pinch of ground cinnamon

1 heaping teaspoon orange paste (available in Naples in gourmet shops), or 1 teaspoon orange extract, or a few drops orange extract, if imported from Italy

2 tablespoons candied orange peel (page 25), cut into small pieces

2 tablespoons candied citron peel, cut into small pieces

3 extra-large eggs

TO BAKE THE *SFOGLIATELLE*

1 extra-large egg, lightly beaten with 1 tablespoon cold water

TO SERVE

Confectioners' sugar

PREPARE THE *PASTA FROLLA*: Arrange the flour in a mound on a cutting board and make a well in the center. Put the granulated sugar, lard, water, salt, lemon peel, and egg yolk in the well. Using your hands or a metal scraper, rapidly mix all the ingredients together and shape them into a ball of dough. This must be done very quickly, without kneading the dough a lot; otherwise the pastry will "burn" and separate when stretched. Wrap the pastry in plastic wrap and let rest in a cool place or on the lower shelf of your refrigerator for at least 1 hour.

PREPARE THE FILLING: Bring the milk to a boil in a casserole over medium heat. Add the salt and immediately pour in all the semolina flour in a stream, stirring constantly with a wooden spoon. Simmer for 10 minutes, then transfer the cooked semolina to a crockery or glass bowl and let rest until completely cool, after 1 hour.

Use the wooden spoon to mix the ricotta, superfine sugar, cinnamon, orange paste or extract, candied orange peel, candied citron, and eggs all together in a large crockery or glass bowl. When the semolina is cool, add it to the ricotta mixture and mix well.

Preheat the oven to 375°F.

Divide the dough into several pieces, about 3 ounces each. Roll out each piece to a round shape, about 6 inches in diameter (see photo, page 240).

At this point, continue by following the steps in the photos.

As the *sfogliatelle* come out of the oven, sprinkle them with confectioners' sugar. Serve warm.

CHAPTER TEN

holiday menus

christmas eve, christmas day, easter, and the local saints' days

In almost every region of Italy, cooking and eating follow the pattern of the seasons, making the best use of the ingredients that are fresh and available in the markets. During the holidays, each region has its own traditional dishes, which each family prepares with its own small variations.

Neapolitans eat *per devozione* (for devotion), meaning that it is almost a duty to eat certain dishes. As a result, every holiday menu is an explosion of dishes served one after the other. These meals are something to remember. If a family does not like hen or capon, they will make a small substitution—in this case, a different fowl—but the style of cooking remains the same because most of the ingredients have a symbolic meaning. For example, pine nuts, almonds, and raisins are used frequently because their oval shape denotes fertility, and raisins are also the symbol of abundance. There are many such symbolic foods or ingredients in Neapolitan cooking.

In general, the holidays are observed not only on a single day, but are extended to include the day before and the day after—and the related holiday dishes are eaten throughout the entire period. In Giovan Battista del Tufo's sixteenth-century traveler's guide, *Ritratto o Modello delle Grandezze, Delizie e Meraviglie della Noblissima Citta di Napoli (Portrait or Model of the Great Delights and Marvels of the Most Noble City of Naples),* the book is divided into seven *ragionamenti* (essays) corresponding to the seven days of the week. These give us a specific list of the dishes prepared and eaten during the different holidays, along with some descriptions of the Neapolitans' amusing "habits"—always with reference to their food. It seems that the bigger the dinner was, the more tidbits *(spassatiempo)* such as toasted squash seeds, fava beans, chickpeas, and so on were consumed after dinner.

Following are sample menus that include traditional Neapolitan holiday dishes. Since Easter is the time of rebirth, we will begin there.

EASTER *(Pasqua)*

- *Fellata* (from the word *fella*, or slice) as an appetizer: A large serving platter with slices of prosciutto and salami.
- A very light soup with seasonal vegetables, such as fresh peas, fresh fava beans, or similar.
- Lamb, generally a stew, with or without egg yolks and lemon juice.
- Vegetables: *Carciofi* (artichokes), boiled or fried or even grilled over charcoal; peas with pancetta (page 51).
- *Pastiera* (Neapolitan Easter Cake, page 248).

CHRISTMAS EVE DINNER *(Vigilia di Natale)*, a dinner without meat.

- *Frittelle di Natale* (*baccalà* fritters, page 253).
- Vermicelli in Clam Sauce (page 158), without tomato sauce.

- Large eels called *capitoni* cooked in different ways: coated with flour and fried, cooked on a skewer over hot ash, or cooked in a light tomato sauce. Traditionally, when eels were fried or cooked on a grill, the leftover was always marinated in wine vinegar and eaten the following day as an appetizer. This marinade, used for *in Scapece*, dates back to the ancient Roman Apicus. Besides eggplant and zucchini prepared with this marinade (pages 39 and 63), other vegetables such as carrots were used.
- As for vegetables, stuffed *scarola* (escarole) is served, sometimes accompanied by a type of *focaccia* or stuffed pizza containing sautéed escarole mixed with olives, capers, and anchovies.
- *Insalata di Rinforzo* (page 252), a salad that was prepared and eaten at least two or three days before.
- A large selection of cookies made just for Christmas Eve, among them:
  - *Roccoco*, small rings of flour and almond flour.
  - *Mustacciuoli*, prepared with flour, sugar, and almonds, and sometimes dipped in chocolate (the name comes from the Spanish *mustaccera*, a cake made with a *savoiarda* pastry).
  - *Susamielli* or *sosamielli*, a cookie with an "S" shape originally made with sesame seeds and honey mixed together. The name comes from *sesamo* (sesame seeds) and *miele* (honey).
  - *Pastidelle*, small, roundish cookies prepared with *uova, zuccaro e cannella* (eggs, sugar, and cinnamon).

LEFT AND RIGHT: *San Gennaro is the patron saint of Naples and a much revered figure who is celebrated on three different feast days.*
PRECEDING PAGES: *It is Christmas all year round in Via San Gregorio Armeno. The street is full of craftsmen making figures and reproductions of small villages from cork for the "presepe," or the crypt. It is here that the beautiful religious figures carved from wood or made from thin china "biscuit" have been made since the 1600s. They also make the celebrated "commedia dell'arte" characters of the Neapolitan comedies and comic operas. Since each of these characters is associated with a different Italian city, it is naturally Naples' own Pulcinella who is the great favorite.*

CHRISTMAS DAY *(Natale)*

- *Menesta Maritata* (page 75).
- *Cappone in Umido con Patate* (page 254), capon stewed in tomato sauce, or in its own sauce with added aromatic herbs and vegetables, and served with potatoes.
- *"Sacicce e Friarelli"* (Sausages and Broccoli Rabe, page 141).
- *Struffoli*, small mounds of dough that are fried, then dipped in honey.

CARNIVAL *(Carnevale)*

- Among a plenitude of festive dishes, the "musts" are *Lasagne di Carnevale* (see *Bugialli on Pasta*, pages 186–187), with the *ragù* sauce prepared with a variety of meats or with just pork and sausages, and *Sartù di Riso* (Stuffed Rice Mold, page 259).

For the saint's day of San Giuseppe, families make *zeppole* (page 229) and exchange them with their friends.

The soft spring wheat kernels that so appropriately represent the season and the earth's return to fertility punctuate the texture of this Easter cake. Many of its ingredients, such as rose water, link the cake through the long centuries to a more primal joy in that season. The *pastiera* is adored by the Neapolitans who, despite all the work involved in making it, tenaciously keep its tradition alive at Easter.

The *pastiera* cannot be completely appreciated unless it is prepared in the authentic manner, with a very thin and delicate covering of *pasta frolla* and the wheat kernels that are at the core of its meaning. Many have tasted commercial travesties, but I have never seen anyone disappointed with the real thing—it's a magnificent representative of the survival of Naples' culinary traditions.

Two additional *pastiere* are prepared in Santa Maria Capua di Venere, a town northwest of Caserta. Undoubtedly the result of foreign influences, these versions ignore the cake's original significance, as one uses rice and the other a thin dry pasta in place of the wheat kernels.

pastiera

NEAPOLITAN EASTER CAKE

SERVES 8

FOR THE STUFFING

- 1/4 pound soft wheat kernels (available in specialty food stores)
- 2 1/2 quarts (about 5 cups) whole milk
- 1/2 cup plus 2 tablespoons granulated sugar
- 2 tablespoons (1 ounce) unsalted butter
- 1 small piece lemon peel
- 1 teaspoon vanilla extract, or 2 or 3 drops if imported Italian extract
- 1 pound whole-milk ricotta
- 2 extra-large eggs, separated
- 1 tablespoon rose water

OPPOSITE: "La ricottina di bufala" *(small individual ricotta made from buffalo milk) is a real Neapolitan specialty. They appear on the market around Eastertime and are served as an appetizer, very lightly scented with fresh basil. However, "Do not put the basil too close to the ricotta!" I was told.*

PREPARE THE STUFFING: Soak the wheat kernels overnight in a large crockery or glass bowl filled with cold water. The next morning, rinse the wheat under cold running water. Drain well and let stand until needed.

Combine the milk, 2 tablespoons of the sugar, the butter, lemon peel, and vanilla in a stockpot over medium heat. When the milk reaches a boil, add the soaked wheat and simmer for about 4 hours. By this time, almost all the milk should be incorporated and the wheat kernels will be completely open. Transfer the cooked wheat to a crockery or glass bowl and let cool completely, about 1 hour.

PREPARE THE PASTRY CREAM: With the ingredients listed here, follow the directions on page 265.

PREPARE THE *PASTA FROLLA*: With the ingredients and quantities listed here, follow the directions on page 238. Wrap the dough in wax paper and place it in the lower part of the refrigerator for about 30 minutes.

Place the ricotta, egg yolks, the remaining 1/2 cup sugar, the rose water, orange extract, and cooled wheat kernels in a large crockery or glass bowl. Mix thoroughly with a wooden spoon. Add the glacéed fruit, cinnamon, and cooled pastry cream, and stir well.

2 teaspoons orange extract, or 2 drops if imported Italian extract

3/4 cup mixed glacéed citron and orange peel, cut into small pieces

Pinch of ground cinnamon

FOR THE PASTRY CREAM

3 extra-large egg yolks

3 heaping tablespoons granulated sugar

2 teaspoons potato starch

1 small piece lemon peel

1 cup cold milk

FOR THE PASTRY (*PASTA FROLLA*)

7 ounces (about 1 1/3 cups) unbleached all-purpose flour

6 tablespoons (3 ounces) unsalted butter

2 ounces (about 1/4 cup) granulated sugar

3 extra-large egg yolks

TO SERVE

About 1/4 cup confectioners' sugar

Preheat the oven to 350°F and butter a 10-inch springform pan.

Roll out the *pasta frolla* between 2 pieces of parchment paper to form a round of dough about 1/8 inch thick. Remove the top piece of paper, then holding the bottom parchment paper at one end, gently flip the dough round into the springform pan and carefully line the inside, allowing the extra dough to hang over the edges.

Using a wire whisk, beat the egg whites in a copper bowl until stiff. Then use a rubber spatula to carefully fold them into the stuffing. Pour the mixture into the dough-lined pan. Use a pastry cutter to cut the dough off at the level of the stuffing. Roll out the remaining pieces of dough, cut them into strips 1/2 to 3/4 inch wide, and place them over the filling in a crisscross pattern.

Place the cake in the oven and bake it for 2 hours, then remove it and let it stand in the pan until cool, about 2 hours.

Open the springform pan, transfer the *pastiera* to a large platter, sprinkle it with confectioners' sugar, and serve, slicing it like a pie.

This dessert is even better if prepared one day ahead.

For this traditional Easter dish, whole eggs in their shells are inserted into the dough before baking. Each is held in place by two strips of dough, which are symbolic of the cross. As the bread bakes, the eggs become hard-cooked.

During Easter time, all the bakeries display large signs asking customers to reserve their *"casatielli"* in advance and to indicate whether they want a lot of lard inside (written in big letters) or (written in tiny, almost illegible letters) no lard at all. Easter is the festivity most loved by the Neapolitans, and shops all over the city decorate their windows with special displays that celebrate the arrival of spring. In the old days, two seasonal vendors would walk all around the city at Easter time: the *ammazzapiecure* (the butcher of lambs) and the *caserecotta*, who sold cheese (*cacio*) and ricotta. Today, still, it is in the weeks before Easter that the *casatielli* vendors begin to appear on the streets.

The association of this *ciambella* (a ring of dough) with the Easter holiday comes from the whole eggs that are inserted into the dough. The number of eggs used depends on the size of the *casatiello*, so there is *casatiello a un uovo* (*casatiello* with one egg), *casatiello a due uova* (with two eggs), and so on.

The *casatiello* was born as a very plain and simple yeast dough, with a bit of added lard. Traditionally made at home, it was meant to be given as a gift, not only to friends, but to those who performed services for the family, like the laundress or the maids, as well. But the wealthy class was not satisfied with the *casatiello* in its simple form, and began to ask that ingredients more suitable to their station be added, leading to a richer (and more expensive) cake. And so, some cooks added sugar, or mixed eggs into the dough—and sometimes a completely different type of dough was used. Today, of the original, only the ring shape and the tradition of inserting the eggs remains.

casatiello

SAVORY EASTER BREAD RING

SERVES 8 TO 10

FOR THE SPONGE

1 cup plus 1 tablespoon unbleached all-purpose flour

1 ounce fresh compressed yeast, or 2 envelopes active dry yeast

1 cup lukewarm water for fresh yeast or warm water for dry

FOR THE DOUGH

3 cups unbleached all-purpose flour

1 heaping tablespoon freshly grated aged local pecorino or Pecorino Romano cheese

4 heaping tablespoons freshly grated Parmigiano

1/2 cup lukewarm water

8 tablespoons (4 ounces) unsalted butter or lard, at room temperature

Fine salt

Abundant freshly ground black pepper

4 extra-large eggs, in the shell

TO BAKE

1 extra-large egg

1 tablespoon water

PREPARE THE SPONGE: Place 1 cup of the flour in a small bowl and make a well in the center. Dissolve the yeast in the water and pour the mixture into the well of the flour. Using a wooden spoon, gradually mix in the flour from the edges of the well until it is incorporated. Sprinkle the remaining 1 tablespoon flour over the sponge, cover the bowl with a cotton dish towel, and let it rest in a warm place away from drafts until doubled in size, about 1 hour.

PREPARE THE DOUGH: Place 2 cups of the flour in a mound on a board and make a well in the center. Place the pecorino, Parmigiano, lukewarm water, and 4 tablespoons of the butter in the well and mix all these ingredients together with a wooden spoon. Then mix in the sponge, and season with salt to taste and a very large amount of freshly ground black pepper.

Start incorporating some of the flour from the rim of the well, then use your hands to work all the flour into the dough. Place the remaining 4 tablespoons butter on the dough and start kneading it with a folding motion, adding the remaining 1 cup flour. Keep kneading until all the butter is completely absorbed and the dough is very homogenous and smooth. Pinch off a piece of dough (about 5 ounces) and set it aside for later use.

Preheat the oven to 400°F and lightly flour a 10-inch ring mold (4 quarts) or an 11- or 12-inch pizza pan. Shape the dough into a ring and transfer it to the prepared mold. If you are using a pizza pan, place a 1-cup metal measuring cup in the center of the dough ring to help it keep its shape. Insert the eggs, still in their shells, into the dough in four different places. Roll out the reserved piece of dough to form a 24-inch-long rope. Cut it into eight 3-inch-long pieces, and crisscross two pieces over each egg to hold it in place. Cover the mold or pan with a cotton dish towel and let it rest until the dough has doubled in size, about 1 hour.

Lightly beat the egg and water together, and brush the top of the *casatiello* with this egg wash. Bake for 45 minutes, or until the bread is golden on top and still very spongy to the touch. Remove from the oven and let the *casatiello* rest for at least 30 minutes before transferring it to a serving platter. *Casatiello* is always eaten at room temperature, sliced like a cake.

The name *Insalata di Rinforzo* has a dual meaning. First, since it is prepared at the beginning of the season, primarily for the family to eat throughout the holidays, every time some is eaten, the salad is "made stronger" (*rinforzare* means to reinforce) by the addition of more and different vegetables. And, since one is eating the salad on top of all the other food that is served during the Christmas dinner, it is said to make your stomach completely full, or "stronger." In the old days, this salad was eaten with *Taralli con i Finocchietti* (*Taralli* with Fennel Seeds, page 221).

insalata di rinforzo

NEAPOLITAN CHRISTMAS SALAD

SERVES 6 TO 8

1 medium-sized cauliflower, about 1 pound, cleaned, all green leaves removed

Coarse-grained salt

Soak the cauliflower in a bowl of cold water for 30 minutes. Bring a pot of cold water to a boil over medium heat and add coarse salt to taste and the clove of garlic. Detach all the florets from the cauliflower and add them to the boiling water, discarding the stem. Boil for about 10 minutes, or until cooked but still quite firm.

- 1 large clove garlic, peeled and left whole
- 1 large bunch curly endive, cleaned, all dark green leaves discarded
- 1/4 pound Gaeta or Calamata olives, pitted
- 1/4 pound green olives preserved in vinegar, pitted
- 3 tablespoons capers preserved in vinegar, drained
- 5 whole anchovies preserved in salt, boned, rinsed under cold running water, and cut into small pieces; or 10 anchovy fillets packed in oil, drained and cut into small pieces
- 1/2 pound *Giardiniera* (mixed vegetables, such as carrots, cauliflower, celery, and peppers), preserved in wine vinegar (see recipe, page 21), drained
- 1 yellow or red bell pepper preserved in wine vinegar, drained, cut into thin strips (see *Peperoni all'Aceto*, page 18)
- Fine salt and freshly ground black pepper
- 1/2 cup extra-virgin olive oil

TO SERVE

- Gaeta or Calamata olives and green olives preserved in vinegar, left whole

Use a slotted spoon to transfer the florets from the water to a serving dish lined with paper towels to absorb excess moisture; discard the garlic. Cover the florets with lightly moistened paper towels to keep them from drying out, and let rest until they are cool, about 1 hour. (The cauliflower may also be boiled several hours in advance.)

Meanwhile, arrange the endive on a large serving platter and cover it with moistened paper towels until needed. Place the Gaeta olives, green olives, capers, anchovies, *giardiniera*, and bell pepper strips in a crockery or glass bowl. Season with fine salt (very little if using anchovies preserved in salt) and pepper, and add the oil. Mix very well and refrigerate, covered, until the cauliflower is ready.

Remove the paper towels from the endive and arrange the cooled cauliflower on top. Distribute the chilled mixed ingredients over all the florets. Scatter the whole olives over the salad and serve.

VARIATION

Sometimes *friselle* (Neapolitan toasted half rolls), lightly soaked in water and vinegar, are used as a base for this salad, which is then called *caponata di Natale*.

frittelle di natale

CHRISTMAS FRITTERS

MAKES ABOUT 20

- Coarse-grained salt
- 1/2 pound soaked *baccalà*
- 1/2 cup plus 1 tablespoon extra-virgin olive oil
- 15 sprigs Italian parsley, leaves only
- 2 small cloves garlic, peeled
- Salt and freshly ground black pepper

OPPOSITE: Insalata di Rinforzo, *a Neapolitan Christmas tradition.*

Bring a pot of cold water to a boil over medium heat, add coarse salt to taste, then add the *baccalà* and cook it for about 10 minutes, or until soft and tender.

Transfer the fish to a crockery or glass bowl and remove any bones, add the 1 tablespoon olive oil, and use a wooden spoon to break the *baccalà* into small pieces. Finely chop the parsley and garlic together on a cutting board and add the mixture to the bowl. Season with salt and pepper and mix very well.

Dissolve the yeast in the milk. Place the flour in a crockery or glass bowl, make a well in the center, and gradually add the dissolved yeast. Mix very well with a wooden spoon, mixing in the flour from the edges until all the flour is incorporated and a rather thick, smooth batter forms. Add the egg and salt to taste, and mix again. Add the *baccalà* mixture to the batter, mix with a wooden spoon, and let rest for 30 minutes.

$^1/_2$ ounce fresh compressed yeast, or 1 envelope active dry yeast

1 cup lukewarm milk for fresh yeast or warm milk for dry

1 $^1/_3$ cups unbleached all-purpose flour

1 extra-large egg

2 cups vegetable oil (preferably a mixture of half sunflower oil, half corn oil)

TO SERVE

Fine salt

1 large lemon, sliced

Heat the vegetable oil and the remaining $^1/_2$ cup olive oil in a large skillet, and when the oil mixture is hot (about 400°F), spoon the batter into the hot oil, 2 heaping tablespoons at a time. Be sure not to crowd the skillet because the *frittelle* will expand a lot. Fry until the fritters are golden all over, then transfer them to a serving platter lined with paper towels to absorb excess oil.

When all the fritters are cooked, remove the paper towels, sprinkle with fine salt, and serve very hot, with the lemon slices arranged all around the fritters.

cappone in umido con patate

STEWED CAPON WITH POTATOES

SERVES 6 TO 8

1 capon, 7 to 8 pounds, cleaned and left whole

1 large red onion, cleaned

2 stalks celery

10 sprigs Italian parsley, leaves only

2 medium-sized carrots, scraped

1 small clove garlic, peeled

10 fresh sage leaves

$^3/_4$ cup extra-virgin olive oil

2 tablespoons (1 ounce) unsalted butter

1 cup dry red wine

Salt and freshly ground black pepper

Small pinch of ground cinnamon

2$^1/_2$ pounds ripe tomatoes, or 2$^1/_2$ pounds drained canned tomatoes, preferably imported Italian

PLUS

3 pounds all-purpose potatoes

Coarse-grained salt

$^1/_4$ cup extra-virgin olive oil

Salt and freshly ground black pepper

OPPOSITE: *A shrine to the patron saint of Naples, San Gennaro.*

Wash the capon very well under cold running water, removing the extra fat in the cavity, and pat it dry with paper towels.

Finely chop the onion, celery, parsley, carrots, garlic, and sage together on a cutting board; they must be so finely chopped that they resemble a paste.

Place a large nonreactive casserole, preferably flameproof terra-cotta or enamel, containing the oil and butter over low heat. When the butter is almost melted, add the chopped mixture and simmer (simmering, not sautéing, because the heat is so low) until the vegetables look like a sauce, about 40 minutes. Add the capon and, keeping the heat low, cook it for about 1 hour, turning it several times. The skin of the capon will be darker after all this cooking, but not golden.

Add the wine to the casserole, raise the heat to medium for 5 minutes, and season with salt, pepper, and the ground cinnamon. If fresh tomatoes are to be used, cut them into pieces; pass the fresh or canned tomatoes through a food mill into a crockery or glass bowl using the disk with the smallest holes. Add the tomatoes to the casserole and lower the heat again.

Continue cooking, mixing, and turning the capon every so often, being careful not to break its skin, until the capon is completely cooked. It will be soft and very juicy, and the sauce dense and very shiny. This should take around 2 hours. (The exact cooking time for capons is difficult to predict, because it depends mainly on the rooster's age when it became a capon.)

As the capon cooks, preheat the oven to 375°F. Peel the potatoes, cut them into 1$^1/_2$-inch cubes, and place the cubes in a bowl of cold water until needed. Bring a pot of cold water to a boil over medium heat and add coarse salt to taste. Drain the potatoes and add them to the boiling water. Cook for 5 minutes.

Drain the potatoes and transfer them to a crockery or glass bowl, pour the oil over them, and season with salt and pepper. Let the potatoes rest until cool, about 30 minutes.

Lightly oil a glass baking dish, arrange the potatoes in it, and bake for 35 minutes. By this time, the potatoes should be golden and almost cooked. Remove the baking dish from the oven and let the potatoes rest until needed.

Thirty minutes before the capon is ready, transfer the potatoes to the casserole containing the bird, or if the pot is not large enough to hold all the potatoes in two layers or less, finish cooking the potatoes in a separate casserole, along with some of the capon sauce from the casserole. The potatoes should simmer in the sauce until they completely soaked in the sauce and rather soft.

This dish can be prepared ahead: Once the capon and potatoes are ready, let them cool in the casserole, if you have used terra-cotta or enamel pots. Otherwise, transfer them to a crockery or glass bowl. Once they are cool, refrigerate them, covered, and reheat before serving.

To serve, arrange portions of capon and potatoes together on each plate.

One of the attractive Christmas cakes from the Naples area, *Rotolo di Natale* is stuffed with walnuts, pignoli, and raisins and flavored with orange and lemon rind and rum. Like some other older recipes, at a certain point within the last two centuries a little chocolate flavoring was added to it.

rotolo di natale

CHRISTMAS FRUIT AND NUT ROLL

SERVES 12

FOR THE SPONGE AND THE DOUGH

6 cups unbleached all-purpose flour

4 ounces fresh compressed yeast, or 8 envelopes active dry yeast

1 cup lukewarm milk for fresh yeast or warm milk for dry

FOR THE STUFFING

1/2 pound raisins

1 cup lukewarm milk

1/2 pound shelled walnuts

1/4 pound pine nuts *(pignoli)*

2 1/4 cups granulated sugar

Grated peel of 2 oranges

Grated peel of 2 lemons

3 tablespoons unsweetened cocoa powder

8 tablespoons (4 ounces) plus about 5 pats unsalted butter

2 extra-large eggs, separated

1/2 cup light rum

Pinch of salt

PREPARE THE DOUGH: Put the flour in a large bowl and make a well in the center. Dissolve the yeast in thc milk and pour the mixture into the well. Mix with a wooden spoon until about a quarter of the flour has been incorporated into the yeast mixture. Cover the bowl with a cotton dish towel, and let it stand in a warm place away from drafts until the sponge has doubled in size, about 1 hour.

PREPARE THE STUFFING: Soak the raisins in the milk for about 30 minutes. Coarsely chop the walnuts and put them in a bowl. Add the pine nuts, 1/2 cup of the sugar, half of the grated orange and lemon peel, and all the cocoa powder. Mix thoroughly with a wooden spoon. Drain the raisins, discarding the milk, and dry them on paper towels. Add them to the stuffing mixture and combine gently but thoroughly.

When the sponge is ready, melt the 8 tablespoons butter in the top of a double boiler and let stand to cool until needed.

Pour the remaining 1 3/4 cups sugar over the sponge. Then add the egg yolks, rum, the remaining orange and lemon peel, and the salt. Stir everything into the sponge with a wooden spoon. Then add the cooled

OPPOSITE AND ABOVE: Rotolo di Natale—*during preparation and the finished cake.*

melted butter and incorporate all but 5 or 6 tablespoons of the unmixed flour. Transfer the dough to a board and knead until the remaining flour is almost all incorporated and the dough is smooth, about 15 minutes.

Using a rolling pin, roll the dough out to a thickness of 1/2 inch, making a rectangle not larger than 9 inches wide.

Beat the egg whites until stiff and spread them on top of the dough. Scatter the stuffing over the egg whites, and place the butter pats on top of the stuffing. Roll the dough up lengthwise.

Butter a 14-inch pizza pan. Transfer the stuffed, rolled dough to the pan and form it into a ring. Cover the pan with a cotton dish towel and let it rest in a warm place away from drafts until doubled in size, about 2 hours.

Preheat the oven to 400°F. When the dough has risen, bake it for about 40 minutes, or until the top is golden brown. Do not open the oven door until at least 25 minutes have passed. Remove the *rotolo* from the oven and transfer it to a rack to cool.

Serve the *rotolo*, cutting it into slices.

Sartù di Riso (opposite) and *Palle di Riso* (page 181) are the only two of the many rice dishes in Cavalcanti that have remained classic. The first one—the "*Sartù*"—is a rather complicated and quite elaborate dish, but the result is worthwhile. Cavalcanti has two *Sartù* dishes, one that has meatballs, as does ours, and the other with fishballs. This latter version has all but disappeared.

Palle di Riso is extremely easy to make and is always served as an appetizer with many other dishes, all fried. The other two famous rice balls are *Arancini*, from Sicily, stuffed with peas, meat sauce, and *balsamella* (béchamel), and *Supplì*, from Rome, stuffed with *fiordilatte* (cow's milk mozzarella). An often told anecdote is that Gugielmo Marconi was seen eating a *Supplì* in a restaurant and looked very uncomfortable dealing with the strings of melted mozzarella. Another customer chided him, saying it was hard to believe that the inventor of the wireless telegraph could not get rid of the mozzarella strings!

Cooking in modern times means shortcuts, so the *Sartù* nowadays is often prepared by mixing all the different ingredients together and baking them in a mold instead of layering the ingredients and reserving the rice to use only as a casing. I have seen one more variation: The rice is mixed with all the ingredients except the meatballs, then the rice mixture is baked in a ring mold and, when ready, is served with the meatballs in the hole of the ring.

We do know that the French word *ragout* became *ragù* and *gratiné* became *grattè*, and so the word *sartout* became *sartù*. But *sartout* in French means a head piece, which is *soprammobile* or "*trionfo*" in Italian, and does not correspond to a dish. On the other hand, in the Livorno area of Tuscany, the dish *Sartù* is well known. At this moment, I cannot make any kind of speculation about the real origin of this word as the name for a dish.

sartù di riso

STUFFED RICE MOLD

SERVES 9 TO 10

FOR THE RICE MOLD

3 quarts cold chicken broth, completely defatted, preferably homemade

Coarse-grained salt

1 1/2 pounds Italian rice, preferably *Carnaroli*

4 ounces (about 1 1/3 cup) freshly grated Parmigiano

3 extra-large eggs

Salt and freshly ground black pepper

3 cups *Ragù di Carne* (page 122)

FOR THE MEATBALLS

1 1/2 slices (2 ounces) white bread, crusts removed

1/2 cup milk

3/4 pound ground beef

2 tablespoons freshly grated Parmigiano

1 extra-large egg

Salt and freshly ground black pepper

1 cup vegetable oil (preferably a mixture of half sunflower oil, half corn oil)

3 tablespoons extra-virgin olive oil

FOR THE CHICKEN LIVERS

3 tablespoons (1 1/2 ounces) unsalted butter

4 chicken livers, cleaned

Salt and freshly ground black pepper

OPPOSITE AND FOLLOWING: *Two views of this traditional stuffed rice mold.*

PREPARE THE RICE: Bring the cold broth to a boil in a large pot over medium heat, add coarse salt to taste, then add the rice and cook for 12 minutes. The rice should still have a strong "bite." Drain the rice, cool it under cold running water, and place it in a large crockery or glass bowl. Add the Parmigiano and eggs, and mix well. Season with salt and pepper, then add 1 cup of the *ragù* and mix again. Refrigerate the rice, covered, until needed.

PREPARE THE MEATBALLS (*POLPETTINE*): Soak the bread in the milk for 10 minutes, then squeeze the bread, pressing out as much milk as possible (discard the milk), and place it in a medium-sized bowl. Add the ground beef, Parmigiano, and egg to the bowl, season with salt and pepper, and mix well with a wooden spoon. Shape the small individual *polpettine*, using 1/2 tablespoon of the meat mixture for each meatball.

Heat the vegetable oil with the olive oil in a medium-sized skillet over medium heat. When the oil mixture is hot, about 375°F, add the meatballs, a few at a time, and cook until they are very light in color, less than 30 seconds piece. Transfer the cooked meatballs to a serving platter lined with paper towels to absorb excess oil, and let rest until needed.

COOK THE CHICKEN LIVERS: Melt the butter in a saucepan over medium heat, then add the whole chicken livers, season with salt and pepper, and cook them for 1 minute. Transfer the chicken livers and all their juices to a plate, then cut them into fourths and let rest until needed.

PREPARE THE PEAS: Place a skillet containing the butter and the olive oil over medium heat, and when the butter is melted, add the onion and sauté for 5 minutes, stirring every so often with a wooden spoon. Add the peas, season with salt and pepper, and cook for 10 minutes, adding a little water if necessary. Let the peas rest until needed.

Place the meatballs, the chicken livers with their juices, and the peas with all their juices in a large casserole over low heat. Add 1 cup of the *ragù* to the casserole, gently mix all the ingredients together, and cook for 2 minutes, stirring every so often. Transfer the stuffing to a crockery or glass bowl and let it rest until cool, about 30 minutes.

Heavily butter the bottom and sides of the mold and coat it with bread crumbs. Place a piece of parchment paper on the bottom of the mold, then butter the paper. Coat it with bread crumbs as well. Reserve the remaining bread crumbs.

FOR THE PEAS

3 tablespoons (1 1/2 ounces) unsalted butter

1 tablespoon extra-virgin olive oil

1 small yellow onion, cleaned and finely chopped

6 ounces (about 1 1/4 cups) shelled fresh peas or frozen " tiny tender" peas (do not defrost)

Salt and freshly ground black pepper

PLUS

Unsalted butter

Very fine bread crumbs to line the mold and to scatter on top

3 hard-boiled eggs, shelled and cut into fourths

6 ounces *fiordilatte* (cow's-milk mozzarella), cut into 1-inch cubes

1/4 pound boiled ham, sliced 1/4 inch thick, then cut into 1/2-inch-wide strips

Take enough of the rice mixture to make a 1-inch-thick layer on the bottom of the mold. Cover the rice with a layer of the stuffing, using one third of it and leaving a 1-inch border of uncovered rice all around the edge. Arrange four egg quarters on top of the stuffing. Then sprinkle one third of the *fiordilatte* cubes and one-third of the ham strips over the stuffing, always leaving the border around the edge.

Now add enough rice mixture around the border to contain all the stuffing. Make another 1-inch-thick layer of rice over the stuffing and the border. Repeat the layers of stuffing, eggs, mozzarella, and ham, and raise the rice edge again. Repeat again for the final layering, using up all the remaining stuffing. Finish with a layer of the remaining rice, and sprinkle some bread crumbs over the top.

Let the *sartù* rest while you preheat the oven to 375°F. When ready, place several pats of butter over the rice, and bake for 45 minutes.

Remove the mold from the oven and let it rest for at least 20 minutes before unmolding the *sartù* onto a large round serving platter. Heat the remaining 1 cup *ragù*, and serve it with the *sartù*, spooned over each serving.

March 19th is the feast day of San Giuseppe (Saint Joseph). In Naples, that means *zeppole*, and according to the "*bungustai*" (gourmands), the place to get the best ones—at least until recently—has been Pintauro, the famous pastry shop located in the "hot spot" that is the Via Toledo. The most celebrated *zeppole* start as a very soft bigné pastry made from water, white wine, flour, and butter or lard; the dough is shaped in small rings and fried until lightly golden, full of air, and not greasy at all.

The writer de Bouchard, in his 1857 book, describes these *zeppole* in such a way that you almost believe you have a plate of these golden delicacies sitting right in front of you. They would have been sprinkled all over with sugar, or golden honey, or—even better—the so-called *giulebbo*, which is a sugar-and-water syrup with flavorings added.

But this is only one type of *zeppole*. There are also the *zeppole* that are prepared and sold by hundreds of "*zeppolajuoli ambulanti*," traveling vendors that fill the streets all over Naples, primarily on St. Joseph's Day. These vendors not only sell fried *zeppole*, but also *zeppole di riso* (rice *zeppole*), *scagliuozzoli* (thick polenta cut into different shapes), *tittoli*, which, if rolled up, are called either *sigari* (cigars) or *fusi* (spools). They even sell small balls of fried dough, called *palle*, either plain or stuffed with a bit of mozzarella. And finally, there are fritters of borage leaves called *vorraccia* or *vurracce*.

De Bouchard's description of *zeppole* ends with the typical Neapolitan mixture of humor tinged with sadness. He says that the *zeppole* eaten in a pastry shop and those bought from a "*zeppolajuolo*" are so different that the distance between them is the same as that between a rich and a poor person.

zeppole di san giuseppe *or* zeppole a bigné

ZEPPOLE FOR SAN GIUSEPPE'S DAY

MAKES ABOUT 16

FOR THE PASTRY CREAM

4 extra-large egg yolks

1/2 cup granulated sugar

Grated peel of 1 orange or 1 lemon

1 tablespoon potato starch

1 1/2 cups whole milk

FOR THE DOUGH

1 2/3 cups cold water

2 tablespoons (1 ounce) unsalted butter

1 tablespoon pure grain alcohol or vodka

Pinch of fine salt

About 3 cups unbleached all-purpose flour

3 extra-large eggs

4 extra-large egg yolks

1/2 tablespoon olive oil

TO FRY THE *ZEPPOLE*

2 cups vegetable oil (preferably a mixture of half sunflower oil, half corn oil), or 4 cups vegetable oil if frying the *zeppole* in 2 skillets

1/4 cup extra-virgin olive oil, or 1/2 cup olive oil if frying the zeppole in 2 skillets

TO SERVE

Amarene (sour Italian cherries in syrup, available at Italian markets or specialty food stores)

Prepare the pastry cream, using the ingredients and quantities listed at left, according to the directions on page 265. Transfer the rather thick cream to a crockery or glass bowl and refrigerate, covered, until needed. The pastry cream may be prepared up to 2 days in advance.

PREPARE THE DOUGH: Place the water, butter, alcohol, and fine salt in a casserole over medium heat. When the butter is completely melted and the water has almost reached the boiling point, add all the flour at once and mix vigorously with a wooden spoon to combine. Keep mixing until a ball of dough forms, about 1 minute. Transfer the dough to a lightly oiled marble slab and use a rolling pin to "beat" the dough. Roll it out, fold it, and beat again until the dough is cooled, about 10 minutes.

Transfer the dough to the bowl of an electric mixer fitted with the paddle attachment. With the mixer set at medium speed, start adding the whole eggs, then the egg yolks, one at a time. Keep mixing until the dough becomes very shiny and smooth and a lot of bubbles form. Let the dough rest for at least 1 hour, then transfer it to a pastry bag with a star tip about 1 inch in diameter.

FRY THE *ZEPPOLE*: Heat the 2 cups vegetable oil and the 1/4 cup olive oil in a deep skillet over medium heat. The oil mixture is ready when it reaches about 280°F. Do not let it get hotter, or the *zeppole* will cook too fast on the outsides while the insides remain very soggy. Actually, it would be better to cook the *zeppole* in two skillets: first in one with the oil at 280°F so the *zeppole* puff up and cook completely inside, and then in a skillet with the oil much hotter, about 375°F, so the *zeppole* become lightly golden. If you choose this method, you will need to double the amount of oil used, putting 2 cups vegetable oil and 1/4 cup olive oil into each skillet.

Squeeze enough dough out of the pastry bag and onto a well-oiled strainer-skimmer to form a ring about 2 1/2 inches in diameter. Gently insert the skimmer into the hot oil to release the dough. The *zeppole* should almost be covered with oil, and only one or two should be fried at a time. They are ready when they are very crisp and puffy. Transfer the cooked *zeppole* to a serving platter lined with paper towels to absorb excess oil. If using two skillets, transfer the *zeppole* from the skillet containing the cooler oil when you see that they are very puffy and completely cooked.

When all the *zeppole* are on the serving platter, remove the paper towels and serve them, spreading some of the cold pastry cream over each and one or two cherries.

basic techniques

HOW TO CLEAN ARTICHOKES

When you buy artichokes be sure they are firm and the outer leaves completely green and unspotted. The bottom of the stem of a fresh artichoke shows the two shades of green of the inner and outer layers that should not have turned dark. The best pot to cook artichokes is glazed terra-cotta, then enamel. Aluminum or cast iron will darken the color of the bright green leaves and change the pale yellow of the heart to black.

Before cleaning, soak artichokes for 30 minutes in a large bowl of cold water with one lemon that has been cut in half.

Cut off a portion of the stem, leaving about 3 inches. Trim off the darker outer ring of leaves. The inner core is the best part because it has the real taste of the artichoke. Remove as many rows of the outer leaves as necessary to arrive at those tender inner rows where you can clearly see the separation between the green at the top and the light yellow at the bottom.

Then remove the top green part. Press your thumb on the bottom of each leaf, the white part, to hold it in place and with the other hand tear off the top green part. As each new row is uncovered, the tender yellow part of the leaves will be bigger. When you reach the rows in which only the very tips of the leaves are green, cut off all the tips together with a knife.

The artichoke then may be cut in pieces or left whole, depending on the recipe. But in either case, the choke must be removed. If you wish to stuff the artichokes whole, first cut off the stems. To remove the hair, fibers, and the choke, use a knife or a long teaspoon, cutting all around the inside of the choke and scooping it out.

HOW TO MAKE BREAD CRUMBS

Unseasoned homemade bread crumbs are the best to use. The bread (preferably homemade or a good quality of packaged commercial white bread) should first be toasted in the oven, then ground in a food processor or blender. Bread crumbs should not be seasoned, not even with salt and pepper.

HOW TO BLANCH TOMATOES

Bring a large pot of cold water to a boil. Add coarse-grained salt and the whole tomatoes and boil for 30 seconds (or 1 minute for large tomatoes). The salt will help the tomatoes to retain their color. Meanwhile, prepare a bowl of cold water. Use a slotted spoon to transfer the tomatoes from the boiling water to the bowl of cold water. Let the tomatoes sit in the cold water for a few minutes if you intend to peel them. To peel the tomatoes, remove the small stem, then use a paring knife to remove the skin, starting at the point where the stem was removed.

HOW TO GRATE ORANGE AND LEMON PEELS

Place a piece of parchment paper over the holes of a hand grater. Hold the paper in place with one hand while moving the orange or lemon back and forth on the paper with the other. Work on different sections of the paper so that the paper does not wear out. Use a rubber spatula to remove the grated orange or lemon peel from the paper. Do not use what is inside the grater or any of the bitter white part of the peel.

HOW TO TIE A PIECE OF MEAT LIKE A SALAMI

To tie a piece of meat like a salami, cut a piece of string six times the length of the meat to be tied. Place the string under one of the short sides of the rolled-up meat (about 1½ inches from the end), and make a knot, leaving only enough string on one side to pull over and knot the first ring in the center. Bring the long end of the string down the meat and another 1½ inches, and hold the string in place with your finger. With the other hand, pull the string under and around again to the point where the string is being held by your finger. Pass the end of the string over and then under (like a sailor's knot). Remove your finger, hold the short end of the string with one hand, and pull the other end tight with the other hand. Continue this process at 1½-inch intervals until you reach the opposite end of the meat. Stand the meat on one end and put the remaining string over the top end to the underside of the meat. As the string intersects with each ring of string, pull under and over, fastening in the same way as was done on the other side (it is no longer necessary to hold the string with your finger or to pull tight on this side). After the last intersections, tie a knot using the two ends of the string. When the meat is ready, you will only need to cut the string in one place in order to remove it.

HOW TO MAKE PASTRY CREAM

The basic, custard-like *crema pasticceria* forms the foundation for many desserts, from the pastry fillings that give it its name to sauces for fruit and the famous Italian ice cream (*gelato*). It is made with egg yolks, sugar, and milk and is lightly thickened, preferably with potato starch or flour (both lighter and less starchy than cornstarch), by cooking over the steam of a double boiler. The insert with the pastry cream should not touch the boiling water but should only be heated by the steam. The technique of making the pastry cream is the same no matter what the amounts of the ingredients given in the individual recipes.

Put the egg yolks into a crockery or glass bowl and add the sugar and potato starch. Stir with a wooden spoon, always in the same direction, until the sugar and the potato starch are completely incorporated and the egg yolks turn a lighter color. Slowly add the milk, then the orange peel, mixing steadily. Bring some water to a boil in the bottom of a double boiler and transfer the contents of the bowl to the top part of the double boiler. When the water is boiling, insert the top part into the bottom. Stir constantly with a wooden spoon, always in the same direction.

Just before it boils, the cream should be thick enough to coat the spoon. That is the moment it is ready. Absolutely do not allow it to boil. Immediately remove the top part of the double boiler from the heat, and continue to stir the contents for 2 or 3 minutes longer. Then remove the orange peel.

Transfer the *crema pasticceria* to a crockery bowl to cool (about 1 hour). This can be prepared several hours in advance and kept, covered, in the refrigerator until needed.

neapolitan dialect: italian/english glossary

NEAPOLITAN DIALECT	ITALIAN	ENGLISH
accio	*sedano*	celery
acetera (from the Spanish *aceitera*)	*oliera*	container for olive oil
aieta	*bietola*	Swiss chard
amenta	*menta*	mint
arancia	*purtuallo*	orange
arucola	*ruca* or *rucola* or *ruchetta*	arugula or rocket
attura (mainly describes coffee beans and seeds)	*tostare*	to toast
bascuglia	*stadera*	scale
burraccia	*boraggine*	borage
butirro caso	*burro cacio* or *formaggio*	butter
cerasa	*ciliegia*	cherry
cerasiello	*peperoncino*	hot pepper
chiapparello	*cappero*	caper
crisommola	*albicocca*	apricot
farenella	*farina gialla* or *farina di mais*	cornmeal
fasano	*fabiano*	pheasant
fasulo	*fagiolo*	bean
frambuase	*lampone*	raspberry
fresella	*biscotto*	toasted half-rolls
magna	*mangiare*	to eat
maruza	*lumaca*	snail
mulignana	*melanzana*	eggplant
ortaglia	*ortaggi*	vegetables
padulano	*venditore di verdure*	fruit man
palummo	*piccione*	squab
pane e casa	*pane fatto a casa*	homemade bread
pane e chiazza	*pane comprato*	store-bought bread
panettiere (from the French *panetier* or the Spanish *panadero*)	*fornaio*	bakery
papara	*papera*	goose
pasta d'ammendula	*pasta di mandorle*	almond paste
pasta siringata	*pasta bigne*	
pastenaca	*carota*	carrot
patana	*patata*	potato
patanella	*patata nuova*	new potato
pecuriello	*agnello*	lamb
pesiello	*pisello*	peas
petrusino	*prezzemolo*	parsley
pignata	*pentola*	to toast
presutto	*prosciutto*	prosciutto
puparuolo	*peperone*	bell pepper
purciello	*maiale*	pig or pork meat
purpo	*polpo*	octopus
saciccia	*salsiccia*	sausage
vasenicola	*basilico*	basil
votapescia	*schiumarola*	strainer

acknowledgments

Preparing a book that will help readers understand the real Naples requires the help and advice of key people who are truly immersed in the traditions, cultures, and life of this great city and the surrounding area. With these credentials in mind, I would like to thank the following individuals and organizations for their generous assistance.

I am grateful to Raffaele Beato, Director of ERSAC; Vincenzo Aita, Assessore of Agriculture in the Campania Region, and Antonio Massimo, President of ERSAC.

Invaluable guidance came from Tony May, the real Neapolitan in New York; Eugenio Magnani, Travel Commissioner of the Italian Government Tourist Board in New York; and Mimmo Magliulo of Buon Italia, importers of Italian food in New York.

In Naples, my deepest gratitude to the Assessore Raffalel Tecce and Dott. ssa Ida Alessio Verni, Avv. Attilio Della Mura, Coordinatore Azienda Autonoma di Soggiorno Cura e Turismo in Naples; Vincenzo Regina of Voyage Pittoresque; Nicola Colandrea, Sergio Amato, and Antonio Roviello from the Voiello pasta factory; and La Marchesa company, producers of buffalo-milk mozzarella. And again, thank you to Tessilarte in Florence for all the beautiful tablecloths and napkins.

Dishes and props from Deruta showroom in New York and fill in blank you left here.

Thank you to Leslie Stoker, my long-time and sympathetic publisher; Marisa Bulzone and Sarah Scheffel, my editors; and Kim Tyner, the production director, all from Stewart, Tabori & Chang. My thanks also to Andy Ryan, photographer, Lynne Yeamans, graphic designer, and Ana Deboo, copyeditor.

My usual thanks to Henry Weinberg for his help and support.

Finally, I'd like to express my immense gratitude to the late Harold Acton for his invaluable books on Naples and for his friendship.

metric conversion charts

WEIGHT EQUIVALENTS

The metric weights given in this chart are not exact equivalents, but have been rounded up or down slightly to make measuring easier.

Avoirdupois	Metric
1/4 oz	7 g
1/2 oz	15 g
1 oz	30 g
2 oz	60 g
3 oz	90 g
4 oz	115 g
5 oz	150 g
6 oz	175 g
7 oz	200 g
8 oz (1/2 lb)	225 g
9 oz	250 g
10 oz	300 g
11 oz	325 g
12 oz	350 g
13 oz	375 g
14 oz	400 g
15 oz	425 g
16 oz (1 lb)	450 g
1 1/2 lb	750 g
2 lb	900 g
2 1/4 lb	1 kg
3 lb	1.4 kg
4 lb	1.8 kg

VOLUME EQUIVALENTS

These are not exact equivalents for American cups and spoons, but have been rounded up or down slightly to make measuring easier.

American	Metric	Imperial
1/4 t	1.2 ml	
1/2 t	2.5 ml	
1 t	5.0 ml	
1/2 T (1.5 t)	7.5 ml	
1 T (3 t)	15 ml	
1/4 cup (4 T)	60 ml	2 fl oz
1/3 cup (5 T)	75 ml	2 1/2 fl oz
1/2 cup (8 T)	125 ml	4 fl oz
2/3 cup (10 T)	150 ml	5 fl oz
3/4 cup (12 T)	175 ml	6 fl oz
1 cup (16 T)	250 ml	8 fl oz
1 1/4 cups	300 ml	10 fl oz (1/2 pt)
1 1/2 cups	350 ml	12 fl oz
2 cups (1 pint)	500 ml	16 fl oz
2 1/2 cups	625 ml	20 fl oz (1 pint)
1 quart	1 liter	32 fl oz

OVEN TEMPERATURE EQUIVALENTS

Oven Mark	F	C	Gas
Very cool	250–275	130–140	1/2–1
Cool	300	150	2
Warm	325	170	3
Moderate	350	180	4
Moderately hot	375	190	5
	400	200	6
Hot	425	220	7
	450	230	8
Very hot	475	250	9

index

(Page numbers in italic refer to illustrations.)

Donzelle
L'Infrascata
Antignano
S. M. di Costantinopoli
Mongibello
Vomero
Villa di Belvedere
Pietracatella
Villa Patrizj
Spiaggia di Chiaja
SCALA
di Cinquecento Tese Parigine
Cinquecento Passi, cadauno di Sette Palmi Napoletani